Excel 365 Essentials

EXCEL 365 ESSENTIALS - BOOKS 1 AND 2

M.L. HUMPHREY

SELECT TITLES BY M.L. HUMPHREY

EXCEL 365 ESSENTIALS
Excel 365 for Beginners
Intermediate Excel 365

102 Useful Excel 365 Functions

WORD 365 ESSENTIALS
Word 365 for Beginners
Intermediate Word 365

EXCEL ESSENTIALS
Excel for Beginners
Intermediate Excel
50 Useful Excel Functions
50 More Excel Functions

EXCEL ESSENTIALS 2019
Excel 2019 Beginner
Excel 2019 Intermediate
Excel 2019 Formulas & Functions

EXCEL 2024 ESSENTIALS
Excel 2024 for Beginners
Intermediate Excel 2024
Excel 2024 Useful Functions

See mlhumphrey.com for Microsoft Word, PowerPoint and Access titles and more

CONTENTS

Excel 365 for Beginners

EXCEL 365 ESSENTIALS - BOOK 1

M.L. HUMPHREY

CONTENTS

Why Learn Excel

Excel is great. I use it both in my professional life and my personal life. It allows me to organize and track key information in a quick and easy manner and to automate a lot of the calculations I need.

I have a budget worksheet that I look at at least every few days to track whether my bills have been paid and how much I need to keep in my bank account and just where I am overall financially.

(Which I shared in *Excel for Budgeting* and which you can also purchase a blank version of via my Payhip store if you're interested. Links available at https://mlhumphrey.com/business-and-personal-finance/)

In my professional career I've used Excel in a number of ways, from analyzing a series of financial transactions to see if a customer was overcharged to performing a comparison of regulatory requirements across multiple jurisdictions.

It's also the quickest and easiest way I've ever found to take rows of raw data and create summaries of that data.

While Excel works best for storing numbers and performing calculations, it is also often a good choice for text-based analysis, especially if you want to be able to sort your text results or filter out and isolate certain entries.

Excel also has very widespread usage. Every single corporate environment I ever worked in used Microsoft Office. I was in banking, finance, and consulting and all of those fields tend to default to Microsoft Office products.

More creative fields tend more towards Apple products, but your bread and butter corporations are very much still users of Office. So learning Excel (and Word and PowerPoint) is an essential skill if you want to be employed in those types of companies.

At least for the foreseeable future. Big companies do not like change.

And honestly, the skills you learn using Microsoft Excel can be applied to similar programs. I use Numbers on my Mac when I need to open a spreadsheet and other than remembering to do Command instead of Control for my shortcuts they work much the same way.

So Excel is definitely worth learning. It will help you with your own life and your career.

Now, real quick, I want to discuss the three main versions of Microsoft Office so you understand where this book fits.

Discussion of Different Office Versions

At this present moment (December 2022), Microsoft Office offers essentially three products that all share the same core functionality.

There is a free version of Microsoft Office that is available online. You can get access to Word, Excel, PowerPoint, and a number of other Microsoft tools by signing up for a free Microsoft account.

We'll call this one Office on the Web.

It has basic functionality that will work for most users, I suspect. But it's also all online. If you have a file on your computer and want to work with it in the free version you have to upload it and store it in a OneDrive account. It also has limited functionality, so it's not going to give you the full range of options as the paid products that Microsoft offers.

Second, are the old-school versions. That's what I have spent the last thirty years or so using. These are static versions of Office that are locked into place at a point in time.

As I write this, the latest static, or as Microsoft likes to call them, "on premise", version of Microsoft Office is Office 2021. The original Office Essentials books I wrote used Office 2013 and I also published a series of titles on Office 2019, but there have been many other versions of Office over the years.

Each of the static versions of Office are released with Office functionality as it exists at that time. They're not supposed to update if there are improvements made later.

(Although I've noticed that they have language about making updates and that sometimes they do seem to make updates, perhaps for security reasons, because I will sometimes notice that my old familiar program isn't working the way it used to.)

But the appearance and tasks do seem to stay fixed.

For example, they changed the appearance of Office with the release of Office 2021, but neither of my laptops, one running Office 2013 and one running Office 2019, were impacted. Also, with Office 2021 it looks like they released the function XLOOKUP to replace VLOOKUP and HLOOKUP, but I didn't get access to it.

One of the disadvantages of working with one of the static or "on premise" versions of Office is that you don't get future improvements like that.

You also, because Microsoft really wants to push people towards their subscription model, are generally limited to having that static version on only one computer. If that computer dies, oh well, you have to buy it again for the next computer. You can't transfer it.

(Again, that's what they say, but when I logged onto my new laptop with my Microsoft account they were ready to let me use Office 2019 on it even though I'd bought it for my old computer. So maybe it's more one computer at a time even though that is not what the license says.)

The advantage to the static versions, though, and the reason I like them, is that they are stable. I buy Office 2019, I figure out how it works, and I'm done until my computer dies.

I don't have to worry that I log in and they've changed things on me overnight. I am not a user who is on the cutting edge who needs the latest and greatest. And I don't collaborate which is where a lot of their more recent improvements seem to be focused so the changes they are making are generally ones that I don't need.

I just want things to stay the same so I don't have to think about anything when I'm ready to work.

Also, I like the static versions because I pay my $300 (or whatever the cost is at the time) once and never have to pay again or worry about losing the ability to edit my files.

But there are good reasons to use the third product option, Office 365, which is the subscription version of Office and the subject of this book.

One is that you can have access to Office across multiple devices. I have a few laptops and having Office 365, if I buy the right option, lets me have Office on my Mac as well as all of my laptops for one monthly fee.

If you're part of a family who all need access that can be a much cheaper option than paying to put Office on each computer.

Also, if everyone is using Office 365 then you know that everyone will be on the same page in terms of compatibility. One of the issues that I ran into professionally a number of years ago was that I was using a newer version of Office than one of my clients. I designed an entire workbook for them that did very complex calculations only to find out that they couldn't use the workbook because the Excel functions I relied on weren't available in the version of Office they were using. I had to redo the whole thing because they couldn't upgrade.

(Of course, that means that if you are going to use Office 365 or even Office 2021, and you're working with someone outside of your organization, you need to be very careful that you don't use something available to you (like XLOOKUP or TEXTJOIN) that that person can't use because they're using an older version of Office.)

Office 365 can also be far more portable if you're willing to put files on OneDrive. (I am not, because I'm a Luddite at heart.) But with Office 365 you can save your files to the cloud and then access them from your other devices.

Also, it can maybe be a much cheaper option for certain programs. I use Microsoft Access and to add that on to a Microsoft 2021 purchase was going to be a couple hundred dollars. But with Office 365 I can have Access along with everything else I need for, at the moment, $8.25 a month. (Go to the business licenses if you need this.)

It also spaces out the cost of the product. You don't have to plunk down all that money on Day 1. But overall Office 365 is probably more expensive for a single user on a single computer than just buying the product with a one-time fee. My laptop that's running Office 2013 is now five years old. If I were paying $8.25 a month I'd have spent $495 which I think is more than I paid up front. And (knock wood) that computer is still going strong.

So it's all about what trade offs you want to make.

To summarize.

There are technically three current versions of Office: (a) the free online one, (b) the static version, the most recent of which is currently Office 2021, and (c) the constantly updating version which is called Office 365.

At the beginner level the differences between the various version should not be significant.

What This Book Covers

Let's talk now about what you will learn in this book, because Excel is an incredibly complex and powerful tool, but it can also get a little overwhelming if you try to cover everything in one go.

So what I've done with the various Excel Essentials series is break that information on Excel down into digestible chunks. And I think I've succeeded at that. (At this point the original *Excel for Beginners* book, which was written for Excel 2013, has over a thousand ratings on Amazon and a rating average of 4.2, so people are generally happy with the level of information covered.)

This book is a version of that book but written for Excel 365. It focuses on the basics of using Excel. We'll cover how to navigate Excel, input data, format it, manipulate it through basic math formulas, filter it, sort it, and print your results.

That should be 95% of what you need to do in Excel day-to-day if you're an average user. I'll also cover at the end how to fill in that last 5% on your own.

(But if you want to keep going with me from there, then there's *Intermediate Excel 365* and *102 Useful Excel 365 Functions* which I'll discuss in a little more detail at the end.)

The other nice thing about Excel is that there are a number of ways to perform the same task. While I do strongly encourage you to learn the control shortcuts (like Ctrl + C to copy) that I mention throughout this book, there will usually be two or three or even more ways to perform a task that we'll cover. So if you have a preference for working in a certain way, it's likely that Excel can accommodate that.

My default is going to be those older ways of doing things because that lets you work across all versions of Excel you may encounter. But when I see that something new works better, I will definitely show that you that method as well.

Okay. So I hope at this point you know that Excel is worth learning.

And I want you to know before we begin that it doesn't have to be hard to learn. Trust me and stick with me through this book and you will have the solid foundation you need.

This book is written to be read start to finish. I want you to read the whole thing. But it's also hopefully organized in such a way that you can come back to it later and use it as a reference for years to come. In the print version there is an index at the end that lists everything we covered and where to find it. (In the ebook version, search will be your friend.)

Now, because this book is about Excel 365, I do need to warn you before we start that Office 365 is a moving target. It is always going to be the latest and greatest. Which means that this book is taking a snapshot of Office 365 as it exists in December 2022, but Office 365 changes monthly.

By the time you read this book, whenever that is, there may be *more* functionality available than I cover here.

Usually, though, that more is not going to impact beginner-level material. For example, the August 2022 update to Excel 365, added a new function (XLOOKUP) and the ability to have "sketched" shapes to make your diagrams and models look hand-drawn, thereby distinguishing ones that were "in progress." Not exactly things that will impact someone new to Excel.

So there will be some changes, but don't worry about them. If I ever think this book isn't a good beginner resource anymore, I will unpublish it or update it. So if you are buying this book new then that means I still think it works for new users and it will still teach you what you need to know to use Excel on a day-to-day basis.

I'm going to be working with the desktop version of Office 365. If you are working online your functionality may be more limited. (That is probably an especially good time to know the control shortcuts.)

Also, your save/open options may be slightly different due to that need to "upload" files or save them to OneDrive.

Okay, one more thing before we get started, which is how to change your appearance, and then we'll dive right in with terminology and absolute basics.

Appearance Settings

Depending on how you have your appearance set, your version of Microsoft Excel may look very different from the screenshots I'm going to use in this book. So before we start I wanted to show you how to change that appearance to match mine in case you want to do that.

If you are absolutely brand new to Excel you may have to come back to this chapter since it relies on having opened an Excel file and knowing some terminology, but I wanted to cover it here before I show you that first screenshot.

To change the appearance of your Office programs, open Excel. That should show you a welcome screen:

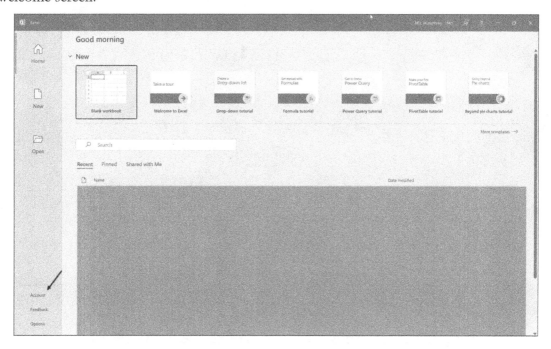

If you don't get that screen, open an Excel file and click on the File option in the top left corner. From there you have two choices. You can either click on Account or Options in the bottom left corner of the screen. Here I've clicked on Account. You can see in the main workspace that there is a dropdown menu for Office Theme. Note that I have mine currently set to Colorful.

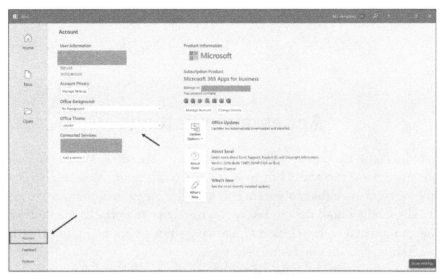

If you click on Options instead, then you can find this same setting under Personalize Your Copy of Microsoft Office in the General section:

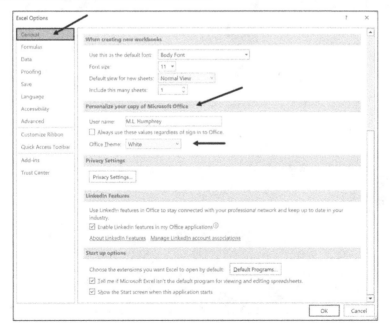

There will be a dropdown menu for Office Theme there as well. Let's look at the different options now.

This is the Dark Gray theme:

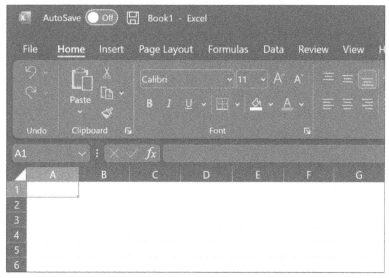

This is the Black theme (which is especially drastic in Word):

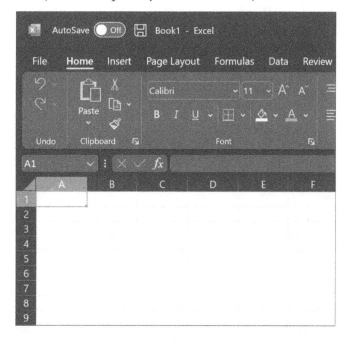

This is the Colorful theme:

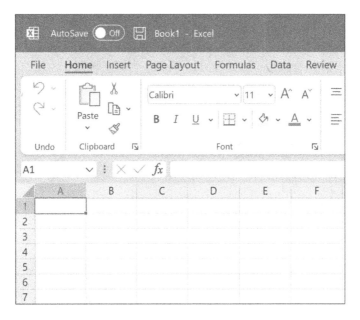

This is the White theme:

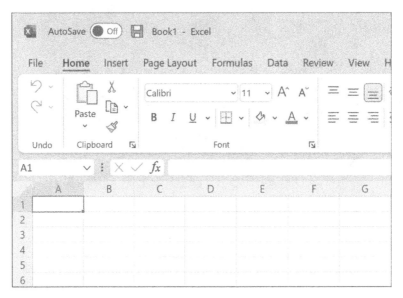

You can't see this in the black and white print version, but the Colorful theme uses blue for the top bar in Word, green for the top bar in Excel, and I would presume orange and red for PowerPoint and Access respectively.

There is also a system settings choice which I presume will be different for everyone based upon the Windows theme they're using. If you have any sort of sight impairment, there are some pretty funky choices you can make in the Windows settings that you may want to explore, but I'm not going to here. One of them for example uses black and bright yellow.

For the rest of this book I'll be using the Colorful theme but it will look just like the White theme most of the time because I won't include the very top of the screen in most of my screenshots.

Whichever choice you make will apply across all of your Office programs, so be careful there. Or be prepared to change it when you move between programs if you have different preferences in different programs.

Okay, now we can cover terminology.

Basic Terminology

Before we can dive in on how to do things, we need to cover some basic terms.

I'm going to assume here you really don't know any of the basics, so you can skim if you think you do, but be sure to at least glance at the headers because I may have my own idiosyncratic way of describing things that you won't have encountered elsewhere.

Workbook

A workbook is what Excel likes to call an Excel file. They define it as a file that contains one or more worksheets. In current versions of Excel a workbook will by default start with one worksheet in it, but you can add more as needed.

Worksheet

Excel defines a worksheet as the primary document you use in Excel to store and work with your data. It can also sometimes be referred to as a spreadsheet, but I will try to avoid using the term spreadsheet here because when I use the term spreadsheet I sometimes actually mean the whole workbook. So better to stick to workbook and worksheet whenever possible.

A worksheet is organized into Columns and Rows that form Cells.

Columns

Excel uses columns and rows to display information. Columns run across the top of the worksheet and, unless you've done something funky with your settings, are identified using letters of the alphabet.

As you can see below, each worksheet will start with A on the far left side for the first column and march right on through the alphabet (A, B, C, D, E, etc.) from there.

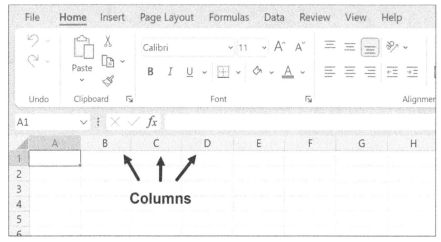

If you scroll far enough to the right, you'll see that the columns continue on to a double alphabet (AA, AB, AC, etc.) and then on to a triple alphabet (AAA, AAB, etc.).

As of right now the very last column in a worksheet is XFD.

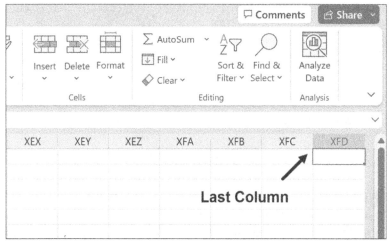

You can reach the very last column in a blank worksheet by holding down the Ctrl key and pressing the End key which is usually also the right arrow key.

If there is already data in that worksheet using Ctrl + End will take you to the last column that has data in it, so you'll need to use Ctrl + End again to go to the last column in the worksheet.

We'll touch on this again, but column letters are basically a way of numbering the columns, not an attribute that is specific to a column. So Column A is always the first column. Column B is always the second column. Etc. And there are always going to be the same number of columns in your worksheet regardless of whether you delete or insert columns.

When you delete or move information in a column you're just moving the data. The grid system doesn't move. So if I take Column A and I delete that column there will still be a Column A because there is still always a first column. And if I were to take all of the data in Column A and move that data three columns over it would now be in Column D.

So think of columns as location information that is actually separate from the data in the worksheet. (We'll work through this more, don't worry.)

Also, columns are one of those areas where you need to be careful if you're working with someone with an older version of Excel because they may not have as many columns in their worksheets in their version of Excel as you do.

For example, I have Excel 2013 on one of my laptops and my last column in that version is IV which means I have far far fewer columns in my version of Excel than anyone using Excel 365 does. This could mean that I would lose data if I open a file from an Excel 365 user in Excel 2013 if that file uses more columns than I have access to.

So always keep in the back of your mind that if you're working with others that aren't set up the same way you are in Office that you can have compatibility issues and one of the main ones you can have is number of rows and columns.

But let's get back to basic terms.

Rows

Rows run down the side of each worksheet and are numbered starting at 1 and up to a very high number. As of now that number is 1048576. That means a single Excel worksheet currently has over a million rows. You can hold down the Ctrl key in a blank worksheet while hitting the down arrow to see just how many rows your version of Excel has.

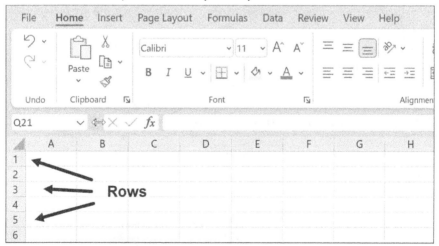

As a comparison, Excel 2013 had only 65,536 rows in a worksheet. Keep this in mind for compatibility issues when working with other users.

And, once more, those row numbers are locational information. The first row will always be numbered 1. The second row will always be numbered 2. And so on and so forth. And at least as of this moment there will always be 1,048,576 rows in every Excel worksheet at all times. So even if you delete or insert rows that will not change that fact.

You are deleting data not the number of rows in the worksheet.

Cells

Cells are where the row and column data all comes together. Think of it as map coordinates. Cell A1 is the first column and first row of the worksheet.

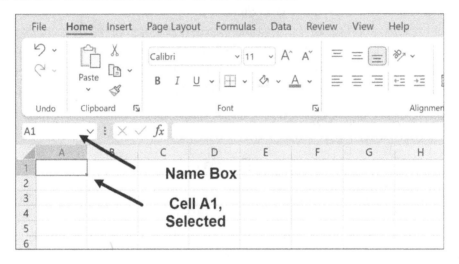

When you click onto a specific cell, like I have above, that cell will be surrounded with a darker border around the perimeter.

You can also look in the Name Box, noted above, to see the cell reference for that cell. These cell references are used when writing Excel formulas or using functions.

And remember, that these are coordinates, they are not fixed to your data. So if you have an entry in the first column of the first row of your worksheet and move that entry to the third column and third row of your worksheet that entry will now be in Cell C3 not Cell A1.

(Again, don't worry too much right now, we will work in Excel and you will see how this happens.)

Click

If I tell you to click on something, that means to use your mouse (or trackpad) to move the cursor on the screen over to a specific location and left-click or right-click on the option. (See the next definition for the difference between left-click and right-click).

If you left-click, this selects the item. If you right-click, this generally displays a dropdown list of options to choose from. If I don't tell you which to do, left- or right-click, then left-click.

Left-click/Right-click

If you look at your mouse you generally have two flat buttons to press. One is on the left side, one is on the right.

If I say left-click that means to press down on the button on the left. If I say right-click that means press down on the button on the right. (If you're used to using Word you may already do this without even thinking about it. So, if that's the case then think of left-click as what you usually use to select text and right-click as what you use to see a menu of choices.)

If you're using a track pad, not all track pads have the left- and right-hand areas visible. In that case, you'll basically want to press on either the bottom left-hand side of the track pad or the bottom right-hand side of the trackpad as needed.

Select

If I tell you to "select" cells, that means to highlight them. If the cells are next to each other, you can just left-click on the first one and drag the cursor (move your mouse or finger on the trackpad) as you hold that left-click until all of the cells are highlighted.

(I will refer to this action as left-click and drag.)

When you do this, all the selected cells will be shaded gray and surrounded by a dark box like below except for the first cell you clicked on which will be within the perimeter of the box but will be white.

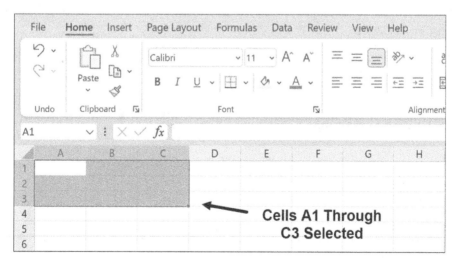

You can also select cells that are not next to each other by holding down the Ctrl key as you left-click on each cell.

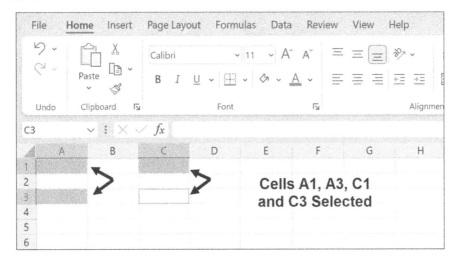

When you do that, each selected cell will be shaded gray except for the last selected cell which will be surrounded by a border but will be white. Above I selected Cells A1, A3, C1, and C3. C3 was selected last.

To select an entire column, click on the letter. To select an entire row, click on the number.

For any row or column where a cell is selected in that row or column, the number or letter for that row or column will be shaded differently. In my version right now with my settings it's shaded a darker gray and the number/letter turns green.

For any row or column where the whole row or column is selected that letter or number will change to a different shading. For my version with my settings it turns light green with a dark green number/letter.

Data

Data is the information you enter into your worksheet. It's the values and text that you input or calculate. I will also sometimes refer to this as information, values, or text.

Data Table

I may also sometimes refer to a data table or table of data. This is just a combination of cells that contain data in them.

One thing to keep in mind with Excel versus Word if you're coming from using Word is that in Word when you create a data table you are adding a specific number of rows and columns into Word to do that. But in Excel the number of rows and columns never changes.

What does change is how many of those rows or columns have your data in them.

Excel is smart enough to only print or focus on the rows or columns with data in them, but if you want something to print out and look like a table you could create in Word you'll want to put borders around your data in Excel. (We'll discuss how to do that, don't worry.)

(This is a question that came up a few times after I released *Excel for Beginners*, so I wanted to mention it here specifically. Data tables as you create them in Word are not the same as data tables as you use them in Excel.)

Arrow

I will sometimes tell you to arrow to somewhere. Or to arrow right, left, up, or down. This just means to use the arrow keys. Using arrows is one way to move between cells within an Excel worksheet.

The other ways are to left-click on a cell. Or you can use Tab and Shift + Tab to move right and left, respectively. And Enter to move to the next row.

Cursor Functions

The cursor is what moves around when you move your mouse or use the trackpad. In Excel the cursor changes its appearance depending on what functions you can perform. You can see this by opening an Excel file and moving your cursor over the cells and then along the edges of a row or column and then up to the menu options up top.

Tab

I am going to talk a lot about Tabs, which are the options you have to choose from at the top of the workspace.

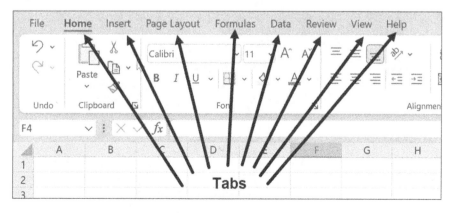

It used to be, in older versions of Excel that when you clicked on one of these options it took on the appearance of a tab like a file folder has. But in the latest versions of Excel that's no longer the case. The selected tab is just underlined. For example, in the image above, I have the Home tab selected which you can tell from the solid line under the word Home.

Each tab has a number of options available. Here is the left-hand set of options available under the Home tab, for example:

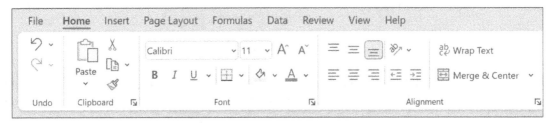

I can Undo, Copy/Paste/Format Sweep, choose my font attributes, choose my text alignment, etc.

The Home tab is the tab that will be selected by default. But you can click on the other tabs to see their available options.

Throughout this book I will often tell you to go to Y section of X tab and choose the task that we're trying to complete. For example, if I wanted you to change the font from Calibri to something else, I would say you could go to the Font section of the Home tab and click on the dropdown menu for font. (I will include screenshots most of the time so you can also see what I'm talking about.)

Dropdown Menus

A dropdown menu is a listing of available choices that you can see when you click on the arrow for that option or right-click in certain places such as the main workspace.

For example, here is the font dropdown menu:

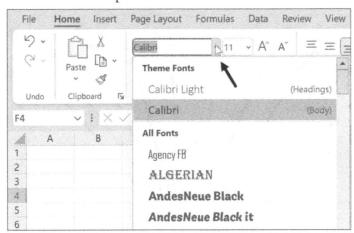

I clicked on the small arrow next to the current font name and that brought up a listing of choices. There are a large number of dropdown menus in Excel as you can see here where we have dropdown menus for Undo, Paste, Copy, Font, Font Size, Underline, Borders, Fill Color, Font Color, and Text Orientation:

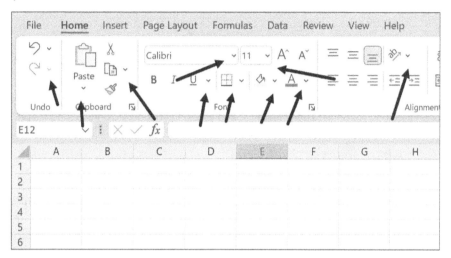

There are many more available in Excel. So any time I tell you to use a dropdown menu or anytime you're trying to find additional options, look for that little arrow to the right of or below the task you're trying to complete or try right-clicking on a worksheet name or in the main workspace.

Help Text

This isn't really a term and we'll discuss it again later, but I just wanted to mention that if you are ever unsure what task an image in the top menu is related to, you can usually hold your mouse over the image and Excel will tell you what it is. Here, for example, I held my cursor over the image of a bucket with a bright yellow line under it and Excel showed me a pop-up box that tells me that's for adding Fill Color and what that does. I can then click on Tell Me More to open Help and learn more about how it works.

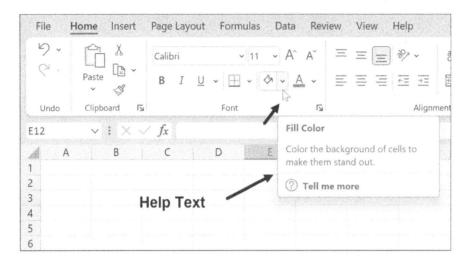

Tell Me More is not always available, but usually you will at least get a brief description of what that image will let you do.

Dialogue Boxes

Dialogue boxes are pop-up boxes that contain additional choices. You will often see one if you click on the arrow in the corner of a section of a tab. For example, here I have clicked on the arrow in the corner of the Font section of the Home tab and that has opened the Format Cells dialogue box.

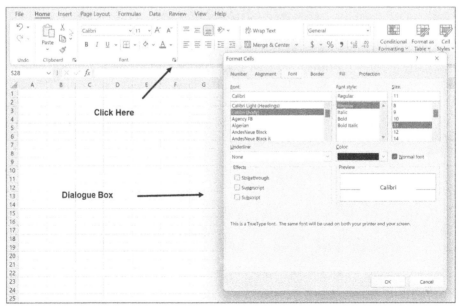

Dialogue boxes often have the most available choices. So if you aren't seeing what you want in the tab choices, then click on that arrow to open the related dialogue box if it exists.

Also, for those who are used to older versions of Excel, dialogue boxes are likely what you're used to working with so using them can sometimes feel more familiar than using the options up top.

You will also sometimes see a dialogue box if you right-click and choose an option from the dropdown menu in the main workspace.

Scroll Bars

When you have more information than will show on the screen, dialogue box, or dropdown menu you can use the scroll bars to see the rest of the information.

The main scroll bars you will see are going to be in the main workspace when there is more data in your rows and columns than can appear on the screen:

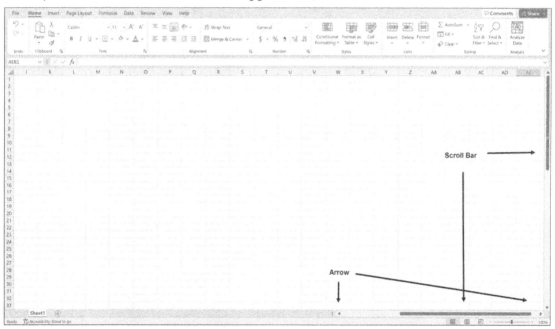

Scroll bars usually appear on the right-hand side or on the bottom of the workspace, dialogue box, or dropdown menu.

In the image above you can see them as darker gray bars. Note that there are also arrows at each end of the scroll bars. And that there is blank space between the arrows and those bars.

The more information involved, the smaller the scroll bars will be and the more space there will be around them.

There are three ways to navigate using the scroll bars.

You can left- click and drag the bar itself. This means, left-click on the bar, hold down the left-click, and move the cursor as you do so. The bar will move and the visible information will change.

If you only want to move a small amount at a time, you can use the arrows. Arrows at the bottom will move one item left or right, arrows on the side will move one item up or down.

You can also, left-click and hold on the arrows to move through multiple items but it will do so one at a time.

The final option is to click into the gray space between the two. One click in that gray space will move you an entire screen's worth. So in the main workspace if I can see Columns A through V and I click in the gray space at the bottom that moves me to Columns W through AR.

In the main workspace, you can only use the scroll bars or click into that gray space to navigate within the area where you have data. But the arrows will let you go past that.

Formula Bar

The formula bar is the long white bar at the top of the main workspace directly below the menu tabs that lets you see the actual contents of a cell, not just the display value.

Here you can see that the value in Cell C1 is 5, but according to what we can see in the formula bar, that value is calculated using the formula =A1+B1, which adds the values in Cells A1 and B1 together:

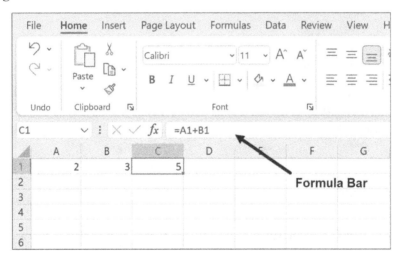

Task Pane

On occasion Excel will open a task pane, which is different from a dialogue box because it is part of the workspace. You can use F1 to see an example of this with the Help task pane which opens on the right-hand side of the workspace.

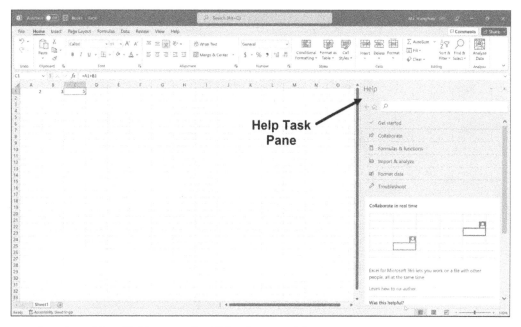

They can be closed by clicking on the X in the top right corner.

Absolute Basics

Before we start working in an Excel workbook, I want to cover the absolute basics of opening, saving, closing, and deleting files.

If you're already familiar with Microsoft Word or another Office program or similar, then this will probably all be familiar to you, but I want to make sure it's here for those who aren't.

Open a New Excel File

If you want to start a brand new Excel file, the first step is to open Excel. How you do this will depend on how you have your computer set up and what version of Windows you're running.

One of the first things I do when I get a new computer is I add my key programs to my taskbar. That way when I want to open Excel I can just click on the icon for Excel and open the program.

In Windows 11, a simple click on that green icon with the X will open Excel.

If you aren't set up with that, then you may have an Excel shortcut on your desktop.

Or you can go to the Start menu in the bottom left corner of your computer (if you haven't moved things around), left-click on that blue window icon and it will show you a menu where Excel may be in your pinned apps. If it's not there you can search for it. Or you can go to All Apps and find it there.

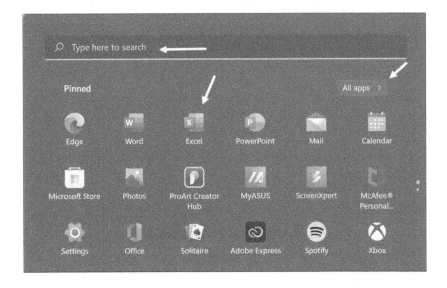

This is Windows 11. Windows 10, you click on the Start menu icon and look for the All Apps listing and then find it that way. They'll probably change it again in Windows 12 or whatever comes next, because they seem to love to do that, which is why I find it once, right-click, and choose to Pin to Taskbar so it's right there when I need it.

Okay. So however you do it, open Excel. If this is your first time in Excel you may have to Activate your account or skip through some screens that want you to activate it. But after you do that, you'll have something like this:

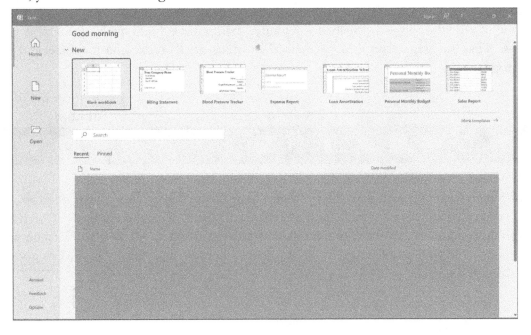

This is the Excel welcome screen. I've grayed out the section with my recent files listed, but otherwise this is what you should see when you first open Excel.

Those appearance settings we talked about before can be changed using Options on the left-hand side, bottom corner.

But if you're there to start a new file, then click on the Blank Workbook choice at the top of the screen.

(You'll see that there are also a number of templates you can choose from, but for what we're going to do in this book you can ignore those for now. If at some point you want to create an expense report, for example, you may want to click on that template and adjust from there.)

You could also click on New on the left-hand side but that just takes you to another screen where you have the Blank Workbook and template choices once more.

Clicking on Blank Workbook will open a new, blank workbook for you that looks like this:

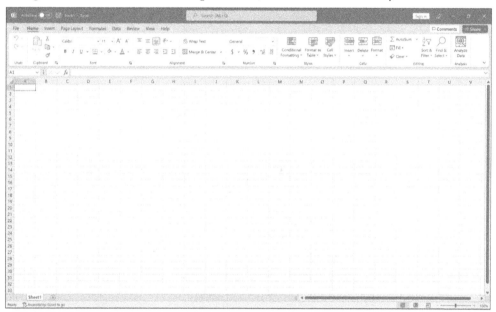

If you are already in an Excel workbook and want to create a new workbook, you have a couple of choices. The easiest is to use Ctrl + N. That will immediately create a new workbook for you.

You can also go to the top of the screen, click on the File option, and then click on Blank Workbook from there.

Open An Existing Excel File

If you already have an Excel file and now want to open that file and work on it, there are a couple of options available.

The first is to find the Excel file wherever you have it saved and double-click on it. That will open the file in Excel and if Excel isn't already open will also open Excel for you.

If you do have Excel open and you've recently used that file, then you should be able to find it in your Recent Files listing on the welcome screen when you open Excel.

You can see in the image below the four most recent files I've opened in Excel and when they were opened last. My screen actually shows eight files and if I scroll down there are two more for a total of ten.

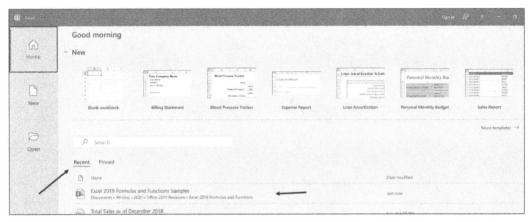

Click on the file name and the file will open.

There may be times when a file is listed in your recent files list but you can't open it from there. This happens if you move the file or change its name outside of Excel.

For a file that you want to open that isn't in that recent files list, click on Open from the welcome screen. You will once more see the Recent Files listing, but there will also be other options. One of those is the Folders option. Click on that and you'll see a listing of any folders that contain files you recently opened.

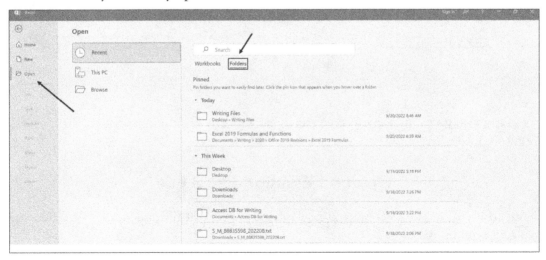

You can see in the image above that I opened files from the Writing Files and Excel 2019 Formulas and Functions folders today and have opened files from my Desktop, Downloads, Access DB for Writing, and a zip file this week.

This can sometimes be the easiest way to find a file you're looking for if you tend to store your Excel files in just a handful of locations. Click on one of those folder options and you'll see a listing of Excel files that are in that folder. You can then click on that file name to open it.

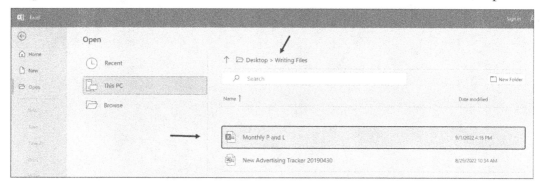

That will often be the best way to find a file. But it doesn't work if the folder the file is in is one you haven't used recently. It also doesn't work if the file you want to open isn't one of the main types of files that Excel can open, namely, .xls, .xlsx, or .csv.

If that's the case, then click on the Browse option instead. This will open the Open dialogue box.

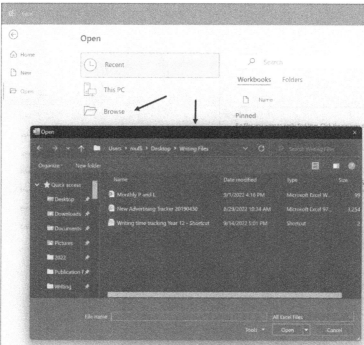

You can then use the options on the left-hand side to navigate to the folder that contains your file and select the file that way.

One of the files I need to open in Excel is a .txt file. By default, Excel will not look for that file type. You can see here that it's not showing any files for me to open.

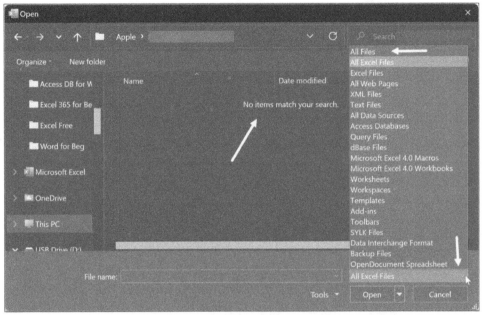

When I need to open one of those Text files, I have to change the file type in the Open dialogue box by clicking on the dropdown menu for file type and changing it to All Files from All Excel Files. Once I do that, I can then see the file I need to open and select that file:

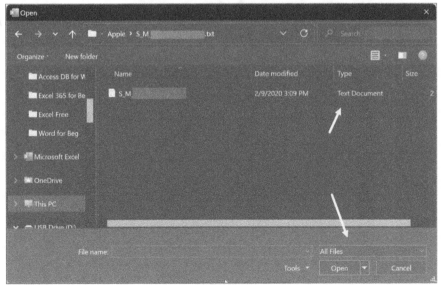

But that's a pretty rare situation, so usually you won't need to worry about that. I just mention it here because for anyone who publishes through Apple, their reports are text files. (That you also have to open with 7-Zip.)

Okay, back to things that matter to most readers instead of just one little subset.

If you already have Excel open and are either working on a file already or are in that main workspace and want to open another file, you can either use Ctrl + O, which will take you to the Open screen, or you can click on File at the top of the workspace and then click on Open.

From there it's the same steps as we just walked through.

Pin A File

If you have a file that you always want readily accessible but that won't stay in your recent files listing because you open enough files that it sometimes falls out of your top ten most recent, then you can Pin that file and it will always be available to you in your Pinned files section.

For example, I have a monthly profit and loss Excel file that I like to review once a month. But it gets lost from my recent files list because when I load all of my sales reports there are more than ten of them. So to make sure I can always find that file, I pin it.

To do this, find the file in your recent files list. Hold your cursor over that listing. You should see the image of a thumbtack appear on the right-hand side, and if you hold your cursor over that image it will say, "Pin this item to the list".

Click on that thumbtack. If you then click onto the Pinned option, that file will be listed there. And it will stay there regardless of what other files you open, so that it's always available to you.

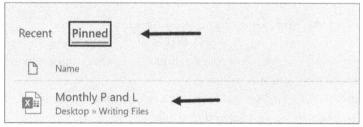

Once you've pinned a file, you can open it by going to your Pinned Files section and clicking on that name.

Close a File

If you ever have an Excel file open and want to close it, you can use Ctrl + W. I personally never remember that particular shortcut, so I instead just click on the X in the top right-hand corner.

You can also click on File in the top menu on the right-hand side and then click on Close from the list of options on the left-hand side of the File screen.

Save a File

If you've made changes to a file and you try to close it Excel will show you a dialogue box that asks if you want to save those changes.

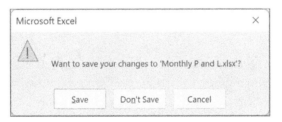

It gives you three options, Save, Don't Save, and Cancel.

Save will overwrite the existing version of the file. You'll keep the same file name, file location, and file type. All changes you made while that file was open will be saved. Whatever the file was like before that, is gone.

Don't Save will close the file but not save any changes you made to the document while it was open. It will be like you never touched that file.

Cancel will not close the file and also not save the changes. Choose Cancel if you want to save the file as a new version and not overwrite the old version.

If you're trying to close a brand new file, choosing Save will actually open the Save As dialogue box, because Excel doesn't know where you want to save the file or what you want to call it.

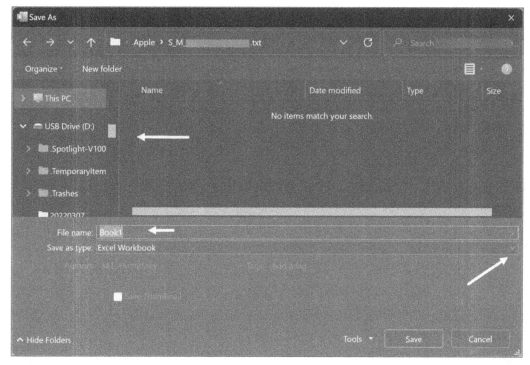

It will default to wherever the last file you opened was saved and the name will be some variation on Book 1. (If you have multiple blank workbooks opened it may be Book 2 or Book 3, etc.)

Type in the new name you want. Use the folders on the left-hand side of the dialogue box to navigate to the folder where you want to save that file. And make sure that the file type is what you want to use. Normally you'll be fine sticking with a file type of Excel Workbook.

But file type is another area where you may run into issues if someone is using an older version of Excel than you are. In that case, change the file type to Excel 97-2003 Workbook.

Be careful doing this, though, because as Excel adds more and more bells and whistles and functionality it makes it more and more likely that the Excel 97-2003 file format is not going to be able to support something you did in your Excel file.

If you're ever looking at file extensions, this is the difference between a .xlsx file and a .xls file. All files before Excel 2007 were .xls files. All files since then are .xlsx. In the past I advised saving to .xls for compatibility reasons, but I think we're far enough along at this point with .xlsx that you don't need to do that by default anymore. And if you're only working on files for yourself or your organization, you absolutely shouldn't need to worry about that.

If that all sounded confusing, don't worry. Just save as Excel Workbook. And if someone ever says, "I can't open that file because I have an older version of Excel," then come back to this section at that point in time.

So that's how you save a file if you weren't being proactive about it and just waited for Excel to remind you to save your file before you closed it.

But it's possible you will want to save that file under a new name or in a new location or as a new file type. Or that you'll want to save as you work so that if your computer crashes you don't lose your work. (Not as much of an issue these days as it was in the past, but it can still happen.)

In that case, let's start with Save first. Save is for a file where you want to save the changes you've made but you don't need to change the name, location, or file type.

The easiest option is Ctrl + S. That will save all of the changes you've made so far and overwrite the former version of the file.

If the file has never been saved before it will take you to the Save As screen under the File tab.

You can also click on the computer disk icon in the top left corner of the screen. Hold your mouse over it and it will say Save (Ctrl + S). Click on that and that too will save any changes you've made so far and overwrite the existing file.

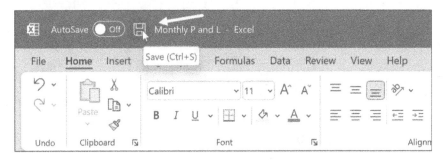

To save the file you're working on under a new name, into a new location, or as a new file type, you need to use Save As. To do that, click on File in the top left corner and then choose Save As.

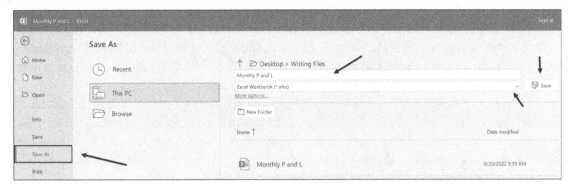

If you just need to change the file name, you can do so right there. Same with the file type. Once done click on Save.

To change the location, click on the Browse option. That will bring up the Save As dialogue box and let you navigate to the new location you want. Clicking on More Options will also bring up that dialogue box.

Keep in mind with Save As that the original file will still exist. So if you want multiple versions of a file, which I sometimes do when I'm building something really complex, that's great. But if what you really wanted was to change the file name or move the file, then you probably don't want to use Save As to do that.

Change a File Name

To change the name of an Excel file you can use Save As as we just discussed but that will leave you with two files. The original file will have the original name and then the newly-saved version will have the new name.

But if you don't need two files, it's better to close the Excel file, go directly to the folder where you have the file saved and change the name there. To do so, click on the file once to select it, and then click on it a second to make the name editable.

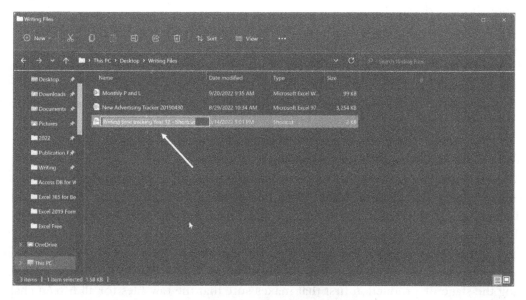

You can see here that I've done that with the third listed file so that the text of the name is now highlighted. I can then click into that field and make whatever change I want to the name. When you're done, hit Enter.

If you change a file name in this way, you will not be able to use the Recent or Pinned file listing to open the file the next time you go to open it in Excel. You will have to open the file directly from where it's saved or use the Browse option.

Delete a File

If you ever want to permanently delete an Excel file. Say, for example, that you did use Save

As but don't need that original file anymore, this has to be done outside of Excel. Close the file in Excel and then go find where you have it saved. Click on the file name once to select it. And then click on the trash can icon at the top of the window. You can also right-click on the file name and click on the trash can from there (for Windows 11) or choose Delete from the dropdown menu (for Windows 10).

File Naming Tip

Before we close out this chapter, I just want to share a file-naming tip I picked up from an efficiency training years ago that's been very helpful for me. I do keep multiple versions of files. For example, when I publish a book there's the original file. And then if I later make an edit because I find a typo or I release a new book in that series that needs to be added to the Also By section, there's another file. Some of my titles have twenty versions because they've been out almost a decade by now.

I want those files to display in an order that lets me quickly find the most recent one. To make that happen, I use a YYYYMMDD naming format.

This book for example would be "Excel 365 for Beginners 20221210". And then if I made an edit on December 15th it would be "Excel 365 for Beginners 20221215". By writing the date in that order–year, month, day–it ensures that when I sort by name, the files sort in proper date order.

(And if I ever for some reason have two on the same day then I add v1, v2, etc. at the end.)

You can use this same trick for folder names as well.

Also, if you have a process that involves multiple files and steps, consider how things will sort there as well. For example, I have put some of my books out as audiobooks. And there are four steps I go through to get to the final file. I have the raw recording, the first pass edit, the Reaper processing, and then the final version. I want to keep all of the raw files together, all the first pass files together, etc. And I want them in order.

So in that case I name the files "Raw 1 Introduction", "First Pass 1 Introduction", etc. By putting the stage of production first that makes sure that the raw files for all fifteen chapters group together. And by using the chapter number next I make sure that the first file in each group is the first chapter.

You will save yourself a lot of headache if you give some thought to your file names up front. And if you don't do so, well, you can always go and rename those files later. Just remember to do it where you saved the files not through Excel.

Okay. Now that we know how to open, close, save, rename, and delete files, let's talk about how to navigate Excel.

Navigating Excel

I want to talk now about how to move around within an Excel worksheet as well as within an Excel workbook and between workbooks.

Move Between Excel Workbooks

Let's start with the easiest one. If you have two Excel workbooks open, the easiest way to move between them is using Alt + Tab. If you have more than two files open just keeping using the Tab key while you hold down the Alt key to cycle through until you reach the one you want.

Alt + Tab lets you cycle through all of your open files or programs, not just Excel.

Items will usually be listed in order of when you last used them, so if you're moving back and forth between two Excel files, even if you have ten items open, those two files should be your first option each time you move. That means just one use of Alt + Tab will take you to the other file.

Another option, is to hold your mouse over the icon for Excel in the taskbar and then choose the file you want that way by clicking on the thumbnail image for the file.

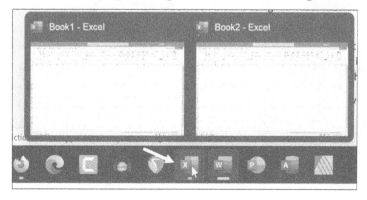

Move Between Excel Worksheets

Within an Excel file it is possible to have multiple Excel worksheets. I usually just click on the name of the worksheet I want at the bottom of the workspace.

You can see which worksheet you are currently on by seeing which worksheet name is white with bolded text.

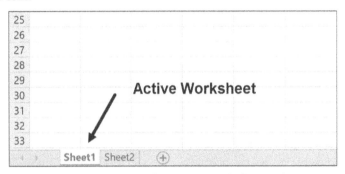

There is also a control shortcut for moving between worksheets that I generally don't use. Ctrl + Page Up will move you one worksheet to the left and Ctrl + Page Down will move you one worksheet to the right. If like on my computer your Page Up and Page Down buttons are combined with your up and down arrows then you may need to use Ctrl + Fn + Page Up and Ctrl + Fn + Page Down.

This does not, as of this moment, cycle through to the start or to the end. Meaning, if you have twenty worksheets and want to get from the first to the last, you would have to use Ctrl + Page Down nineteen times. Just using Ctrl + Page Up isn't an option. (It would be nice if it was, though, so maybe they'll do that someday.)

If you have more worksheets in your file than can be displayed at the bottom of the workspace, there will be little … at the end of the visible worksheet names.

Click on that … to see more worksheets. You can also use those left and right arrows on the bottom left corner of the workspace to move left or right and show more worksheets.

Using Ctrl and left-clicking on one of those two arrows will take you all the way to the first sheet or all the way to the last sheet, depending on which arrow you click on.

You can also right-click on one of those arrows to bring up an Activate dialogue box listing all of your worksheets in your workbook. From there click on the name of the worksheet you want and then click on OK and Excel will take you to that worksheet.

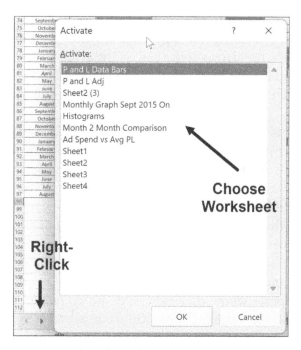

(If you don't want to try to remember those last two, holding your mouse over the arrows will tell you that as well. When in doubt in Excel, try holding the cursor over something because often there will be additional help text that appears.)

Move Within An Excel Worksheet

Any brand new Excel workbook is going to open on Sheet 1 and in Cell A1. To move from there, as we discussed briefly in the terminology section, you have a few options.

You can simply use the arrow keys to move one cell in any direction. So, right arrow moves you right one cell to Cell B1. Or if you used the down arrow it would move you down one cell to Cell A2. And then once you're not pinned into a corner in Cell A1, you can also use the left arrow to go left one cell and the up arrow to go up one cell.

The Tab key will also let you go right one cell. And using Shift and the Tab key will let you go left one cell.

Enter will also move you down one cell. Although, sometimes if you're entering data Enter will actually move you down one row but over to the beginning of where you were entering your data. So, for example, if I put "a" in Cell A1, "b" in Cell B1, and "c" in Cell C1, and then hit Enter that will take me to Cell A2. This can be very useful when entering multiple rows and columns of data directly into Excel.

Page Up and Page Down will take you one full screen's worth of rows up or down. (You may need to use Fn + Page Up and Fn + Page Down depending on how your computer is set up.)

You can also simply left-click into whichever cell you want if it's visible in your workspace.

As discussed more fully in the terminology section, to move greater distances within a file, you can use the scroll bars, the arrows at the end of the scroll bars, or click on the gray space between those arrows and the scroll bars. But be careful using those, because what you see will adjust, but until you click into a cell in the worksheet, you will still be in the last cell you were clicked into or edited.

This has occasionally tripped me up when I have my panes frozen (something we'll talk about later) and then I scroll far down in my data, but forget to click into one of the cells I can see on the workspace and so hit enter and am suddenly back at Row 2 instead of Row 2,354 or whatever.

Also, as mentioned before, according to Microsoft's help, Ctrl + End and Ctrl + Page Down will move you to the end of a range of data or the end of your worksheet, depending on if there's data in the worksheet.

Likewise, to go from somewhere in your worksheet to the top or the left-most edge, you can use Ctrl + Page Up and Ctrl + Home.

For me, with a computer where my arrow keys are combined with my Page Up, Page Down, Home and End keys I just have to use the arrow keys. I don't need to add the Fn key in to this one to get to Page Up, Page Down, Home, and End. So you may need to experiment around a bit to see how your particular computer acts.

Also, the help text on this one seems to differ from how it actually works. The help text says it takes you to the outer range of any existing data, but from testing it, what it actually does is takes you to the end of the next set of data in that particular row or column.

So if Column A has data for six rows and Column B has data for ten rows, depending on which column you're in when you use the shortcut you may go six rows or you may go ten.

If you do use this, and it can be very handy especially when paired with Shift so that you select those cells at the same time, watch out for gaps in your data. If there is an empty column or an empty row, Excel will stop at that gap. You'll need to use the arrow/page up/page down/home/end key again to grab the full range of your data if that happens.

Freeze Panes

If you have a lot of information in a worksheet, Freeze Panes will save you. Because it lets you keep certain information, such as a header row, visible in your workspace while you scroll down to see more data. Without freeze panes you end up with a screen full of data but nothing that tells you what that data is.

Here, for example, is a few rows of data from one of my Amazon reports:

	A	C	E	F	G	H	I	J	K	L
68	2021-01-26	Author A	Amazon.com		70% Standard	1	0	1	4.99	4.99
69	2021-01-26	Author F	Amazon.com		35% Free - Price Match	1	0	1	0.99	0.00
70	2021-01-26	Author A	Amazon.com		70% Standard	2	0	2	4.99	4.99
71	2021-01-26	Author D	Amazon.com		70% Standard	1	0	1	3.99	3.99
72	2021-01-25	Author A	Amazon.com		70% Standard	3	0	3	4.99	4.99
73	2021-01-25	Author B	Amazon.co.uk		70% Standard	1	0	1	3.99	3.99
74	2021-01-25	Author A	Amazon.com		70% Standard	1	0	1	2.99	2.99
75	2021-01-25	Author B	Amazon.com		70% Standard	1	0	1	4.99	4.99

If you wanted to use one of those columns to know the total number of units sold, which one would you use? And which one would show list price of the book? Versus which one shows what a customer actually paid for the book? Some of it is self-explanatory, but not all of it.

This particular report also has 15 columns, which means that I either would need to Zoom Out and make the text smaller to see everything or I'm going to not be able to see the left-most columns when I'm looking at the right-most column.

Which is a problem. I have it hidden right now, but Column B is Title and looking at how much I earned in the second-to-last column doesn't do me much good if I don't know which book it is.

But Freeze Panes lets me solve this issue. Because I can set up this worksheet so that Row 1 is always visible even when I'm on Row 250. And I can also set it up so that my title column is always visible, too.

Like so:

	A	B	N	O	P
1	Royalty Date	Title	Royalty	Currency	
224	2021-01-06	Book Title	2.76	USD	
225	2021-01-06	Book Title	3.96	USD	
226	2021-01-06	Book Title	2.05	USD	
227	2021-01-06	Book Title	5.90	USD	
228	2021-01-06	Book Title	2.76	USD	
229	2021-01-06	Book Title	5.83	USD	
230	2021-01-06	Book Title	2.76	USD	

See how it goes from Row 1 to Row 224? And how it shows Columns A and B and then Columns N and O? All of the other rows and columns are still visible, but I've scrolled down and over to see this information.

So how do you set this up?

If all you want is to freeze the top row of your worksheet or the first column, go to the Window section of the View tab and click on the dropdown arrow for Freeze Panes. Choose either Freeze Top Row or Freeze First Column.

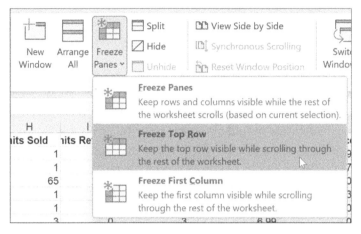

You can do one or the other this way, but not both. If you want to freeze more than one column, more than one row, or columns and rows both at the same time, then you need to first click into your worksheet at the first cell that you are okay *not* seeing.

In other words, below the rows that you want to freeze in place and to the right of the columns that you want to freeze in place.

So in our example worksheet, I want to keep the first row visible and I want book title visible, which is in the second column. That means I need to click into Cell C2.

	A	B		C	E	F
1	Royalty Date	Title		Author Name	Marketplace	Royalty Type
2	2021-01-31	Book Title		Author A	Amazon.com	70%
3	2021-01-31	Book Title		Author B	Amazon.com.au	70%
4	2021-01-31	Book Title		Author C	Amazon.com	70%
5	2021-01-31	Book Title		Author D	Amazon.com	70%
6	2021-01-31	Book Title		Author C	Amazon.fr	70%
7	2021-01-31	Book Title		Author C	Amazon.ca	70%

In the image above you can see that I've shaded the first row gray as well as the two columns on the left gray so that I can make it more clear which data will remain visible.

I can then go to the Freeze Panes dropdown and choose the first option, Freeze Panes, to keep both that top row and the left two columns visible.

Now, honestly I don't care about keeping the date visible, but with freeze panes you don't get to be that specific. So it's everything to the left and everything above the cell you choose. Which means if I want book title I am also going to get date.

(I could hide a column or move a column to fix that, but it's not that big a deal to me.)

To remove freeze panes, just go back to that same dropdown menu. The top option will be Unfreeze Panes now and you can just click on it to remove any freeze panes that are in effect.

Now, one thing to be careful of, that I do more than I should. If you are clicked into Row 1 and have freeze panes in effect and have scrolled down to Row 10,522 but not clicked into any cell in that row or in that part of your data, you are still on Row 1 as far as Excel is concerned. And so if you use your down arrow you will go to Row 2 and the rows you see on your workspace will change to Rows 2 through…37 or so. And then you'll have to scroll all the way back down to Row 10,522 again.

Also, don't try to freeze too many rows or columns at a time. If you freeze the majority of your screen then you'll only be able to scroll maybe one record at a time which is very inefficient.

Hide Columns or Rows

Sometimes when I'm working with data in Excel there will be rows of data or columns of data I really don't need to see at all. So it's not that there's so much information on the screen I can't see it all, it's more that I want what's in Column B next to what's in Column F. Maybe I'm inputting data into those two columns, but there are calculations between the two that I want to stay where they are. So while I'm adding my information I don't need to see the calculation columns, just the columns where I'm putting in information.

When that happens I hide those rows or columns I don't need to see.

To hide a row or column, right-click on the letter or number for that column or row, and choose Hide from the dropdown menu.

When you hide a column it still exists, so you will see that the letters or numbers skip that missing column or row. It will go from Column C to Column E, for example, if you've hidden Column D like I have in the screenshot above.

To unhide hidden columns or rows, select the columns or rows on either side of the hidden entries and then right-click and choose Unhide.

* * *

Now let's talk about inputting data after which we'll talk about inserting and deleting rows, columns, and cells as well as a bit more about working with worksheets.

Input Data

At its most basic, inputting your data is very simple. Click in the cell where you want to input information and then type. But there are some tricks to it that you'll want to keep in mind.

First, let's take a step back and talk about one of the key strengths of using Excel and that's the ability to sort or filter your data.

For example, I publish books and every month I get reports from the places where my books are published listing all of the sales of my books at those locations.

But what if I only care about the sales of book A? How can I see those if I have a couple hundred rows of information in the report they've given me?

Well, if the site where I sold those books is nice and helpful and they understand data analysis, they've given me my sales listings in an Excel worksheet with one header row at the top and then one row for each sale or for each book.

If they've done that, then I can very easily filter my data on the title column and see just the entries related to title A. Or create a pivot table of that data so I can see all sales for that title grouped together.

If they haven't, then I'm stuck deleting rows of information I don't need to get to the data I want.

Which is all a roundabout way of saying that you can input your data any way you want, but if you follow some key data principles you'll have a lot more flexibility in what you can do with your data once it's entered.

Those principles are:

1. Use the first row of your worksheet to label your data.

2. List all of your data in continuous rows after that first row without including any subtotals or subheadings or anything that isn't your data. Keep all data for a specific item on one row. (So a customer buys something from you on July 1st, have all of the information related to that transaction on one single line if transactions are what you care about. Or have all information related to sales of Widgets on one line per transaction if what you care about is your widgets.)

3. To the extent possible, format your data in such a way that it can be analyzed. (Which means rather than put in a free-text field, try to use a standardized list of values instead. A column that uses a 1 to 5 point ranking scale is better for analysis than a column that uses a free text field where anyone can say anything.)

4. Standardize your values. Customer A should always be listed as Customer A. United States should always be United States not USA, U.S.A., or America.

5. Store your raw data in one location; analyze or correct it elsewhere.

I wrote an entire book on this subject, *How to Gather and Use Data for Business Analysis*, so if you really want to explore this topic, that's where you need to go. In the interim those were just my high-level rules to follow when possible.

Of course, some of the ways in which I use Excel don't conform to those principles. And that's fine.

My budgeting worksheet is more of a snapshot of information than a listing of data, so it doesn't follow most of these rules because it's a report. But my worksheet that lists all vendor payments for the year? You bet it's formatted using this approach.

I bring this up because it's important before you start collecting and entering data into Excel that you think about how you might use that data. Are you just wanting to display this information? Or do you want to analyze it?

When in doubt, assume that you'll want to analyze your information at some point and structure everything accordingly. Here is a good example of data that is formatted in a way that in can be easily analyzed:

	A	B	C	D
1	Customer Name	Amount Paid	Date	Customer Satisfaction Rating
2	Customer A	$ 250.00	January 1, 2020	3
3	Customer B	$ 125.00	February 3, 2022	4
4	Customer C	$ 132.00	June 1, 2021	5
5	Customer D	$ 287.00	July 8, 2020	3
6				
7				

It's not that you can't work with data that isn't set up using the rules above, it's just that it's harder to do.

Okay, now that we have that out of the way, what are some tricks you should know to make inputting or deleting data easier?

Enter Information In A Cell

To enter information or data into a cell in Excel, click into that cell and just start typing or paste in whatever it is you want to enter.

Edit Information In A Cell - F2

If there is already data in that cell and you want to edit it, I find using the F2 key helps. The F2 key will take you to the end of the contents of that cell. And then you can use the arrow keys to move within the contents of the cell and make whatever edits you need to make.

This is useful for when you don't want to completely overwrite what's already in there. For example, I sometimes will forget a closing paren when I enter a formula. Going to that cell, using F2, and then typing that closing paren is the quickest way to fix that issue.

However, not every computer is set up to have F2 be the default. I've had to change that on each new laptop I've bought over the last five years or so. If that's the case and your key that says F2 is actually controlling the volume on your computer, then you'll need to use the Fn key and the F2 key together.

Edit Information in A Cell – Other Options

Another option is to click on the cell and then click into the formula bar and edit the text that way. Once more, you can use the arrow keys to move through what's already there once you're clicked into that cell. Or you can click into the point in those cell contents where you want to make your edit.

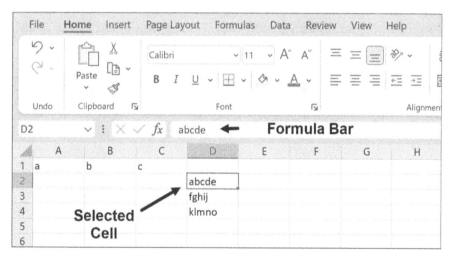

If you are working with formulas and cell references, when you click into the formula bar each cell reference will be color-coded and the corresponding cell in the worksheet will share that color.

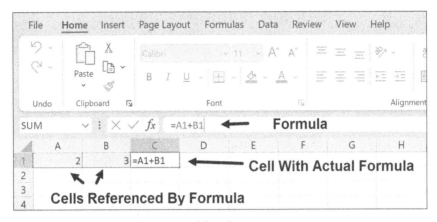

Undo

To undo something when you make a mistake, use Ctrl + Z. Learn this one.. Trust me.

I sometimes think I've done something the right way and as soon as I finish, I realize I was mistaken. Ctrl + Z quickly gets me back to where I was before I made that mistake.

And sometimes undoing what you did (like a bad sort that didn't include all columns) is the only way to safely fix things.

If you don't want to use that control shortcut, you can also click on the Undo option in the Undo section of the Home tab. It looks like an arrow pointing counter-clockwise.

That also gives you the option, if you click on the dropdown arrow instead, to undo multiple steps at once.

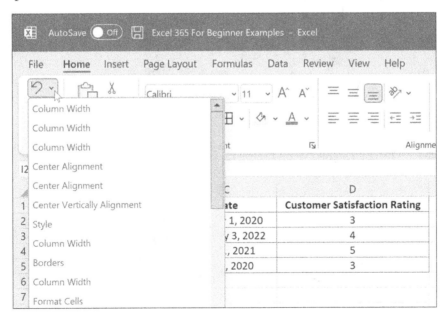

You can see the steps I took to create that data table in the image above. If I click on one of the items at the bottom of that list, Excel will undo every step from that point forward. So if I scroll down and find "Typing 'Customer Name' in A1" and click on that, it erases the table entirely and the worksheet goes back to how it was at that point in time.

Redo

Of course, you may find that you undo something that you didn't want to undo and have to bring it back. That's what Redo (Ctrl + Y) is for. That will bring back one step. But you can also go to the Undo section of the Home tab and click on the dropdown for Redo, which is an arrow rotating clockwise, and then choose from that list to bring back as many steps as you need to.

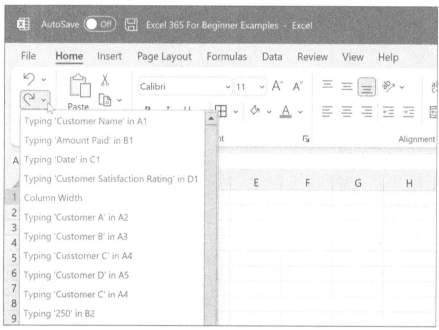

So I would scroll to the end of that list there and choose the very last option to restore my entire table.

Esc

Another handy tool to keep in mind is using the Esc key. Sometimes I will start entering information in a cell and then accidentally click somewhere I don't want to or in some other way get stuck doing something I don't want to be doing. If I'm mid-mistake, I use Esc to back up.

It basically says, "Oops, just kidding, let me stop doing this and go back, thanks." It comes in especially handy when working with formulas when an inadvertent click can change a formula in a way you did not want.

Use Auto-Suggested Text

If you're inputting a lot of data directly into Excel and that data is repetitive, auto-suggested text can save you a ton of time.

What it does is looks at the values you've already entered into a column and suggests how to complete an entry for you.

So if I'm selling Widgets, Whatchamacallits, and Whatsits and I have five hundred rows of data to enter, I don't have to type each full word each time.

I can start to type Widgets, W-I, and Excel will suggest that word for me if I've already used it. Like here:

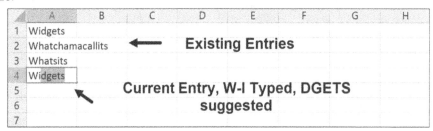

For that fourth entry, all I've typed so far are the W and the I, but Excel looked at the list of entries I already made and tried to complete the entry for me. I can ignore it and just keep typing or I can hit Enter to accept the suggestion. I only had to type two letters instead of seven, which is a great time-saver.

Now, there are some caveats here.

It tends to only look at entries that are connected. Meaning, if I had tried to type W-I in Row 5 but left Row 4 blank, Excel wouldn't make a suggestion. Unless I had a column next to this one that already had continuous entries in Rows 1 through 5. Basically, Excel needs some way to presume that the cell you're entering data into now is connected to the one above it before it will make a suggestion.

Also, what you type has to be unique for Excel to make a suggestion. So when I type W-I, Excel says "Widgets". But if I type "W-H" it's not going to do anything because that could be either Whatsits or Whatchamacallits. I'd have to type W-H-A-T-S or W-H-A-T-C before Excel suggested a word for me.

If you can, keep this in mind when creating your values. Because using Customer A, Customer B, Customer C doesn't save you any time. But using A Customer, B Customer, and C Customer would. (And if you find that funky, you could always later use data manipulation to turn "B Customer" into "Customer B" after you'd saved yourself a bunch of time inputting those entries.)

Excel also doesn't tend to be very good with pulling in rare values. Here, for example, I entered Whatchamacallit as my value for about 440 entries and then tried to type Widgets. I had to type W-I-D-G-E-T before Excel finally suggested Widgets as my value.

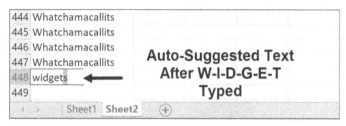

Excel also won't make suggestions for numeric values. So even if you have an entry like 123TRE, it won't even try to suggest a value until that first letter is typed. But once the first letter is typed it will look for a word to suggest.

Again, keep this in mind when coming up with values that you might input. You will save more time if you have TRE123 instead of 123TRE as the customer identifier as long as TRE is somewhat unique and you don't use TRE123, TRE456, TRE789. In which case you'd be better off sticking with 123TRE, 456TRE, and 789TRE.

Despite how confusing I probably just made that sound, it really is helpful when inputting values.

Copy Patterns or Repeated Entries

In the next chapter we'll discuss copying data in detail, but this is more of a tip related to inputting your data, so I wanted to cover it here.

Excel has the ability to recognize patterns. For example, let's say that you wanted to create a data table that shows your income for each month of a year. So you want Column A to have January, February, March, etc.

That is a pattern that Excel can recognize. Which means you do not have to enter all twelve months. You can actually type just January into the first cell, click back onto that cell, and then left-click and drag down from the bottom right corner. Your cursor should look like a little black plus sign as you do this and as you drag past each cell Excel is going to show you the value it predicts for that cell.

Here, for example, I have dragged down to Row 4 and Excel is telling me that will be April. As I dragged past Row 2 it showed February and for Row 3 it showed March.

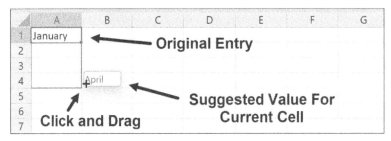

When I let up on that left-click and drag, Excel will then populate all of those fields for me. Like so:

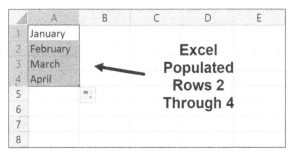

All I had to do was give Excel the start of the pattern. It took it from there.

Now that was click and drag. But if you already have other entries in your data table, then you don't even have to do that. You can double-left click on that bottom right corner and if Excel can see how far to take the entries down it will populate all those rows for you.

Here, for example, I have twelve rows that already have a year entered:

	A	B	C	D	E	F	G
1	January	2020					
2		2020					
3		2020					
4		2020		**Double-Left Click**			
5		2020		**Here to Have Excel**			
6		2020		**Complete Row 2**			
7		2020		**Through 12**			
8		2020					
9		2020					
10		2020					
11		2020					
12		2020					

All I have to do is double left-click in the bottom right corner of the cell that says January in it and Excel does the rest for me.

Sometimes, though, you may just want to copy values down instead. For example, when I bring in my monthly sales reports from my various vendors I always add two columns, one for Month, and one for Year. In the first row of my data I put the Month and Year values. I then highlight both of those sells and double-left click in the corner.

Excel does its thing and populates the values for Month and Year for the rest of the entries in that table (which can be hundreds of entries). But it tries to turn them into a series. So January 2020 is followed by February 2021, etc.

	A	B	C	D	E	F	G
1	Month	Year	Date				
2	January	2020	1/2/2020				
3	February	2021	1/2/2020				
4	March	2022	1/2/2020				
5	April	2023	1/2/2020				
6	May	2024	1/2/2020				
7	June	2025	1/2/2020		Change To		
8	July	2026	1/2/2020		Copy Cells to		
9	August	2027	1/2/2020		Copy Down		
10	September	2028	1/2/2020		First Row		
11	October	2029	1/2/2020		Values		
12	November	2030	1/2/2020				
13							
14			○ Copy Cells				
15			◉ Fill Series				
16			○ Fill Formatting Only				
17			○ Fill Without Formatting				
18			○ Fill Months				
19							

That's not what I want. But it's an easy fix. I can click on the dropdown arrow for that Auto Fill Options that shows at the bottom right side of the series in the workspace and change the option from Fill Series to Copy Cells. That immediately changes all those values to January 2020 which is what I want. It's faster than copying the top entries, selecting all the other cells, then pasting, especially when there are a lot of entries. Although that works, too. (And is discussed in the next chapter.)

The examples I just showed you are for copying a pattern down a column, but it works just as well across a row. So you could write Monday in Cell A1 and then click and drag to the right from the bottom right corner of that cell to get the rest of the days of the week.

Excel can also recognize custom patterns, but you usually have to give it more than one entry for that. And it seems to be better with numbers than letters. So I can enter Customer 123, Customer 124, Customer 125, and then get it to predict Customer 126 and so on, but if I use Customer A, Customer B, Customer C, it can't see that pattern.

So sometimes it will help, sometimes it won't. But when it does help it's very helpful.

Display the Contents of a Cell As Text

Excel tries to be helpful, but sometimes it fails miserably. There's a reason there are numerous jokes on the internet about Excel mistaking things for dates. If you get anywhere close to entering information that it thinks might be a date, it will transform that entry into a numeric date and format it accordingly.

For example, I sometimes want to have "January 2020" in a cell in my worksheet as a label. As soon as I type that into that cell and hit Enter, Excel turns it into a date with a day of the week included.

My text entry of "January 2020" displays as Jan-20 in that cell and in the formula bar you can see it listed as 1/1/2020.

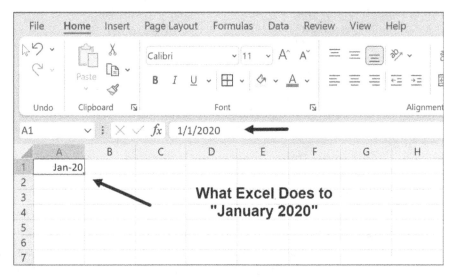

Not what I want.

The other time this happens is if you ever try to start an entry in a cell with a dash (-), a plus sign (+), or an equals sign (=), all of which Excel interprets as the beginning of a formula.

So if I want to use "- Item A" in a cell, I can't just type that in that cell. Excel will get very confused and give me a #NAME? error.

To keep Excel from reacting this way, you can type a single quote mark (') before the contents of the cell. If you do that, Excel will treat whatever you enter after that as text and will keep the formatting type as General. It also won't think that you're entering a formula in that cell that requires it to make a calculation.

For example, if you want to have June 2020 display in a cell in your worksheet, you need to type:

'June 2020

Not just

June 2020

If you want to have

- Item A

display in a cell, you need to type it as

'- Item A

The single quote mark will not be visible when you look at that cell in your worksheet or when you print the data from your worksheet. It is only visible in the formula bar when you've selected that cell. Like so:

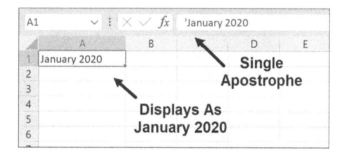

Include Line Breaks In a Cell

Another thing you might find yourself wanting to do is to include text in a cell but have it break across lines. So, for example, you may want an entry that looks like this:

where the A, the B, and the C are all on separate lines. You can't just use Enter because that will take you to the next cell. What you have to do is use Alt + Enter. So hold down the Alt key as you hit Enter and that will create a line break within the cell.

Delete Data

To delete information you've entered into a single cell, simply click into that cell and use the Delete key. You can delete the text in more than one cell at a time the same way. Just select all of those cells and then use the Delete key.

This deletes the contents of the cell, but leaves the cell where it is.

You can also double-click on a cell or use F2 to get to the end of the contents in a cell and then use your computer's backspace key to delete the contents of a cell one character at a time.

Or you can click on a cell and then go to the formula bar and select a portion of the cell contents and then use Delete or Backspace.

Clear Cell Formatting

When you delete the the contents of a cell that does not remove the formatting that's been applied to that cell.

To delete the contents of a cell as well as the formatting, select the cell(s), go to the Editing section of the Home tab, click on the dropdown next to the Clear option, and choose to Clear All.

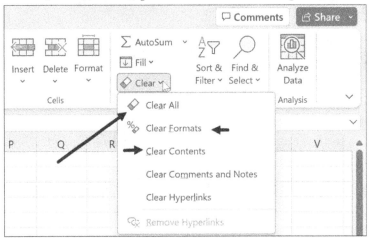

You can also choose to just Clear Formats or Clear Contents using that same dropdown menu.

Find and Replace

Find will locate whatever it is you're searching for. Replace takes that one step further and locates that entry and then replaces it with whatever you designate.

I don't use replace often in Excel, because I'm usually dealing with data entries and I don't want to risk messing those up. But I do use find fairly often to get to a particular entry in a data table.

(Another option, which we'll cover more later, is filtering. That one is best for displaying a subset of your data, especially when find would return more than one result.)

But back to find and replace. Let's walk through an example using replace.

Above I mentioned that typing in A Customer instead of Customer A would let Auto-Suggested text work in your favor. But having entries that say "A Customer" feels awkward. I could enter all of my entries using A Customer and then use Replace to change those over to Customer A. That's one way to fix that after the fact.

Here are some random entries to work with:

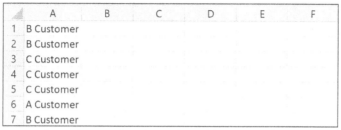

I actually have 51 rows of entries randomly assigned between A Customer, B Customer, and C Customer. I want to change those over to Customer A, Customer B, and Customer C.

Either Ctrl + F or Ctrl + H will open the Find and Replace dialogue box. Ctrl + F will open it to the Find tab, Ctrl + H will open it to the Replace tab.

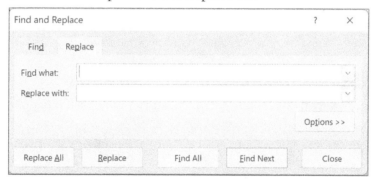

If you don't want to use the control shortcuts or you forget them, you can go to the Editing section of the Home tab and click on the dropdown arrow for Find & Select and then choose either Find or Replace from there.

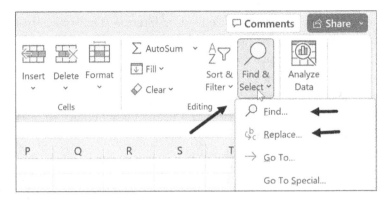

That will also open the same dialogue box.

The entries we're dealing with here are very basic. So we could probably just type A Customer in the Find What field and Customer A in the Replace With field and be fine clicking on Replace All.

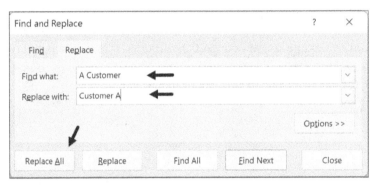

And, sure enough, that worked just fine on the 19 entries in my list that said A Customer. You can see two of those entries here are now Customer A.

But you have to be careful with Replace. Because it is not, by default case sensitive. And it also does not, by default, look for whole words. So if I'd had entries that were AA Customer, for example, and I did a replace for A Customer, those entries would be changed, too. I would end up with entries that said ACustomer A, which is not what I want.

The way to make sure that Excel only replaces what you want it to replace is to click on that Options button to expand the Find and Replace dialogue box. Here is what that will look like:

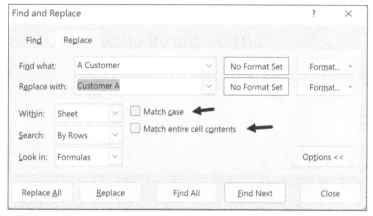

If I check the box for Match Entire Cell Contents, that addresses the issue with AA Customer versus A Customer. And if I check Match Case, that makes sure that if I have a paragraph of text in that worksheet that discusses "how a customer may want to...", I don't inadvertently replace that and end up with "how Customer A may want to..."

Replace in Excel is a fairly blunt tool as it currently exists. It is far more refined in Word where I do use it often. But wherever you use it, be sure you've really thought through what the replacement you're making will actually do to your contents.

When in doubt, you can use the Find option first to see which entries your current criteria capture. Here I clicked over to the Find tab, typed in my text, B Customer, under Find What, and then clicked on Find All. The Value column shows the contents of each cell in its entirety.

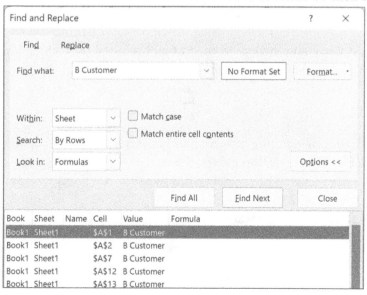

You can click on each entry in that list to go to it.

If you just want to walk through your results, you can use Find Next instead.

Turn Off Scroll Lock

On occasion I will find that navigating in Excel isn't working the way I'm used to. I arrow and things don't move like they should. When this happens, it's usually because Scroll Lock somehow was turned on. The way to turn it back off is to click on the Scroll Lock key on your keyboard.

Unfortunately, I haven't had a computer with a Scroll Lock key in probably a decade, so you have to open a virtual keyboard to do this. Use the Windows key (the one with four squares to the left of your spacebar) + Ctrl + O to open it.

(Another option is to go through your Start menu to Settings and search for keyboard there and then toggle the on-screen keyboard to on.)

The keyboard will appear on your screen. The Scroll Lock key (ScrLk) should be colored when it's turned on. It's one of the right-hand-side options on the keyboard:

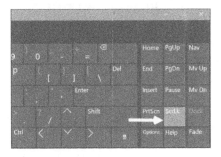

Click on it to turn it off and then close the virtual keyboard by clicking on the X in the top corner. Excel will return to acting normally.

* * *

Okay. That's the basics of entering information into Excel. I do still want to talk about how you enter formulas in Excel, but I'm going to save that for its own chapter where we discuss formulas at a very high-level. (For the detailed discussion you'll want to read *102 Useful Excel 365 Functions*.)

Now let's talk about copying, pasting, and moving data around.

Copy, Paste, and Move Data

Now that you know how to enter data into an Excel workbook it's time to talk about how you can move that data around.

Before we dive in on copy, cut, paste, etc. I want to refresh you on how to select cells. It was covered in the terminology section, but in case anyone skipped that...

Select Data

To select one cell, click on it or arrow to it.

To select multiple cells that are next to one another, go to a cell at the outer end of that range, hold down the Shift key, and then use the arrow keys to select your cells. Or left-click and drag with your mouse to select the remaining cells you want. You can select across rows, columns or both rows and columns.

To select multiple cells that are not next to one another, click on the first cell you want, and then hold down the Ctrl key as you click on the other cells you want. You cannot use the arrow keys for this one.

To select an entire column, click on the letter for that column.

To select an entire row, click on the number for that column.

To select multiple rows or columns it works the same as for cells. Shift and arrow or left-click and drag if they're next to each other, Ctrl if they aren't.

Select All

If you want to select all of the data in a worksheet, go to that worksheet and then use Ctrl + A.

If you don't want to use Ctrl + A, you can also click in the top left corner where the columns and rows meet.

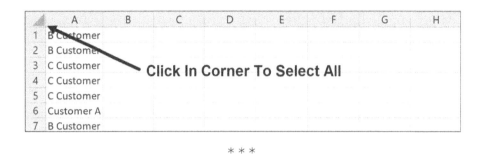

* * *

Now that you know how to select cells, rows, columns, or data, we can talk about copy, paste, and moving things around.

Copy and Move Data As Is To One Location

Let's start with copying data from one location to another without any special changes to that data.

When you Copy you leave an original version of the data where it was and you take that exact same data and you put a copy in a different location.

By default that data will transfer with all of its formatting. And if there were any formulas in the data you selected those formulas will move as well. (We'll come back to formulas more in the formulas section.)

So to copy and move data as is, first, select the data you want to copy.

Next, the easiest way to copy is to just use Ctrl + C. (If you only memorize a handful of Ctrl shortcuts, make this one of them.) That will take a copy of your data for you.

Go to where you want to put that data, click into the first cell in that range, and hit Enter.

Here, for example, I have copied the data from Cells A1 through A6 to Cells E1 through E6.

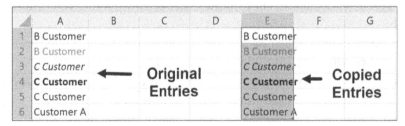

So I selected Cells A1 through A6, used Ctrl + C, went to Cell E1, and hit Enter. All of the text and all of the formatting copied over.

If you didn't want to use a Ctrl shortcut there are a number of other ways to access the copy option. One is to right-click on the selected cells and choose Copy from the dropdown menu.

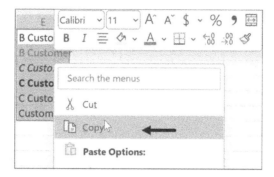

Another is to go to the Clipboard section of the Home tab and click on the Copy option from there.

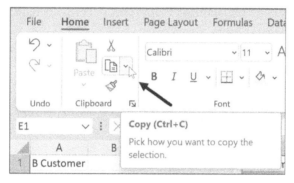

Copy and Move Data As Is To Multiple Locations

If you want to copy and move the same data but to multiple locations, then you'll want to use the Paste function instead of Enter to place the data in each new location.

So copy it the same as before, but when you click into the first cell of the new range use Ctrl + V instead to paste the data. (This is another Ctrl shortcut you should absolutely memorize.)

Look at these copied and pasted entries. It may be a little hard to see, but the copied entries have a dotted line around them:

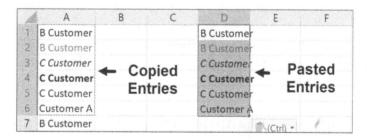

This means that they are still copied even though I pasted them once into Column D, so I can go to another location and paste them again. As long as I use Ctrl + V (or one of the other ways to paste that I'll discuss in just a moment) I can put that copied data into as many locations as I want.

When you are done copying your data, use the Esc key to turn that off. Typing into a new cell will work as well.

Just like with Copy, Paste can also be found by right-clicking on the selected cell(s) or going to the Clipboard section of the Home tab.

Move Data To A New Location

If you don't want to take a copy of your data, but instead want to move that data to somewhere new so that there's just that one copy of the data in the new location only, then you need to use Cut. It works the same as Copy, you select your data, Cut, and then go to the new location, and put the data there.

The control shortcut for this is Ctrl + X. (Another good one to memorize.) And it works with either Enter or Ctrl + V at the new location.

But with Cut you are moving that data and you can only move it once. So both Paste and Enter place the data and you're done.

Here is data I Cut from Cells A1 through A6 and Pasted into Cells C1 through C6:

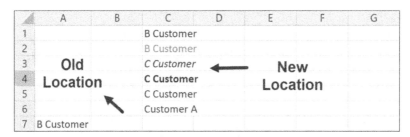

I went to Cells A1 through A6 and selected them, used Ctrl + X, clicked into Cell C1, and used Ctrl + V. Note that there is now no content in Cells A1 through A6. It is only in Cells C1 through C6.

Cutting also takes the cell formatting with it. So if I type a new value in Cell A2 which previously had red text in it, that text is black not red.

You can Cut by selecting the cells and then right-clicking and choosing Cut from the dropdown menu or by going to the Clipboard section of the Home tab. Cut is shown as a pair of scissors in the Clipboard section.

Copying or Cutting Cells With Formulas

If you have formulas in the data you're moving you need to be more careful because the choice to Cut versus the choice to Copy will impact your result, but I'm going to save that for the

Formulas chapter. Just note for now that there is an issue there that you need to be aware of.

Copy and Move Data With Changes

Sometimes you will want to copy just the contents of a cell without keeping any of its formatting. Or you will want to take a list of values in a column and put them into a single row instead. Or maybe you want the results of a formula, but you don't want to keep the formula anymore.

That's where the Paste Special options come in handy.

First, know that you can only use Paste Special if you've copied the contents of a cell (Ctrl + C). These options do not work if you've cut the contents of a cell (Ctrl + X).

To Paste Special, you either need to right-click in the new cell and choose from the Paste Options section in that dropdown menu

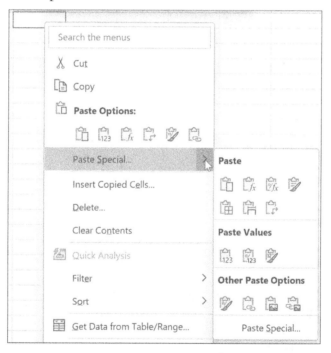

Or you need to click on the dropdown arrow under Paste in the Clipboard section of the Home tab.

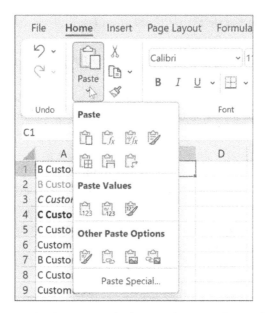

Clicking on Paste Special at the bottom of either of those lists will open the Paste Special dialogue box, but you're rarely going to need that.

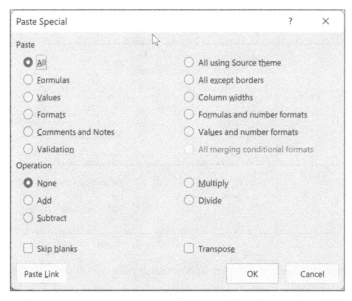

If you use the dropdown menu you can actually see what the result will be by holding your mouse over each option. Here, for example, I have my cursor over Paste Values and you can see that it will paste in the text that I've copied from Column A but without any of the formatting such as bolding, italics, or red text color.

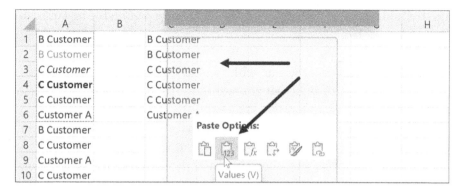

And here is what Paste Transpose looks like in preview:

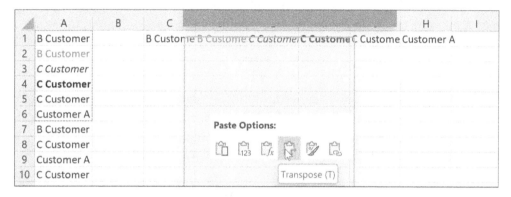

Those are the two paste options I use the most.

Paste Values has a 123 in the bottom corner of the clipboard image and what it lets you do is copy entries and then just paste those values. This is incredibly useful when working with formulas. For example, I would've probably fixed that transform B Customer to Customer B problem using one of two functions, TEXTJOIN or CONCATENATE. But that means I would've been doing so using a formula. And that formula would have depended on the content of cells in two different columns that I would have wanted to delete.

The only way to delete those columns but keep my "calculation" result would be to copy that column with my final calculation and then paste-values so that I keep the result of the "calculation" but not the formula.

It's also useful when you want the contents of a cell, but would prefer to use the formatting in the destination cell(s). For example, if you're copying from one Excel file to another.

Another way I use it is when I've run a set of calculations on my data, found my values, and now want to sort or do something else with my data but don't want to risk having the values change on me.

I will highlight the entire data set, copy, and then paste special-values right over the top of my existing data. (Just be sure to type Esc after you do this so that the change is fixed in place.)

I often do that when dealing with pivot tables. I'll create a pivot table to summarize my data, but then I copy that table and paste-special so that it's no longer a pivot table but just the calculated values.

The Paste Transpose option—the one with two sets of arrows in the bottom corner—is very useful if you have a row of data that you want to turn into a column of data or a column of data that you want to turn into a row.

Like in the screenshot above where you can see that my six entries that were in a column would be in a single row across six columns if I chose that option.

Just be sure before you paste that there isn't any data that will be overwritten when you paste your entries, because Excel won't warn you before it overwrites it.

There are a lot more paste options available, but those are the two main ones I use. I do also use paste formatting, but I do that through the Format Painter option in the Clipboard section of the Home tab. We'll discuss that more when we talk about how to format your data.

* * *

Now let's talk about another way to move around your data which is by inserting cells, rows, and columns. Also, I want to talk about worksheets a bit more, namely renaming them to reflect what they contain and also moving or copying them.

I'm going to start with worksheets, because that's the easiest part.

Rename a Worksheet

To rename an Excel worksheet, double-click on the worksheet name, and then start typing the new name you want to use. If you change your mind, use the Esc key to back out.

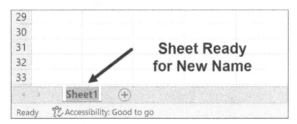

You can also right-click on the tab with the name and choose Rename from the dropdown menu.

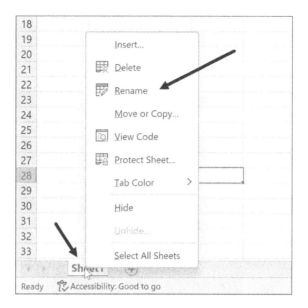

There are rules to naming worksheets. It can't be blank. It also has to be 31 character or less. And those characters cannot include / \ ? * : [or] and the worksheet name cannot begin or end with an apostrophe ('). Also, no worksheet can be named History because behind the scenes Excel already has one of those in each worksheet.

Don't worry too much about those rules. In more recent versions of Excel they just won't let you type those prohibited characters. And if you accidentally leave the name blank it will show a dialogue box telling you there's an error with the name. You just need to click OK on that and type in an actual name. Use Esc to go back to the original name.

Add a Worksheet

To add a new worksheet you can click on the little plus sign next to the last existing worksheet. That will add a worksheet to the right of the last worksheet you were clicked on.

Or you can go to the Cells section of the Home tab, click on the dropdown arrow under Insert, and choose Insert Sheet. That will insert a worksheet to the left of the one you were clicked on before you chose that option.

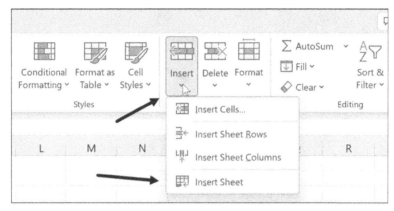

Move a Worksheet

To move a worksheet, left-click on the tab for the worksheet name and drag the worksheet to where you want it. As you move the worksheet there will be a little arrow pointing at the spot between the two worksheets where it would move to.

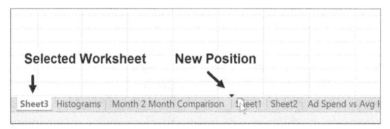

You can also right-click on the worksheet name and choose the Move or Copy option. That will bring up the Move or Copy dialogue box.

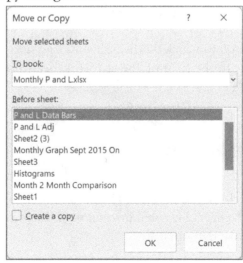

Click on the name of the worksheet you want to place the worksheet *before* and then click on OK. If you want to move a worksheet to another workbook you can do that from the Move or Copy dialogue box as well. Just change the option under To Book using that dropdown. Your available options will be a new Excel workbook or any Excel workbooks that are currently open.

Copy a Worksheet

You can also use the Move or Copy dialogue box to make a copy of a worksheet. I often will do this to put a copy of a worksheet I create in one workbook in a new workbook. To do so, click on the Create a Copy checkbox.

Here I've done so and selected to copy it to a new workbook using the dropdown menu choices. I just need to click OK to make that happen.

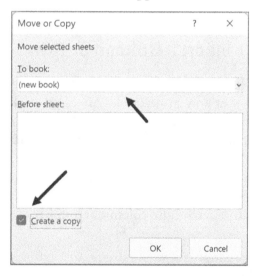

If you are moving or copying a worksheet to a new workbook and it includes formulas that reference other worksheets in the old workbook it will continue to reference to the old workbook. So be very careful about that, because if someone doesn't have access to the old workbook, those formulas aren't going to work for them.

(In general, I think it's best to keep everything contained in one workbook when working with formulas, but I know there are situations where that isn't possible. All I can say is, if you're going to have formulas that work across workbooks do so deliberately not just because it was a sloppy error.)

Delete a Worksheet

You can also delete a worksheet. To do so, right-click on the worksheet name and choose Delete from the dropdown menu.

Or you can go to the Cells section of the Home tab, click on the dropdown arrow for Delete, and choose Delete Sheet from there.

If the worksheet was blank, Excel will just delete it. If it contains any data Excel will show you a pop-up window asking you to confirm that you want to delete that worksheet. Be sure you really want to delete that worksheet, because you won't be able to undo it if you change your mind later.

* * *

That was worksheets, now let's talk about inserting and deleting columns, rows, and cells.

Insert a Column or Row

You only need to insert a column or row if you already have data in your worksheet and realize that you want a new column or row in the midst of that data that already exists. (Because, remember, the number of columns and rows in a worksheet is constant. So when you "insert" a column or row what you're really doing is just shifting around your existing data on that column and row map. You're taking data in Column A and moving it to Column B, but the total of columns in the worksheet isn't going to change.)

You have a number of options for this one.

I usually right-click on the letter for the column or number for the row and choose Insert from the dropdown menu.

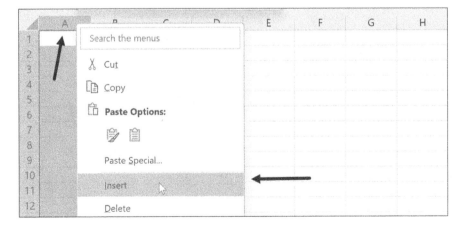

This will, for columns, insert a new column where I right-clicked and shift all of the data that was in that column previously or that was in any column to the right of that column over by one column. So if I right-click on Column B, all data that was in Column B is now in Column C, all data from Column C moves to Column D, etc.

You can insert multiple columns using this approach. Left-click on the column where you want to insert those new columns and then drag until you've selected the desired number of new columns to insert. Right-click and choose Insert from the dropdown. That should insert X number of columns and shift everything to the right.

Here you can see this for rows.

I selected Rows 2 through 6, then right-clicked and chose Insert. That moved the values from Rows 2 and 3 (the numbers 6 through 10 and 11 through 15) down that many rows so that they are now in Rows 7 and 8. Rows are always added above the selection, so everything shifts down.

You can also insert a column or row by right-clicking in a single cell that's in that row or column and choosing Insert from the dropdown menu. Excel won't know whether you want to insert a cell, row, or column, so it will show you the Insert dialogue box.

Click Entire Row or Entire Column and then choose OK to insert a row or column, respectively.

Your final option is to select a row or column or click into a cell in that row or column and then go to the Cells section of the Home tab and choose Insert Sheet Rows or Insert Sheet Columns from the dropdown menu.

Insert a Cell

Inserting a cell works much the same way. Click where you want to insert that cell, right-click, and choose Insert. Or click where you want to insert that cell and go to the Cells section of the Home tab, click on the Insert dropdown arrow, and choose Insert Cells.

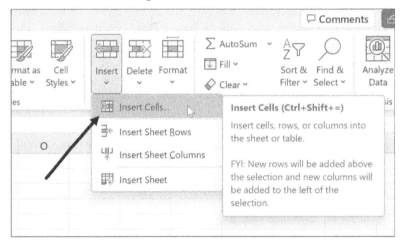

There is one quirk with inserting cells, however, and that's that you have to tell Excel whether to shift things to the right or to shift things down to make room. So you will always see the Insert dialogue box.

If you choose to Shift Cells Right, all data in that row with that cell will move to the right one column. If you choose to Shift Cells Down, all data in that column with that cell will move down one row.

Which you want will depend on the data you already have in your worksheet and why you're adding this cell.

You can insert multiple cells at once, which is what I often do. Just select the cell range first (left-click and drag) and then choose to insert.

Be careful when adding cells into a worksheet as opposed to entire rows or columns. I have, more than once, added say five cells and shifted my data but forgotten that I had other data in that same column or row in my worksheet and accidentally moved my data out of alignment.

So when adding cells, check first to see what is impacted. And check again after to make sure everything looks okay. If you get it wrong, Ctrl + Z, for Undo, is your friend. It will undo what you just did and let you try again. (Ctrl + Y is Redo if you ever undo something and decide that wasn't necessary.)

Delete Rows, Columns, or Cells

Deleting works just like inserting. Select the row, column, or cells that you want to delete and then either right-click and choose Delete from the dropdown or go to the Cells section of the Home tab, click on the dropdown for Delete, and choose your option there.

As with inserting cells, when you delete cells you should see a dialogue box that looks just like the insert one except it's talking about deleting. You will again need to decide whether to shift cells, this time left and up are the two choices.

So look at your other data and decide what to do. You may need to delete a range of cells instead of one single cell to keep everything in alignment.

If you select a range of cells and try to use the Delete key that will just delete your data, but the cells will remain there so none of the rest of your data will move.

Also, be careful with deleting rows, columns, or cells that have data in them. Check any formulas in your worksheet to see if deleting that data impacted those formulas. It will usually show up as a #REF! error.

Here, for example, I had a value in Cell A1 and a value in Cell B1 that were then added together in Cell C1. When I deleted Column A, that removed that value that was being used in the formula so the formula no longer works.

Note also that the value that was in Cell B1 moved to Cell A1 and that my formula that was in Cell C1 moved to Cell B1. Everything shifted one column. (One of the nice things about Excel is that the formula automatically updated to reflect that shift. So the formula now shows A1 not B1 for that second value location.)

Formulas and Functions

We've touched on formulas and functions a couple of times now, but I've set that aside each time. If you really want to dig in on formulas and functions in Excel I wrote a whole book about it that includes over a hundred different Excel functions and how each one works, *102 Useful Excel 365 Functions*.

But formulas are such a key part of working in Excel that I also want to talk about them here. So some of what I'm going to cover here duplicates the introductory material in that book. But it's a higher-level discussion than you get there. And we certainly are not going to cover a hundred functions here.

Cell Notation

Before we can move forward with a discussion of formulas, we need to talk in more depth about cell notation because cell notation is how you tell Excel where your data is for your formula.

I already discussed in the terminology section how each cell is identified by the combination of its Column and Row and that you should think of that as map coordinates. So Cell A1 is the first column, first row of a worksheet.

Within Excel when you are referencing that cell, you leave off the Cell portion. So you just write A1.

You can also reference multiple cells at once. To reference a cell range, so all the cells between X point and Y point, you use a colon to separate the first coordinate from the last. If I write

A1:A25

that's all cells between Cell A1 and Cell A25. If I write

A1:B25

that's all cells in Columns A and B and from Rows 1 through 25.

If you want to reference cells that aren't touching or that don't form a clean rectangular shape, then you need to use commas to separate the cells or ranges.

$$A1,B2,C3$$

would be referencing Cells A1, B2, and C3. And

$$A1:A3,B1:B6$$

would be referencing the combination of Cells A1 through A3 and Cells B1 through B6.

Excel also has ways of identifying which worksheet those cells are in if you're referring to cells in a different worksheet. This is done by writing the name of the worksheet followed by an exclamation point before the cell reference.

$$Sheet2!C19$$

is referring to Cell C19 in the worksheet called Sheet2.

You can also identify which workbook a cell is in using brackets.

$$[Book1]Sheet3!E11$$

is referring to Cell E11 in the worksheet called Sheet3 in the workbook called Book1.

I have never bothered to memorize how to reference worksheets or workbooks, because Excel will write that for you if you start a formula and then go to that workbook or worksheet and select the cells you want to use. So I always let Excel do that heavy lifting for me.

You can also reference an entire column using the : like so:

$$A:A$$

is referencing Column A and

$$A:C$$

is referencing Columns A, B, and C.

Same goes for Rows.

$$1:1$$

is referencing all cells in Row 1

$$1:5$$

is referencing all cells in Rows 1 through 5.

Okay, now that you have an understanding of how to tell Excel where your data is located, let's define formulas and functions.

Definition of Formulas and Functions

For our purposes I'm going to define a formula in Excel as anything that is started with an equals sign and asks Excel to perform a calculation or task.

(Technically, you can start a formula with a plus or a minus sign as well, but I'm just going to ignore that because unless you're coming from a specific background where you learned to do things that way, you shouldn't do that. Also, Excel transforms those formulas into ones that use an equals sign anyway.)

I define a function as a command that is used within a formula to give instructions to Excel to perform a pre-defined task or set of tasks.

Think of a function in Excel as agreed-upon shorthand for some task.

Examples of Formulas and Functions

A formula in Excel could be as basic as:

=A1

It starts with an equals sign and is telling Excel that this particular cell where we've written our formula should have the exact same value as Cell A1. The "task" Excel completes here is pulling in that value.

But usually a formula will be more complex than that. For example:

=SUM(A1,B1,C1)

which could also be written as

=SUM(A1:C1)

is telling Excel to take the values in the specified cells and sum them together. So if the value in Cell A1 is 2, and the value in Cell B1 is 3, and the value in Cell C1 is 4, then this formula would return a value of 9.

You can also combine multiple functions or calculations within a single formula. Each cell can only hold one formula, but that formula can perform multiple tasks. For example,

=ROUND(RAND()*100,0)

is a formula that combines three steps to randomly generate a number between 0 and 100. It includes two functions, RAND and ROUND, as well as one mathematical calculation.

RAND generates a random number between 0 and 1. The *100 part takes that result and turns it into a value between 0 and 100. ROUND takes that result and rounds that number to a whole number.

How to Create a Formula

The basic rules of building a formula are to (a) start with an equals sign, (b) always use an opening paren after a function name, and (c) if you use an opening paren make sure that it's paired with a closing paren.

Functions always require opening and closing parens, but you can also have opening and closing parens when doing pure math, too. So

$$=234*(123+345+(2*3))$$

is a perfectly valid Excel formula that is telling Excel to multiply 2 times 3 and then add that to 123 and 345 and then take that total and multiply it times 234. It's straight out of math class.

Functions normally require additional inputs, but not always. In our example above with ROUND and RAND, RAND is a function that does not use other inputs. It just has an opening paren followed by a closing paren.

But ROUND does have inputs. And everything between that opening paren after ROUND and the closing paren at the end of that formula are those inputs. In the case of RAND the first input is the number to be rounded. In this case, that was the randomly generated number times 100. The second input is how many places to round that number to. Since I wanted a whole number that was 0.

For each function you use, Excel will help you with which inputs are required. If I type

$$=ROUND($$

into Excel, the minute I type that opening paren it tells me what the inputs are that are required for that function. Like so:

If that isn't enough information for me, because maybe I'm not familiar with the function, I

can click on the function name in that little display box and it will open a dialogue box or Help text on the function that gives more information.

Formulas do not have to start with a function or a calculation.

$$=A1+SUM(B1:B5)$$

is a perfectly legitimate formula that takes the value in Cell A1 and adds that to the values in Cells B1 through B5.

Your Result

After you enter your formula in your cell, hit enter or leave the cell by arrowing, using the tab key, or clicking away. That will be when Excel tries to calculate your result.

The cell where you entered your formula will then display the result of the formula.

The formula can still be seen and edited via the formula bar. So if you click back on that cell you will see the value in the cell, but the formula in the formula bar. Like so:

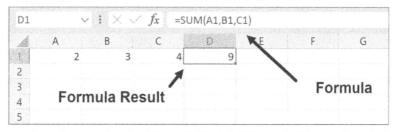

Here you can see that the result of adding Cells A1, B1, and C1 was 9 and that the formula used for that was

$$=SUM(A1,B1,C1)$$

You can also double-click into the cell with the formula or into the formula bar and Excel will color code each cell reference within the formula and within the worksheet so that you can make sure that the right cells were referenced in the formula.

It's a little hard to see in print, but Cells A1, B1, and C1 are each shaded a different color which corresponds to the color they are in the formula bar. This makes it easy to see which cell is being used in which part of a formula. That becomes especially helpful when dealing with very complex formulas.

Be careful moving away from a cell that has a formula in it. The best bet is to exit the cell using Esc. Otherwise sometimes Excel will try to select a new range of cells to use in the formula instead of just leaving the cell. This is especially an issue when using the arrow keys.

When you exit a cell that contains a formula, the cell will return to showing the calculated value not the formula.

Basic Math Calculations

Now let's talk about how to perform some basic math calculations in Excel.

Addition

If you want to add two numerical values together in Excel, you can use the plus sign (+) to indicate addition.

Here I'm adding 2 to 3:

$$=2+3$$

If those values were already showing in other cells, let's say Cells A1 and B1, you could write the formula to reference those cells instead:

$$=A1+B1$$

If you use cell notation, like in the second example there, then any change you make to the values in Cells A1 and B1 will also change the result of your formula because your formula is no longer performing a fixed calculation, like 2+3, but is instead performing a conditional calculation based on what's in Cells A1 and B1.

If you have more than two numbers to add together you can keep using the plus sign, so:

$$=A1+B1+C1$$

would add the values in Cells A1, B1, and C1. But it's better at that point to use the SUM function which will add all values included in the function. So:

$$=SUM(A1:C1)$$

adds the values in Cells A1, B1, and C1 together.

$$=SUM(A:A)$$

adds all the values in Column A.

$$=SUM(1:1)$$

adds all the values in Row 1.

If you ever forget how to write a cell range or to refer to an entire column or row, just start your formula, like this:

$$=SUM($$

and then go select the cells you want. Excel will write the reference for you and then you just need to close out the function with the closing paren.

Subtraction

To subtract one number from another you use the minus (-) sign. There is no function that will make this one easier, because the order of the values matters. Two minus three is not the same as three minus two.

However, you can combine the minus sign with the SUM function. So:

$$=A1-SUM(B1:D1)$$

is the equivalent of

$$=A1-B1-C1-D1$$

Multiplication

To multiply numbers you can use the asterisk (*) sign. Or you can use the function PRODUCT. All of the following will get the same result:

$$=A1*B1$$

$$=PRODUCT(A1:B1)$$

$$=PRODUCT(A1,B1)$$

Division

To divide two numbers you use the forward slash (/). There is no corresponding function because, again, order matters. Two divided by three is not the same as three divided by two. So:

$$=A1/B1$$

is the value in Cell A1 divided by the value in Cell B1.

* * *

To summarize:

Calculation	Numeric Symbol	Function	Examples
Addition	+	SUM	=A1+A2 =SUM(A1:A2)
Subtraction	-		=A1-A2
Multiplication	*	PRODUCT	=A1*A2 =PRODUCT(A1,A2)
Division	/		=A1/A2

A Quick Tip

Often when I just need to see the sum of values in a range of cells, I won't even write a formula or function. I'll just select those cells and look in the bottom right corner of my workspace. By default Excel displays the average, count, and sum of a range of selected cells in the very bottom right corner of the workspace.

(You can right-click where the values are displayed and also choose to have it display minimum and maximum values.)

Where To Find Functions

To find the functions available in Excel, you can go to the Formulas tab. There is a section called Function Library that lists various categories of functions. Mine shows Recently Used, Financial, Logical, Text, Date & Time, Lookup & Reference, Math & Trig, and then there's a dropdown for More Functions that shows the categories Statistical, Engineering, Cube, Information, Compatibility, and Web.

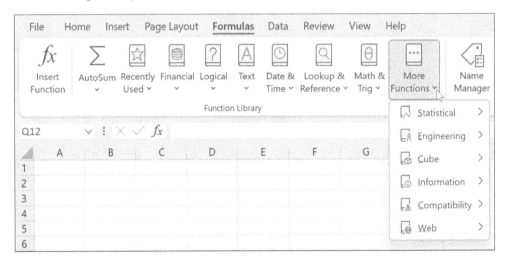

Click on the dropdown arrow under any of the categories and you'll see a listing of functions that fall under that heading. But, unless you know what you're looking for, that listing probably won't help you much because the functions are named things like ACCRINT and IFNA.

You *can* hold your cursor over each of the names and Excel *will* provide a brief description of the function for you, but for some of the lists that's a lot of functions to look through.

Each description also includes a Tell Me More at the end of the description. If you click on that option, the Excel Help task pane should appear. You can then click on the category for that function and choose the function from the list you see there to see further discussion of the function and examples of how to use it.

The level of detail provided varies by function. Sometimes it is very useful to read the Help section for a function and sometimes…it is not.

The approach I normally take instead is to click into the cell where I want to add my formula and then use the Insert Function option available on the far left-hand side of the Formulas tab.

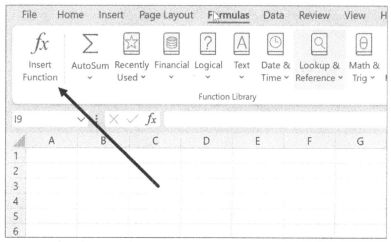

That brings up the Insert Function dialogue box.

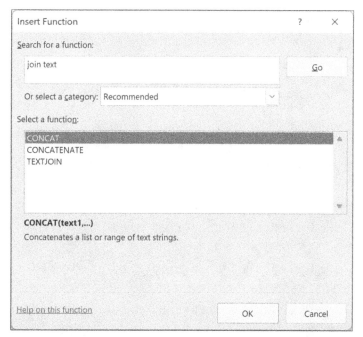

In the top section where it says "Search for a function" you can type what you're looking to do and then click on Go like I have above with "join text". (Be sure that the category dropdown right below the search box is set to All unless you know for sure what category your function falls under. After you click on Go that will turn into Recommended like it did in the image above.)

Excel will provide a list of functions that it thinks meet your search criteria. Sometimes this list is very far off, so don't just accept the first choice blindly.

You can left-click on each of the listed functions to see a brief description of the function directly below the box where the functions are listed. In the image above, that's showing for the CONCAT function.

You will also see in the description for each function a list of the required inputs for that function. For CONCAT that's at least one text entry.

If you need more information on a function, you can click on the "Help on this function" link in the bottom left corner of the dialogue box which will bring up help specific to that function.

Otherwise, you can just click on the function you want and choose OK, which will insert the function into whichever cell you were clicked into before you chose Insert Function. Excel will also open a Function Arguments dialogue box that lists the inputs your function needs and provides a location for you to input those values so that Excel can build your formula for you.

Here is the Function Arguments dialogue box for the TEXTJOIN function:

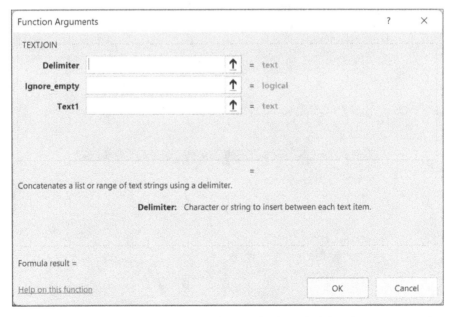

If you use the dialogue box, click into each input field and either input numeric values, cell references, or select the cells you want to use for each field. As you do so, Excel will show you a sample result based upon the inputs you've chosen at the bottom of the dialogue box next to Formula Result.

If you use the dialogue box, when you're done, click OK and the calculated value will appear in your cell.

If you don't want to use the dialogue box, close it out by clicking on OK and then OK on the error message that will appear.

This will give you the function in your cell in a formula format but without any of the required inputs, like so:

=TEXTJOIN()

Your cursor will be in the empty space between the opening and closing parens and you can then manually add the inputs at that point. Excel will show you which inputs are required and in which order.

If you X out the dialogue box instead, you'll just have a blank cell with no function or formula started.

* * *

That's about all I want to cover on how to write formulas and functions in this book. You can do a lot with basic addition, subtraction, multiplication, and division in Excel. And you now have an idea of where to look if you want to get fancier than that. And, of course, the third book in this series, *102 Useful Excel 365 Functions*, is almost two hundred pages long and covers over a hundred of the most useful functions in Excel.

But the other thing we need to cover when it comes to formulas is what makes them really powerful, and that's how you can copy formulas so that they apply to multiple cells.

Let's do that now.

Copying Formulas

The way in which formulas copy in Excel is key to what makes them so powerful. That's because you can write a formula once, copy it, and paste it to thousands of cells, and Excel will automatically adjust that formula to each new location

It's fantastic.

Let's say, for example, that I want to calculate total cost based upon units sold and price per unit for a thousand rows of data. Here are what the first few rows look like:

	A	B	C
1	Units	Cost Per Unit	Total Cost
2	2	$1.65	
3	4	$1.32	
4	3	$6.95	
5	6	$7.80	
6	9	$4.90	

I have units in Column A, cost per unit in Column B, and I want a total cost for each row in Column C.

The formula for Cell C2 in that first row is:

$$=A2*B2$$

Now, here's where the beauty of Excel comes in. I click on Cell C2 where I wrote that formula and then I double-left click in the bottom right corner of that cell and Excel copies my formula down for me.

(I could also use Ctrl + C, select the cell range and then use Ctrl + V or Enter to copy and paste my formula.)

Here's what I now have:

	A	B	C
1	Units	Cost Per Unit	Total Cost
2	2	$1.65	$3.29
3	4	$1.32	$5.28
4	3	$6.95	$20.84
5	6	$7.80	$46.81
6	9	$4.90	$44.11
7	3	$0.82	$2.47

Let's go to the Formula Auditing section of the Formulas tab and click on Show Formulas so we can see what Excel did for us.

	A	B	C
1	Units	Cost Per Unit	Total Cost
2	2	1.6452643749914	=A2*B2
3	4	1.3203471105506	=A3*B3
4	3	6.9475273087147	=A4*B4
5	6	7.80121230326684	=A5*B5
6	9	4.90149762880339	=A6*B6
7	3	0.824543582413774	=A7*B7

As Excel copied that first formula from Cell C2 down to Cells C3, C4, etc. it changed the formula. When the formula was copied one cell down from the original the cell references were updated to also reference cells one down.

So the original formula in Cell C2 used

$$=A2*B2$$

but when that was copied down to Cell C3 Excel changed that to

$$=A3*B3$$

Each cell reference in the formula adjusted relative to the original position.

Which is great for our thousand rows of data. It means we can write that formula once and copy it down and it works for all thousand rows of data.

Perfect.

But there are going to be times when you don't want Excel to adjust your formula for you. When that happens you need to either use fixed cell references or cut the formula and move it instead of copy and paste it. Let's start with fixed cell references.

Fixed Cell References

Let's take this scenario we've been working with and add a fixed 5% tax that needs to apply to every transaction. Here's our new data table:

	A	B	C	D	E	F	G	H
1	Units	Cost Per Unit	Total Cost	With Taxes		Tax Rate	5%	
2	2	$1.65	$3.29	$3.46				
3	4	$1.32	$5.28					
4	3	$6.95	$20.84					
5	6	$7.80	$46.81					
6	9	$4.90	$44.11					

Column D is calculating for that first transaction the total cost when we include a 5% tax. The formula is:

$$=C2*(1+G1)$$

where C2 is the cost before tax and G1 is the tax rate. If I copy that down to the other cells right now, Excel will adjust the cell references for both C2 and G1. I want it to do so for C2, but not for G1. I want every formula in my worksheet to continue to reference that tax rate in Cell G1.

To tell Excel to keep a cell reference fixed, I need to use dollar signs ($). That tells Excel, don't change this one. Keep it as is. And since I want to refer to that one specific cell, then the way to write that is:

$$=C2*(1+\$G\$1)$$

That means don't change the column or the row from G1 when you copy this.

Once I make that change to my formula, I can copy that formula down to all my other rows and have no issue.

	A	B	C	D	E	F	G
1	Units	Cost Per Unit	Total Cost	With Taxes		Tax Rate	0.05
2	2	1.6452643749914	=A2*B2	=C2*(1+$G$1)			
3	4	1.3203471105506	=A3*B3	=C3*(1+$G$1)			
4	3	6.9475273087147	=A4*B4	=C4*(1+$G$1)			
5	6	7.80121230326684	=A5*B5	=C5*(1+$G$1)			

Here you can see that I've double-clicked on Cell D4 to confirm that the formula is still referencing my tax rate in Cell G1. Perfect.

You can fix either the column reference for a cell, the row reference for a cell, or both. Just use the $ sign in front of whichever part of the cell reference you want to fix.

Moving a Formula

What happens if you're perfectly happy with a formula as written, but you just don't want it to display in the cell it's currently in? Sometimes, for example, I'll write a formula below a table of data and then later decide that I'd rather have all calculations off to the side of the table instead of below it.

I can't just copy that formula, because when I copy the formula and move it, all the cell references will change.

The way to get around this is to Cut the formula instead. So click on the original location, Ctrl + X, go to the new location, Ctrl + V. Esc. Or Ctrl + X, go to the new location, Enter.

If you just want the text of the formula as it exists right now but you don't want to move the original calculation, click on the cell, go to the formula bar, use Ctrl + A to select all of the text, use Ctrl + C to copy the selected text, Esc to exit that cell, click on the new location, and then use Ctrl + V to paste the text. (This is, for example, how I've copied the formulas into this book from the sample Excel worksheets where I wrote the formulas.)

* * *

Okay. Now that we've covered inputting your data and formulas, let's talk about how to make your data presentable. Because raw data in Excel is not pretty.

Formatting

If you're going to spend any amount of time working in Excel then you need to learn how to format cells, because inevitably your column won't be as wide as you want it to be or you'll want to have a cell with red-colored text or to use bolding or italics or something that isn't Excel's default.

That's what this section is for. It's an alphabetical listing of different things you might want to do to format your data in Excel.

You can either format one cell at a time by highlighting that specific cell, or you can format multiple cells at once by highlighting all of them and then choosing your formatting option. In some cases, you can also format specific text within a cell by clicking into a cell, selecting that text, and then choosing your formatting option.

There are basically four main ways to format cells or text in current versions of Excel.

First, you can use the Home tab and click on the option you want from there.

Second, you can use the Format Cells dialogue box. Either right-click from the main workspace and select the Format Cells option from the dropdown menu or use Ctrl + 1 to open the dialogue box.

Third, you can right-click from the main workspace and use the mini formatting menu that appears above or below the dropdown menu.

Finally, some of the most popular formatting options can be applied using control shortcuts. For example, Ctrl + B to bold text, Ctrl + I to apply italics, and Ctrl + U to apply a basic underline.

Okay, let's dive right in.

Align Text

By default, text within a cell is left-aligned and bottom-aligned. This won't be noticeable at the default row height and column width, but is definitely noticeable if you change either of those enough.

The easiest way to apply alignment to a cell is to go to the Alignment section on the Home tab. There are two rows of lines there on the left-hand side that visually show your choices. The top row contains Top, Middle, and Bottom alignment choices. The second row contains Left, Center, and Right. You can choose one option from each row.

In the screenshot below I've clicked on Cell B2 where I've chosen Middle Align and Center. You can see those options selected in the Alignment section of the Home tab.

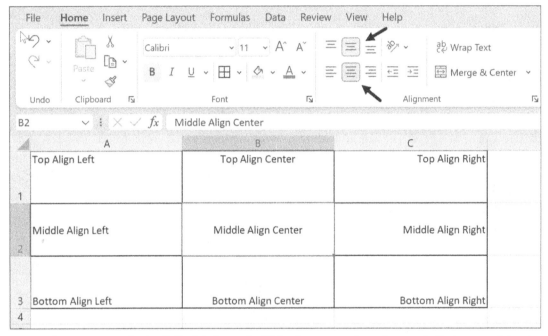

You can also see examples in Cells A1 through C3 in the screenshot above of all nine combinations.

The second-best choice for applying alignment is to use the Alignment tab of the Format Cells dialogue box. The Horizontal and Vertical alignment dropdown menus will give you the same choices as well as a few others that you're unlikely to use.

The mini formatting bar includes an option for centering your text, but that's the only alignment option it includes.

Angle Text

You can choose to angle your text in various ways using the dropdown menu under the angled "ab" with an arrow under it on the top row of the Alignment section of the Home tab.

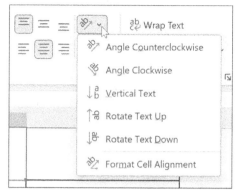

It has a handful of pre-defined options for changing the direction of text within a cell. You can choose Angle Counterclockwise, Angle Clockwise, Vertical Text, Rotate Text Up, and Rotate Text Down.

(It also offers another way to access the Alignment tab of the Format Cells dialogue box by clicking on Format Cell Alignment at the bottom of that dropdown menu.)

The Format Cells dialogue box lets you specify an exact degree for angling your text. So if you want to angle text at say a 30 degree angle, you'd need to do that in the Format Cells dialogue box. You can either enter that value in the Degrees field or click on a point in the Orientation box.

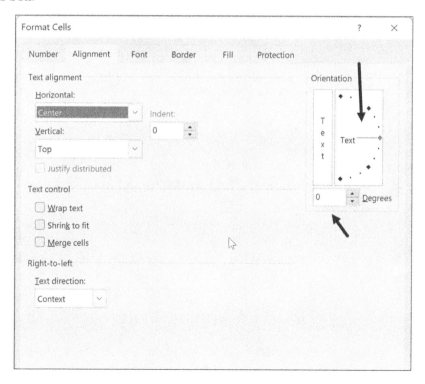

Bold Text

You can bold text in a number of ways. For each option below, select the text within a cell that you want to bold or the entire cell or cells first.

My default is to use Ctrl + B.

Another quick option is to click on the large capital B in the Font section of the Home tab.

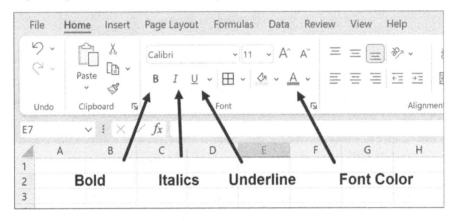

Or you can choose the capital B from the mini formatting toolbar.

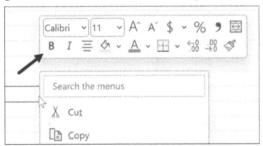

Your final option is to go to the Font tab of the Format Cells dialogue box and choose Bold from the Font Style options listing. If you want text that is both bolded and italicized, choose Bold Italic.

To remove bolding, you use the same options again (Ctrl + B or click on the capital B). If the selected text is only partially bolded when you do so, Excel will bold everything first so you'll have to do it twice. You can also go to the Format Cells dialogue box and change the Font Style to Regular.

Borders Around Cells

Placing borders around your data allows for better distinction between each cell and is something I do almost always when I create a data table. It's also very helpful when you print data from Excel, because that background grid that you see when working in Excel isn't actually present when you print.

Let me show you.

Here are those alignment choices pictured above as seen in Excel with no border around the individual cells. You can see that there is a faint line around each cell, right?

	A	B	C	D	E
1	Top Align Left	Top Align Center	Top Align Right		
2	Middle Align Left	Middle Align Center	Middle Align Right		
3	Bottom Align Left	Bottom Align Center	Bottom Align Right		
4					
5					
6					

Here is the print preview of the first two columns of that image:

Top Align Left	Top Align Center
Middle Align Left	Middle Align Center

Note how the borders are no longer showing on the page? That's because the default cell borders that you see when working in Excel do not print. You have to add your own borders if you want your data to print with borders around it.

For the final comparison, this is that same information in print preview with a border added:

Top Align Left	Top Align Center
Middle Align Left	Middle Align Center

(Print preview, which we'll discuss in the chapter on how to print, is the best way to see how your data will actually appear when printed without wasting paper actually printing the document.)

There are three main ways to add borders around a cell or set of cells.

The easiest is also the newest.

If all you want is a simple basic border around a range of cells, go to the Font section on the Home tab and click on the dropdown arrow for the Borders dropdown option. It's a four-square grid with an arrow next to it that's located between the U used for underlining and the color bucket used for filling a cell with color.

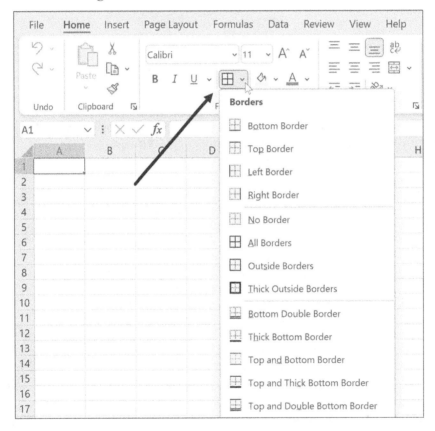

Go to the bottom of the dropdown menu and choose Draw Border Grid:

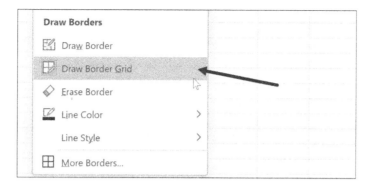

Click on it and then select the cells that you want to apply borders to.

Excel will apply the default line color and line style around all four edges of each cell you select. When you're done, use the Esc key to turn it off or click on the Border icon in the Font section of the Home tab.

For me, with the computer I'm working on and in Excel 365 as it exists in December 2022, the default line thickness isn't as dark as I would prefer it to be. I find myself wanting to change that line thickness to something I can see better on the screen.

But...

And here's where it gets weird, that line thickness is just fine in print preview. And when I choose the darker line that looks best to me on the screen, it's way too thick in print preview.

Now, I don't know if this is because of the computer I'm using which has better graphics than computers I've used in the past, or if this is part of the new streamlined appearance they rolled out with Office 2021.

But it's something to check on your own computer. Because if I were in an office environment where I was designing worksheets that others had to use and print, I'd need to be very careful that I didn't set the appearance of my worksheets to what I visually prefer since those settings will not print well.

Let me show you what I'm seeing. This is what the thick line option looks like on my worksheet:

Not bad, right? But this is what it looks like in print preview:

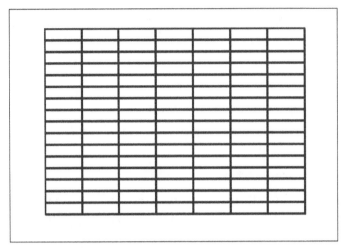

Horrible. That thick border is best for outlining a table, not for interior lines.

Which is all to say, if you're going to add borders to a document in Excel using Excel 2021 or Excel 365 and that document will be printed, be sure to look at that document in print preview before you print or provide it to others and adjust your borders accordingly.

Okay. Now, how do you adjust those lines from the default?

Go to the bottom of the Borders dropdown menu and choose one of the options from the Line Style secondary dropdown menu:

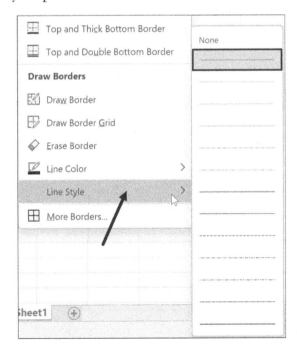

To change the line color, use the Line Color secondary dropdown menu.

The key, though, is that you need to change your line style or line color *before* you apply any borders to your cells.

That means since I don't like the default line style anymore that step one for me is to choose my line style from the dropdown. Step two is to then choose Draw Border Grid from the dropdown. Step three is to select the cells I want to add a border to. Step four is to hit Esc when I'm done.

Excel will keep that changed line style as the current default as long as that file is open.

If you have specific edges of cells where you want a border, you can use the Draw Border instead of the Draw Border Grid option. Simply select it and then click on the edge of a cell where you want to place a border line.

Draw Border when used on a range of cells at one time will apply a border around the perimeter of those selected cells but leave the inner cell borders alone.

So here, for example, I used Draw Border Grid with the default line style, highlighted my cells, and then changed the line style to the thickest option, chose Draw Border, and highlighted those exact same cells again.

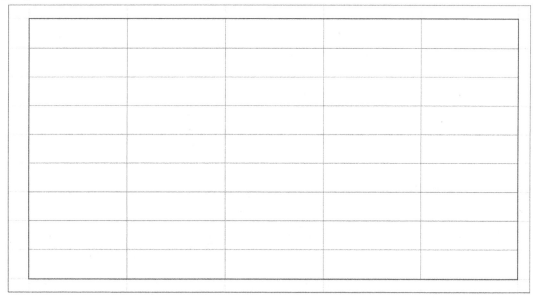

That combination gave me a table with interior lines that were thin and a dark exterior border.

Be sure each time that you choose Draw Border Grid or Draw Border that you see a pencil shape before you start highlighting your cells. There were a few times I clicked on that option and it didn't turn into the pencil for me so didn't work.

Also, hit Esc when you're done to turn off that pencil.

That is the easiest way I think to draw a table in current versions of Excel. But there are a couple other ways to do it.

That same Border dropdown menu has a number of choices at the top that you can use. With those options, though, you first need to select the cells you want to format and then choose the option you want from the dropdown.

All Borders is one I've used often as well as Thick Outside Borders. But if you use both together like I could have to create the table in the screenshot above, be sure to apply them in the right order. All Borders first, Thick Outside Borders second.

The other option for applying borders is to select your cells and then go to the Border tab of the Format Cells dialogue box either by clicking on More Borders at the bottom of the borders dropdown menu or by right-clicking on the selected cells and choosing Format Cells from that dropdown. Here is that Border tab:

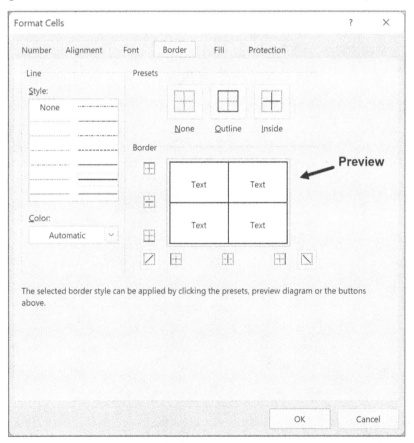

The image in the Border section of the dialogue box that shows four cells with Text in them, will show the current formatting for the selected cells.

To change that formatting, choose your line style and color on the left-hand side and then either click on the presets (none, outline, inside) above the preview or on the individual border thumbnails around the perimeter. You'll see the preview update as you click on each option.

The Format Cells dialogue box is the only way I know of to place a slanted line in a cell.

As I've done a few times in the examples above, you can combine different line styles and line colors in the same table. You just need to think through the order of applying them and make any color or line style choice first before trying to apply it to your entries.

Here is an example where I'm using three different line styles (thick, medium, and dotted line) as well as two line colors. Each of those had to be applied separately with changes to the style and/or color made before I chose the line position.

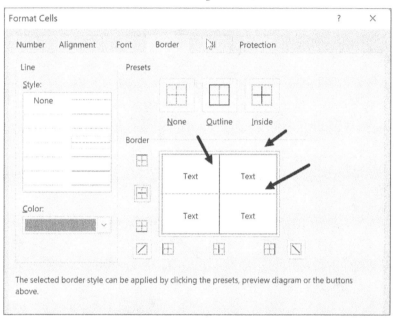

If you're in the Format Cells dialogue box and want to clear what you've done and start over, you can select None from the Presets section. The corresponding option in the dropdown menu is No Border. This does not, however, reset your line style and color choices, so if you changed those you'll need to manually change them back before you draw new borders in that worksheet. (Or close the worksheet and reopen it to reset to the default choices if you're not sure what they are.)

Color a Cell (Fill Color)

You can color (or fill) an entire cell with any color you want. I do this often when building tables. I will add fill color to the header rows of my tables and also to any columns that are either labels or non-input columns.

Like here with this example of the MAXIFS function where the header rows in each table have a green fill color, the cells with calculated results have a gray fill color, and the cells with the text of the formulas used have a blue fill color.

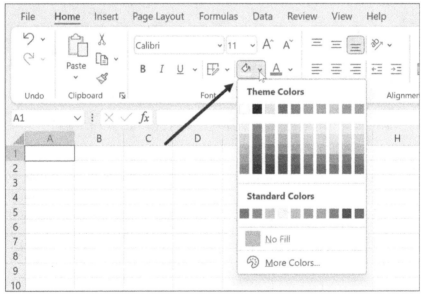

	A	B	C	D	E	F	G	H
1	Score	Teacher	Gender	←				
2	50	Smith	F					
3	49	Barker	M			F		M
4	68	Vasquez	F			98.00	Smith	94.00
5	75	Smith	M			90.00	Barker	93.00
6	90	Barker	F			68.00	Vasquez	76.00
7	94	Smith	M					
8	93	Barker	M		Cell F4:	=MAXIFS($A$2:$A$13,$B$2:$B$13,$G4,$C$2:$C$13,$F$3)		
9	91	Smith	F		Cell H4:	=MAXIFS($A$2:$A$13,$B$2:$B$13,$G4,$C$2:$C$13,$H$3)		
10	76	Vasquez	M					
11	82	Smith	F					
12	64	Barker	M					
13	98	Smith	F					
14								

To add fill color to a cell(s), highlight the cell(s) you want to color, go to the Font section of the Home tab, and click on the arrow to the right of the paint bucket that by default has a yellow line under it.

This should bring up a colors menu with 70 different colors to choose from, including many that are arranged as complementary themes. If you want one of those colors, just click on it.

(If you just wanted the default yellow color you could click on the paint bucket image without needing to bring up the dropdown menu. After you choose a color that option will change to show the last color used, so you can always click on the image to apply whatever color is shown without needing to use the dropdown menu.)

For more color options or to specify a specific color, click on More Colors at the bottom of the dropdown menu to bring up the Colors dialogue box.

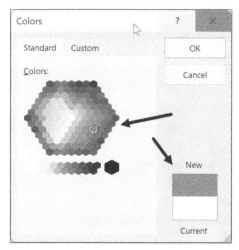 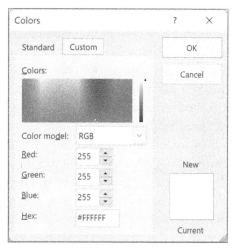

The first tab of that box, Standard, has a honeycomb-like image in the center that includes a number of colors you can choose from by clicking into the honeycomb. Shades of black, white, or gray can be selected just below that.

When you select a color it will show in the bottom right corner in the top half of the rectangle there under the heading New.

The second tab is the Custom tab. Click on it and you'll see a rectangle with a rainbow of colors that you can click on to select a color.

It also allows you to enter specific RGB, HSL, or Hex code values to get the exact color you need. (If you have a corporate color palette, for example, they should give you the values for each of the corporate colors. At least my employers always have.)

RGB is the default option, but you can change that in the dropdown menu.

Or you can enter a specific Hex code at the bottom if you have that.

On the Custom tab, you can also use the arrow on the right-hand side to darken or lighten your color.

If you like your choice, click on OK. If you don't want to add color to a cell after all, choose Cancel.

If you add Fill Color to a cell and later want to remove it, select the cell, go back to the dropdown menu, and choose the No Fill option.

Column Width

If your columns aren't the width you want, you have three options for adjusting them.

First, you can right-click on the column and choose Column Width from the dropdown menu. When the box showing you the current column width appears, enter a new column width. (I don't use this one often because I'm not a good judge of how wide I need to make a column in terms of a specific numeric value.)

Second, you can place your cursor to the right side of the column name—it should look like a line with arrows on either side when you have it in the right spot—and then left-click and drag either to the right or left until the column is as wide as you want it to be.

Or, third, you can place your cursor on the right side of the column name and double left-click. This will make the column as wide or as narrow as the widest text currently in that column. (Usually. Sometimes this one has a mind of its own. But it almost always works with shorter text entries.)

To adjust all column widths in your document at once, you can highlight the entire worksheet (Ctrl + A or click in the top left corner) and then apply one of the above options. A double-left click on any column border will adjust each column to the contents in that column. (Usually. See comment above.) Manually adjusting the width of one column or setting a Column Width using the dropdown menu, will apply that width to all columns in the worksheet.

Currency Formatting

Currency has two main formatting options, Currency and Accounting, but there are a number of other choices available as well.

To format cells using one of the currency options, highlight the cell(s) you want formatted, and then go to the Number section of the Home tab, and either click on the $ sign (which will use the Accounting format) or click on the dropdown arrow for General and choose Currency or Accounting.

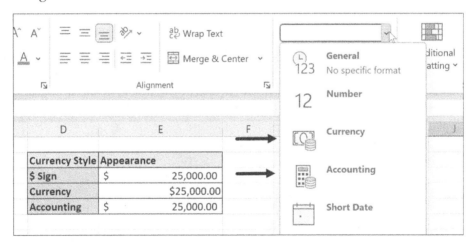

As you can see in the image above, the main difference between the two options is where they place the $ sign relative to the numbers. The Currency option places the $ sign right next to the number, the Accounting option left-aligns the $ sign and right-aligns the numbers.

The $ sign option in the Number section of the Home tab has a dropdown menu where you can choose other common currencies. Also, if you just want your currency to display as whole numbers you can click on the Decrease Decimal option twice, which is located in that same row.

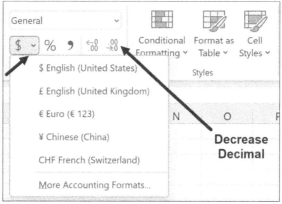

If those options aren't enough for you, you can go to the Number tab of the Format Cells dialogue box and then either use the Currency or Accounting category:

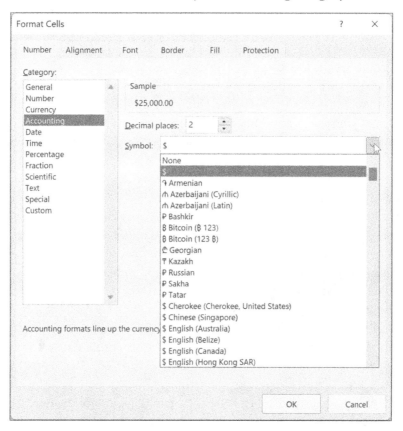

That gives a much larger range of currencies to choose from. The Currency category also includes multiple choices for how to distinguish negative values.

You can also use Ctrl + Shift + $ to apply the Currency format to a selected cell or range of cells.

Date Formatting

Not only does Excel sometimes like to format things as a date that aren't but it also sometimes has a mind of its own about how to format dates. Here are a few examples:

Input Value	Excel Default Displayed Result	Excel Short Date
3/6	6-Mar	3/6/2022
January	January	January
January 2020	Jan-20	1/1/2020
3/6/20	3/6/2020	3/6/2020

In the first column you can see the text I entered. In the second column you can see what Excel did with that text. The third column is the date, when applicable, that Excel assigned to what I'd entered.

So that first entry 3/6, Excel automatically interpreted as the date March 6th (for me, here in the United States with U.S. settings) but rewrote it as 6-Mar and added the current year to the date, which was 2022 when I was writing this so stored that date as March 6, 2022.

The second one, January, it left alone and did not turn into a date.

The third, January 2020, it converted into a date, rewrote as Jan-20, and stored as January 1, 2020.

The fourth, 3/6/20, it reformatted slightly, and treated as March 6, 2020. (Again, for me, here in the United States where month is written first.)

This demonstrates a key thing you need to remember about Excel and dates. It will always insist on having a month, day of the month, and year for every date. If you don't provide that, Excel will do it for you. And it is over-eager to turn anything that may possibly be a date into a date.

The other thing to know is that once Excel decides something is a date, you can't really change that with formatting. So with that first entry there I tried to change that to a Text format and it showed it as the number 44626 which is how Excel really stores dates behind the scenes. (As the 44,626th day since Excel's start date.)

Which means that if Excel ever turns an entry of yours into a date and you didn't want it to, the best thing is to Undo and then retype the entry using that single apostrophe at the start of the cell to keep Excel from converting the entry on you.

But let's say you did want that to be a date. How can you control the date format that Excel applies to your date?

Click on the cell with your date in it, go to the Number section of the Home tab, click on the dropdown menu which should show General by default, and then choose either Short Date or Long Date from there. You will be able to see examples of what that date will look like when chosen:

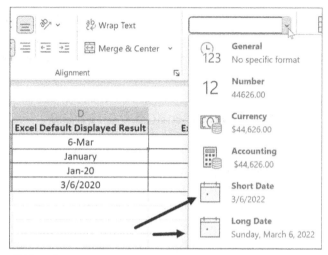

Usually, Short Date will be the one you want.

But if neither of those work for you, go to the Number tab of the Format Cells dialogue box, and click on the Date category. There will be about a dozen options to choose from there.

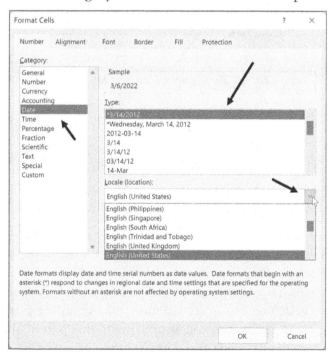

Note that there is also a Locale dropdown menu that lets you choose formats used in other countries. For example, here in the United States 3/6 is March 6th, but in many other parts of the world 3/6 is June 3rd, so if you're going to use that Short Date format understand that it is a regional format that may be misinterpreted by others on a printed document. (I believe Excel adjusts the display for the local country settings, so it won't be an issue when looking at the Excel file, but be careful there just in case.)

You can also use Ctrl + Shift + # to apply a date format that uses day, month, and year. For me the format was 2-Jan-20 for January 2, 2020.

Font Choice and Font Size

The current default font choice in Excel is Calibri and the default font size is 11 point.

You may have strong preferences about what font you use or work for a company that uses specific fonts for its brand or just want some variety in terms of font size or type within a specific document. In that case, you will need to change those settings.

There are a few ways to do this. Each requires selecting your text or cells first.

Once you've done that, option one is to go to the Font section on the Home tab and select a different font or font size from the dropdown menus there by clicking on the one you want.

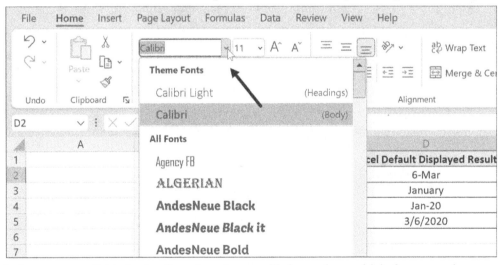

Which fonts are available in the font dropdown will depend on which fonts you have on your computer. Most people have a number of fonts already available. I have a large number of additional fonts so you may see different fonts listed there than I do.

Excel shows your theme font at the top and then the rest of your fonts are shown in alphabetical order below that. You can either use the scroll bar on the side to scroll down or you can start typing the name of the font you want to get to that part of the list.

Each font will display in the list using that font. You can see this in the screenshot above where Agency is a very different font from Andes Neue and Algerian.

The font size dropdown only has the most common sizes listed. It lists 8, 9, 10, 11, and 12 pt but then starts jumping up in numbers. If you have a specific font size you want that isn't listed, you can just type it in.

You also have the option to increase or decrease the font one listed size at a time by clicking on the A's with little arrows that are shown next to the font dropdown box. The bigger of the two, on the left, increases the font size. The smaller one decreases the font size.

All of these options are also available in the mini formatting menu if you right-click in the main workspace after selecting your cells.

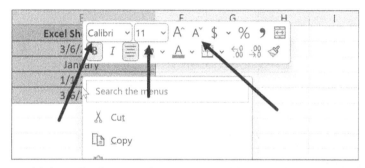

Your other option, which really doesn't give you any additional functionality, is to use the Font tab of the Format Cells dialogue box.

Font Color

The default color for all text in Excel is black, but you can change that if you want or need to. (For example, if you've filled a cell with a darker color you may want to change the font color to white to make the text in that cell more visible.)

You have three options. All require selecting the text or cells first.

After that, the first option is to go to the Font section on the Home tab and click on the arrow next to the A that by default will have a red line under it. (Or click on the A if you want the color shown.)

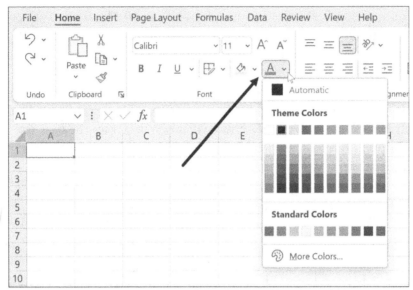

You can then choose from one of the 70 colors that are listed, and if those aren't enough of a choice you can click on More Colors and select your color from the Colors dialogue box. (See Coloring a Cell for more detail about that option.)

Second, you can use the mini formatting menu.

Third, you can use the Color dropdown in the Font tab of the Format Cells dialogue box.

Indent Text

If you want your text within your cell to be indented from the edge of the cell, you can increase the indent to make that happen by selecting the cell, going to the Alignment section of the Home tab, and clicking on the Increase Indent option that's located to the left of the Merge & Center option.

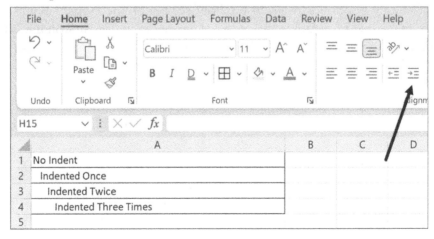

You can see how that would impact text placement in the screenshot above.

To decrease the indent, use the Decrease Indent option located to the left of the Increase Indent option.

You can also use the Indent field in the Alignment section of the Format Cells dialogue box. It will accept a whole number for the number of times to indent the text.

Italicize Text

To italicize text, highlight the text selection or cells containing text you want to italicize, and then use Ctrl + I or click on the slanted I in the Font section on the Home tab or in the mini formatting menu.

You can also change the Font Style option in the Font tab of the Format Cells dialogue box to Italic or Bold Italic.

To remove italics from text or cells that already have it, select that text and then use Ctrl + I or click on the slanted I in the Font section of the Home tab or the mini formatting menu. You may have to do this twice if you select text that is only partially italicized since Excel will apply italics to the entire selection first.

You can also remove italics by changing the Font Style back to Regular in the Format Cells dialogue box.

Merge & Center

Merge and Center is a specialized command that can come in handy when you're working with a table where you want a header that spans multiple columns of data. (Don't use it if you plan to do a lot of data analysis with what you've input into the worksheet because it will mess with your ability to filter, sort, or use pivot tables. It's really for creating a finalized, pretty-looking report.)

What it does is merges the cells you select and then centers your text across those merged cells.

You can merge cells across columns and down rows. So you could, for example, merge four cells that span two columns and two rows into one big cell while keeping all of the other cells in those columns and rows separate. But what I usually am doing is just merging X number of cells in a single row.

If you're going to merge and center cells that contain text, make sure that the text you want to keep is in the top-most and left-most of the cells you plan to merge and center. Data in the other cells that are being merged will be deleted. (You'll get a warning message to this effect if you have values in any of the other cells.)

To use this option, first select all of the cells you want to merge.

Next, go to the Alignment section of the Home tab and choose Merge & Center. This will combine your selected cells into one cell and center the contents from that left-uppermost cell across the selection.

Like so:

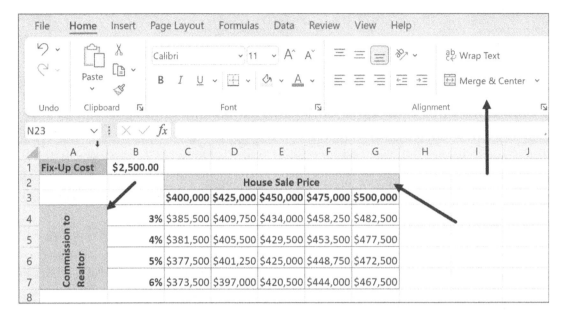

In the screenshot above I've merged and centered the text "House Sale Price" across Columns C through G in Row 2. I've also merged and centered the text "Commission to Realtor" across Rows 4 through 7 in Column A. (You'll note that I also changed the alignment of the commission text.)

That is the option I use most often, but there are additional choices available if you click on the dropdown arrow for Merge & Center. You can also choose to Merge Across (which will merge the cells in each row of the selected range separately and will not center the text) or to Merge Cells (which will merge all of the selected cells but won't center the text).

If you ever need to unmerge merged cells you can do so by selecting those cells and then clicking on the Unmerge Cells option from that dropdown.

You can also merge or unmerge cells by using the Merge Cells checkbox in the Alignment tab of the Format Cells dialogue box.

Merge & Center is also an option in the mini formatting menu. It's located in the top right corner of the menu. Clicking on it for previously merged cells will unmerge those cells.

Number Formatting

In addition to date and currency formatting, which we already discussed, you can apply other basic number formatting to your cells.

The first option is to use the Number section of the Home tab. The second option is to use the mini formatting menu. And the final option is to use the Format Cells dialogue box.

There are three default number styles in the dropdown menu on the Home tab that you may want to consider. If you already have values entered, the dropdown menu will show you a sample of how each one will look.

Here, for example, I used 10000 as my entry and you can see how General, Number, and Scientific would display that number:

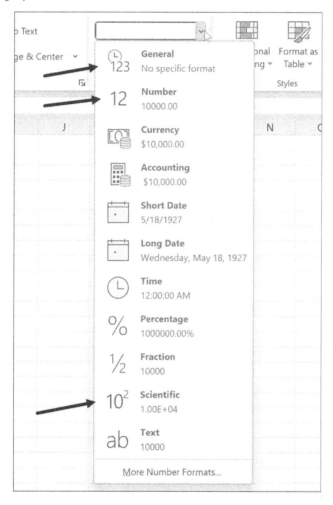

I often prefer to use the Comma Style option that's available below the dropdown and is just shown as a big comma because that one includes a comma for thousands where Number does not:

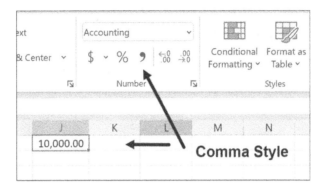

It is also available in the mini formatting menu.

Ctrl + Shift + exclamation mark (!) will give a similar but not identical result to the Comma Style option. (The spacing within the cell is different.)

And, as with all other number formatting options, there is a more detailed option in the Number section of the Format Cells dialogue box, in this case using the Number category.

You can also use the Increase and Decrease Decimal options in the Number section of the Home tab or in the mini formatting menu to change the number of decimal places for your values, just be sure to do that after you've applied your number format, not before.

Percent Formatting

To format numbers as a percentage, your first option is to highlight the cell(s), and click on the percent sign in the Number section of the Home tab or the mini formatting menu. This will convert the value to a percent with no decimal places.

Your second option is to use the dropdown menu in the Number section of the Home tab and choose Percentage from there. This will format the value as a percentage, but also include two decimal places.

Your final option is to use the Percentage category in the Number tab of the Format Cells dialogue box which will let you specify the number of decimal places to use.

With any of the above options, be sure that your numbers are formatted correctly or it won't work properly. In other words, 0.5 will translate to 50% but 50 will translate to 5000% so you want your entries pre-formatting to be .5 not 50 if you're looking for 50%.

(You can fix this by dividing those entries by 100, copying that result, and then pasting special values over the original values.)

Row Height

If your rows aren't the correct height, you have three options for adjusting them.

First, you can right-click on the row you want to adjust, choose Row Height from the dropdown menu, and when the box showing you the current row height appears, enter a new row height.

Second, you can place your cursor along the lower border of the row number for the row you want to adjust until it looks like a line with arrows above and below. Left-click and hold while you move the cursor up or down until the row is as tall as you want it to be.

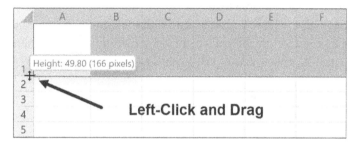

Third, you can place your cursor along the lower border of the row, and double left-click. This will fit the row height to the text in the cell. (Usually. Sometimes in the past it would not work with really large amounts of text and the only option was to manually resize the row height.)

To adjust all row heights in your document at once, highlight the entire worksheet (Ctrl + A or click in the top left corner) first and then use one of the options above. Entering a specific row height or clicking and dragging will keep all rows the same height. Double-left-clicking will resize each row to its contents. (Theoretically.)

Underline Text

Underlining text works much the same way that bolding and italics work.

For a basic single-line underline select the text or cells with text that you want to underline and then use Ctrl + U or click on the underlined U in the Font section of the Home tab.

You can also use the Underline dropdown in the Font section of the Format Cells dialogue box.

There are other underline types such as a double underline. For that, use the dropdown arrow next to the underlined U in the Font section of the Home tab or choose one of the options in the Format Cells dialogue box which includes single accounting and double accounting options as well.

To remove underlining from text or cells that already have it, highlight the text and then use one of the above options again. If you applied a special underline type, then using Ctrl + U or clicking on the underlined U in the Font section will first change the underline to a single underline, so you have to do it twice to completely remove the underline.

Wrap Text

Wrap text is an essential one to learn if you want to use text in your worksheet and be able to see all of the text in that worksheet without expanding the width of your columns to make that happen.

To Wrap Text in a cell, select the cell(s), go to the Alignment section of the Home Tab, and click on the Wrap Text option in the top row.

Or you can go to the Alignment tab in the Format Cells dialogue box and check the box for Wrap Text in the Text Control section.

Here is an example of a FINRA regulation in the left-most column and then an analysis column next to it. The content of the cells in Rows 1 through 3 are the same as those in Rows 6 through 8. In Column A, Rows 2 and 3 did not wrap the text but Rows 7 and 8 did.

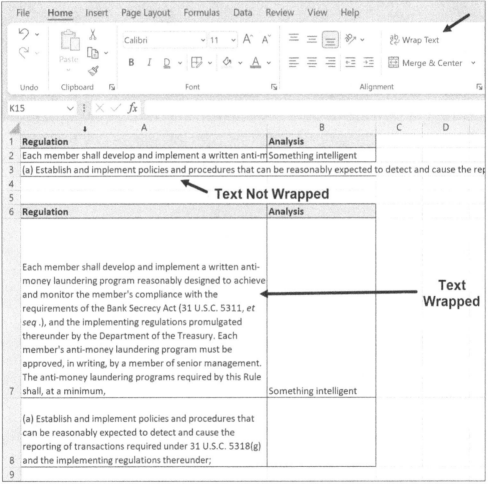

Note a few things. In the example at the top where the text is not wrapped, the text stops at the next column when there is content in that next column. You can see that in Cell A2. But when there isn't text in that next column, the text is visible on the screen. You can see that in Cell A3.

But when text is wrapped, like in Cells A7 and A8, the text moves to a new line when it reaches the border with the next column and as long as the row height is high enough, you can see the full text in that cell, regardless of what text may or may not be in any other column.

It also just looks much better when it's contained to the cell it belongs to.

(Excel does seem to have a maximum row height which will limit the amount of text you can display in one cell, so if you have any cells with lots of text in them, check to make sure that the full contents of the cell are actually visible. You may have to manually adjust the row height or it just may not be possible to see all of the text.)

* * *

Okay. That was our alphabetical discussion of the various formatting options, but before we move on to sorting and filtering, I wanted to cover a couple more formatting tricks.

Copy Formatting From One Cell To Another

I find this one incredibly useful, although I use it more in Word than in Excel.

If you already have a cell formatted the way you want it, you can use the Format Painter located in the Clipboard section of the Home tab to sweep the formatting from that cell to other cells you want formatted the same way.

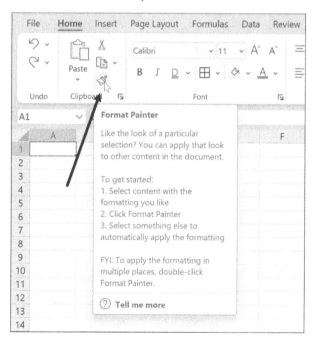

The help text sort of says it all.

First, select the cell(s) that have the formatting you want to copy (if the formatting is identical, just highlight one cell).

Next, click on the Format Painter. Double-click if you have more than one place you want to apply that formatting.

Finally, click into the cell(s) you want to copy the formatting to.

The contents in the destination cell will remain the same, but the font, font color, font size, cell borders, italics/bolding/underlining, and text alignment and orientation will all change to match that of the cell that you swept the formatting from.

If you double-clicked, use Esc or click on the Format Painter again to turn it off when you're done.

You can also find the Format Painter tool in the mini formatting menu.

You need to be careful using the Format Painter because it will change all formatting in your destination cells. So, if the cell you're copying the formatting from is bolded and has red text, both of those attributes will copy over even if all you were trying to do was copy the bold formatting. (This is more of a problem when using the tool in Word than in Excel, but it's still something to watch out for especially if you have borders around cells.)

Also, the tool copies formatting to whatever cell you select next, which can be a problem if the cell you're copying from isn't next to the one you're copying to. DO NOT use arrow keys to navigate between the cells. You need to click directly on the cell you're transferring the formatting to.

Remember, Ctrl + Z is your friend if you make a mistake. But if you format sweep and then undo, you'll see that the cell(s) you were trying to format from are surrounded by a dotted border as if you had copied the cells. Be sure to hit the Esc key before you continue to turn that off.

Clear Formatting

I don't use this often, but it can be handy if I had a lot of formatting in a worksheet and deleted the contents but the formatting is still there and I don't want it anymore.

To clear formatting, select the cells where you want to do this (or the entire worksheet with Ctrl + A), and then go to the Editing section of the Home tab and click on the dropdown arrow under Clear.

The Clear Formats option will remove all formatting from the selected cells. Clear All will remove contents and formatting at the same time.

* * *

Okay, that was formatting. We have three more topics to go: Sorting, Filtering, and Printing. And then we're done with this introduction. Yay. The end is in sight.

Sorting and Filtering

Two of the most common and basic ways I analyze or use data in Excel is by sorting or filtering. (The other option I use frequently is PivotTables, which are covered in the next book in this series.)

Sorting

Sorting allows you to display your information in a specific order. For example, by date, value, or alphabetically. You can also sort across multiple columns, so you can, for example, sort first by date, then by name, then by amount.

To sort your data, select the data, including your header row if there is one, and all columns of related information.

And do be sure that you select *all* columns of your data. Because this is one of those areas where if you choose the first five columns out of ten and sort those five, there's no way to return things to an order that matches those five columns that were sorted with the ones that weren't.

So you have to be a little careful here because sorting is one of the ways to irretrievably break a data set.

If you set your data up with the first row as the header and all of the rest as data with no subtotals or grand totals, the best thing to do is just use Ctrl + A or click in the top left corner of your worksheet to select all of the cells in the worksheet. Excel will then figure out the limits of your data from there.

If you have a table of data that starts lower down on the page or that has a summary row or that is followed by other data, be sure to only select the cells in the data set that you want to sort, because Excel will sort everything you select whether it makes sense to do so or not.

(I often mess this up and end up sorting my data so that my summary row is included, for example, so instead of seeing my best-selling title at the top I see a value for all sales of all books instead. It's not the end of the world if that happens, but it is mildly annoying and something to fix before anyone else sees your data.)

Once you've selected your data, go to the Editing section of the Home tab. Click on the arrow next to Sort & Filter, and choose Custom Sort.

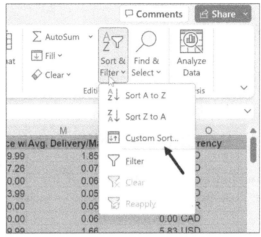

(The Sort A to Z and Sort Z to A options are ones I try not to use simply because that gives a little too much control to Excel about how it sorts the data. It seems to default to sorting by values in the first column when you choose that option, but I'm not always clear on where it goes from there and I've had it not work for me. Also, I often am not interested in sorting by the first column, so I just default to Custom Sort from the beginning. Less thought required.)

You can also go to the Sort & Filter section of the Data tab and click on the Sort option there. That's the one I tend to use.

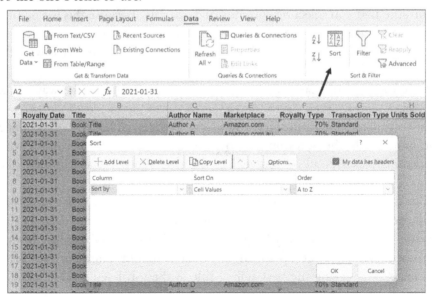

Either option will open the Sort dialogue box that you can see in the screenshot above.

The first thing you need to do is tell Excel whether or not your data has headers. It will guess the answer, but review to make sure it got it right.

If your data does have headers that box in the top corner that says, "My data has headers" should be checked.

If you indicate that there is a header row, it will not be included in your sort and will remain the first row of your data. Also, the Sort By dropdown will use the text in that first row for the dropdown menu choices. Like so:

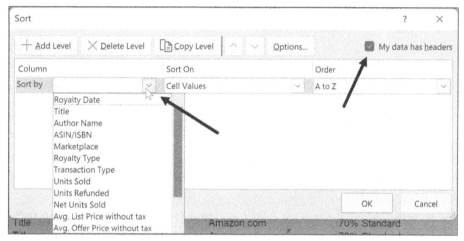

If you don't have a header row, the listed field name choices for Sort By will be the generic column names (Column A, Column B, etc.) and all of your selected data will be sorted, including the first row. Which makes sense to have happen if, for example, you are sorting a subset of your data.

When might you do this?

I have a worksheet that tracks my advertising spend where I need to do this because when I input the advertising spend I just do it in the order it's shown on my reports. However, when I'm matching that spend up to sales to see if my ads were profitable it's easier to do that if I sort alphabetically by title. But I only want to do that for the current month. That worksheet tracks advertising spend back to 2013. I only select the rows for the current month and then sort by title.

So it can happen that you don't have a header row to include for your sort.

The next step is to choose your sort order.

Decide what the primary criteria you want to sort by is and then choose that column from the Sort By dropdown menu.

After you've done that, choose what to sort on for that sort option. For a basic sort, like mine above where I want to sort by title, you'll generally leave this alone because you want to sort by the values in each cell.

There are also options to sort by cell color, font color, and conditional formatting icon which will only be useful to you if you've manually applied color to certain entries or used conditional formatting to do so. (Conditional formatting is covered in the next book in this series.)

Finally, you have to specify the Order that will be used for your sort. The choices there are going to depend on the type of data.

For text use A to Z to sort alphabetical or Z to A to sort reverse alphabetical. I also sometimes use the Custom List option when I have a column with the months of the year or the days of the week in it because Excel already has those set up.

For numbers it's Smallest to Largest or Largest to Smallest.

For dates it's Oldest to Newest or Newest to Oldest.

The default choices are A to Z, Smallest to Largest, and Oldest to Newest. But if you want to use a different option you can change this using the dropdown arrow.

If all you want is to sort by one column, then you're done. Click OK and Excel will sort your data.

If you want to then sort by another column, you need to add that second column to the Sort dialogue box.

(For example, maybe you sort first by year, then month, then Customer so that all of the sales for a particular month are grouped together and then within that month the information is sorted by customer name.)

To add a second sort level, click on Add Level and select your next column to sort by and your criteria for that sort.

Here for example, I have four total sort levels:

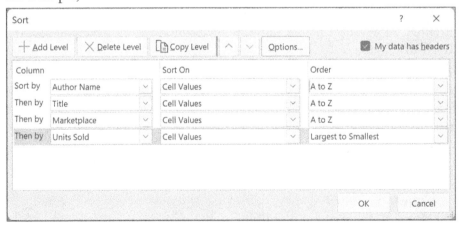

The data will first be sorted by author name, then by title, then by marketplace, and finally by units sold in reverse order from largest to smallest.

If you add a level you don't need, like I just did here with units sold which should only have one value per marketplace, title, and author, click on it and then choose Delete Level from the top of the dialogue box.

Also, if you have multiple levels but decide that they should be sorted in a different order, you can use the arrows at the top to move the selected sort level up or down.

The default for sort is to sort top to bottom, so down a column, but you can click on Options to sort left to right or to make your sort case-sensitive. (Something I rarely need, but have used once or twice.)

If you change your mind about sorting your data, click Cancel or the X in the top right corner of the dialogue box. Otherwise, when you're done with your sort options, click OK and Excel will sort your data.

If you get a sort that has a mistake in it, use Ctrl + Z to undo and try again. Don't try to fix a bad sort, just undo it and start over.

Filtering

The other thing I do often is filter my data. Sometimes I just want to look at a quick subset of a data table. For example, all of the sales for Author A. The data in the table is just fine, I don't need to summarize it in any way, I just want the rest of the entries hidden while I look at that subset.

Filtering allows you to do that as long as your data is set up the right way. (Ideally, a header row at the top, rows of data below, no subtotals or blank lines or blank columns.)

To turn on filtering for your data table, the first step is to click on any cell in the first row of the table and then go to the Editing section of the Home tab, click on the arrow next to Sort & Filter, and choose Filter.

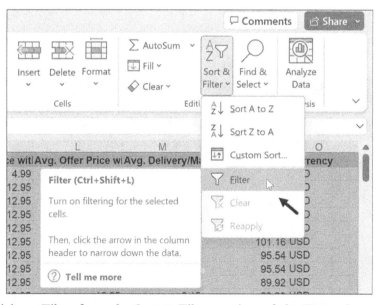

You can also click on Filter from the Sort & Filter section of the Data tab.

(It's possible that Excel will now appropriately apply filtering as long as you've clicked on any cell in the data table or selected the whole worksheet even if you don't click in a cell in the first row of the data table, but in older versions of Excel this could be an issue so I still as a best practice try to click on a cell in the header row before I apply filtering.)

Once filtering has been applied, you should see little arrows in the bottom right corner of each cell in that first row of the data table. If there was a gap in the columns in the table, only the columns on that side of the table will have the filter option. Like here:

F	G	H	I	J	K	L
Royalty Typ ▾	Transaction Ty ▾	Units Sold ▾			Avg. List Price witl	Avg. Offer Price wi
70%	Free - Price Match	65			4.99	0.00
60%	Standard - Paperba	21			12.95	12.95
60%	Standard - Paperba	21			12.95	12.95
60%	Standard - Paperba	19			12.95	12.95
60%	Standard - Paperba	18			12.95	12.95
60%	Standard - Paperba	18			12.95	12.95

I clicked into Cell H1 before I turned on filtering. So all of the columns on that side of the gap have a filter option now. But see that Cells K1 and L1 do not, because Excel doesn't see them as part of the same data table due to that gap.

You can overcome this by selecting the entire worksheet before you apply filtering. If you do that, Excel will apply a filter option to every column in that first row, up to the point where the last column with text is.

From here on out, I'm going to talk about filtering as it exists in Excel 365 as of December 2022. This is one of those areas where you need to watch out for compatibility with older Excel versions. If you are working with someone who has an older version of Excel, I highly recommend that you never share with them a file that has filtering already applied, because there are types of filtering you can do now that you could not do in the past.

Okay, then.

If you click on the arrow for any given column, you should see a list of all potential values in that column. Here, for example, are all of the potential values for Column C in this data table, which contains author names.

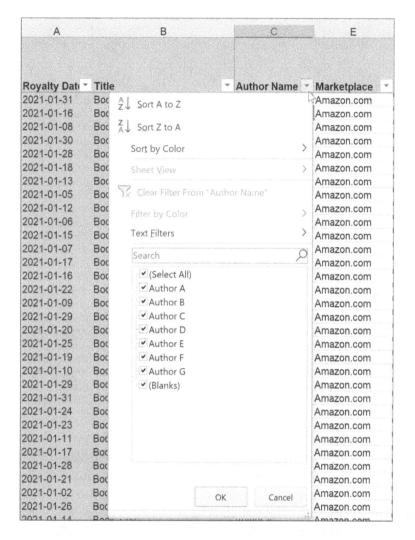

Note that there are checkboxes next to each value and that by default they are all checked.

For really long data sets (tens of thousands of rows) that have a lot of potential values this may not be a complete listing. (It definitely wasn't in older versions of Excel.)

If there are any values you don't want displayed, you can simply uncheck the box next to that value. Usually I want just one out of that list or maybe a few. The easiest way to accomplish this is to click on the box next to Select All. That removes all of the checks for all of the entries. You can then go through and check the boxes for the ones you want to see.

Like here where I now am only going to see results for Author A:

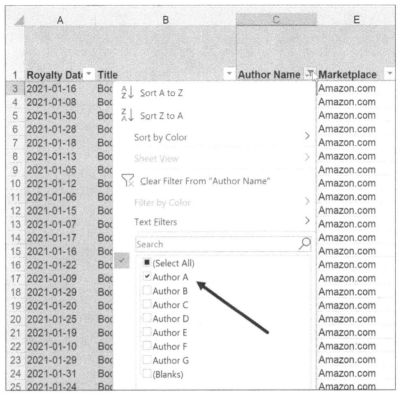

If the list of potential values is really long, you can start to type the name of the value you want to filter by into the Search field to make it appear within the visible list of entries.

Another option is to use filter criteria to narrow down what information is displayed. Depending on the type of data you're filtering and how it's formatted, the option will say Number Filters, Text Filters, Date Filters, etc. In the image above the filter option is Text Filters. It's located directly above the Search field.

Click on the arrow next to the filter name to open a secondary dropdown menu with available choices.

You should see options like "Equals" or "Does Not Equal" or "Begins With" or "Between" etc. The options differ depending on the type of data.

You can use these filter criteria to select only the rows where those criteria are met. So, for example, if I only want to see entries where the number of units sold is greater than 5, I can choose the Greater Than option under Number Filters in the Units Sold column.

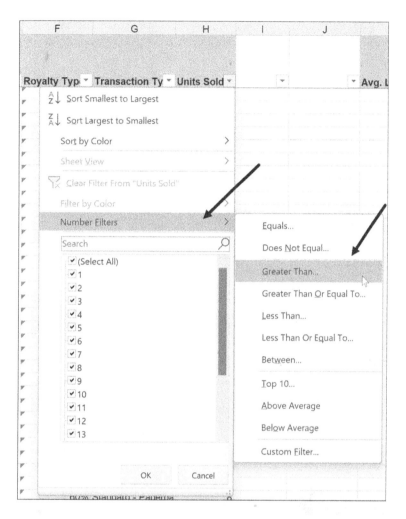

That brings up a dialogue box where I can enter my filter value and then click OK.

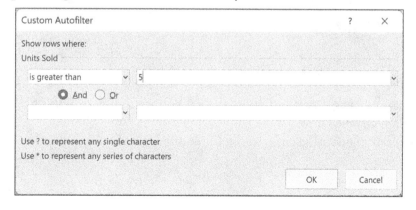

My data will now be filtered to only show those rows that meet the filter criteria I specified.

If you've color-coded cells using font color or cell color, you can also filter by those criteria, using the Filter by Color option.

When cells in your worksheet are filtered, the row numbers in your worksheet will be colored blue or aqua (depending on your theme settings), and you'll see that the row numbers skip since some rows are hidden.

	A	B	C	E
1	Royalty Dat	Title	Author Name	Marketplace
3	2021-01-16	Book Title	Author A	Amazon.com
5	2021-01-30	Book Title	Author A	Amazon.com
7	2021-01-18	Book Title	Author A	Amazon.com
8	2021-01-13	Book Title	Author A	Amazon.com
9	2021-01-05	Book Title	Author A	Amazon.com
10	2021-01-12	Book Title	Author A	Amazon.com
11	2021-01-06	Book Title	Author A	Amazon.com

For example, in the screenshot above Rows 2, 4, and 6 have been filtered out. The numbers for Rows 3, 5, 7, etc. are blue.

Columns where filtering is in place will show a funnel instead of an arrow in the corner of the header row like you can see above for Royalty Date and Author Name.

To remove filtering from a specific column, click on that filter image, and select Clear Filter from [Column Name].

	A	B	C	E
1	Royalty Dat	Title	Author Name	Marketplace
3	2021-01-16	Boc	A↓ Sort A to Z	Amazon.com
5	2021-01-30	Boc	Z↓ Sort Z to A	Amazon.com
7	2021-01-18	Boc		Amazon.com
8	2021-01-13	Boc	Sort by Color >	Amazon.com
9	2021-01-05	Boc		Amazon.com
10	2021-01-12	Boc	Sheet View >	Amazon.com
11	2021-01-06	Boc		Amazon.com
12	2021-01-15	Boc	⧖ Clear Filter From "Author Name"	Amazon.com
13	2021-01-07	Boc		Amazon.com

To remove all filtering in a worksheet, go to the Editing section of the Home tab, click on Sort & Filter, and then choose Clear.

To turn off filtering entirely, click on the Filter option in that dropdown once more.

Printing

Alright, so that was the basics of how to work with your data within Excel. But there are going to be times when you want to print your results. Excel can be especially problematic that way, simply because what looks good on the screen doesn't always print well.

Basic printing in Excel is as simple as going to File, Print, (or using Ctrl + P) and then clicking on the Print icon. But don't do that. Take a moment before you do that to check all of your settings and look at your print preview first.

Here is what the Print screen looks like:

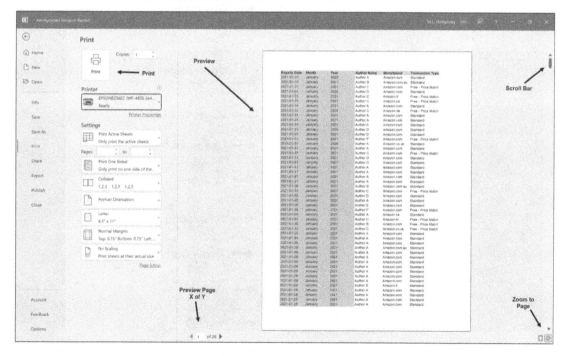

The image of a printer on the top under Print is what you ultimately will click on to print your document.

The preview in the right-hand side of the screen shows you what that document will look like when printed, page-by-page. You can see here how the first page of this document would look if I were to print it right now.

Down below that you can see what page this is and how many total pages will print. There are arrows there for moving between pages. You can also use the scroll bar on the right-hand side to move to the other pages.

In the bottom right corner are options to show margins and zoom to page. Zoom to Page can be useful if you can't read text or see what's on the page well and want to zoom in a bit. But generally I leave those alone.

Now let's look at the print options on the left-hand side:

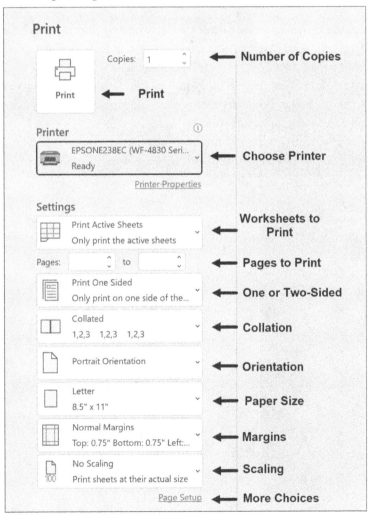

Print

Once you're ready to print your page, you can click on the button on the top left with the image of a printer that says Print to print your document.

Number of Copies

The Copies field is located to the right of the Print button. If you want to print more than one copy, change your number of copies in the Copies field using the up and down arrows or click into the field and type the desired number of copies.

Printer

This should display your computer's default printer, but if you want to use a different printer than that one or print to a PDF, click on the arrow next to the printer name and choose from the listed options. If the printer you want isn't listed, choose Add Printer from the dropdown menu and add the printer.

You generally won't need to click on that Printer Properties link that you can see below the dropdown.

Print Active Sheets / Print Entire Workbook / Print Selection

My version of Excel defaults to Print Active Sheets. This will generally be the worksheet you were working in when you chose to print.

However, you can select more than one worksheet by holding down the Control key and then clicking on another worksheet's name. When you do this, you'll see that the names of all of your selected worksheets are highlighted, not just one of them.

You can also right-click on a worksheet and choose Select All Sheets to select all of the worksheets in your workbook at once. (Be careful doing this because an edit to one worksheet will be an edit to all of them.)

I would only print multiple worksheets together if you're satisfied that each one is formatted the way you want it formatted already.

Also, choosing to print more than one sheet at a time either with Print Active Sheets or Print Entire Workbook, results in strange things happening to your headers and footers if you use those. For example, your page numbering will be across worksheets.

If you mean each worksheet to be a standalone report with numbered pages specific to that report, then you need to print each worksheet separately.

As I just alluded to, the Print Entire Workbook option prints all of the worksheets in your workbook.

Print Selection allows you to just print a highlighted section of a worksheet.

(Or worksheets. I happened to have three worksheets selected at once and when I highlighted the first twenty cells in one of those worksheets, the selection it was ready to print was those twenty cells in each of the three worksheets. So again, be careful that that makes sense to do.)

The dropdown also has an Ignore Print Area option which you could use if a worksheet has a print area set and you want to print everything on the worksheet not just the print area. (A print area lets you permanently specify which cells in a worksheet should be printed instead of the default of all cells with data in that worksheet.)

Pages

Just below the Print Active Sheets section is a row that says Pages and has two boxes with arrows at the side. Using this section, you can choose to just print a specific page or a subset of pages rather than the entire worksheet. To figure out which page(s) to print, look at the print preview.

For a single page use the same page number in both boxes. For a range of pages, put the first page of the range in the first box and the last page of the range in the second box.

In Excel you can only do a range of pages unlike Word where you can print a series of non-adjacent pages.

Changing the values in this section will NOT update your print preview.

Print One Sided / Print on Both Sides (long edge) / Print on Both Sides (short edge)

This option will only be available if you have a printer chosen that can do this.

The default is to just print on one side of the page. If you have a printer that can print on both sides of the page you can change your settings to do so either on the long edge or the short edge.

You generally will want the long edge option if your layout is going to be portrait style and the short edge option if your layout is going to be landscape style. (See below.)

Collated / Uncollated

This only matters if what you're printing has more than one page and if you're printing more than one copy.

In that case, you need to decide if you want to print one full copy at a time, x number of times, or if you want to print x copies of page 1 and then x copies of page 2 and then x copies of page 3 and so on until you've printed all pages of your document.

In general, I would choose collated, which is also the default, which prints one full copy at a time.

Portrait Orientation / Landscape Orientation

You can choose to print in either portrait orientation (with the short edge of the page on top) or landscape orientation (with the long edge of the page on top). You can see the difference in what will print on each page by changing the option in Excel and looking at your print preview.

Which option you choose will depend mostly on how many columns of data you have.

Assuming I'm dealing with a normal worksheet with rows of data across various columns, my goal is to fit all of my columns on one page if possible.

Sometimes changing the layout to landscape allows me to do that because it allows me to have more columns per page than I'd be able to fit in portrait mode.

If I have just a few columns of data, though, but with lots of rows I'll generally stick with portrait orientation instead.

You'll have to decide what works best for you, your specific data, and where the printed document will be used.

Letter / Legal / Statement / Etc.

This is where you select your paper type. Unless you're in an office or overseas, chances are you'll leave this exactly like it is. I'm sure my printer could print on legal paper, but I don't have any for it to use so it's a moot point for me.

In an office you may have the choice of standard paper, legal paper, and even other larger sizes than that. Just make sure whatever you choose is in fact an available option for you.

Normal Margins / Wide Margins / Narrow Margins / Custom Margins

I would expect you won't use this, but if you need to then this would be where you can change the margins on the document. The normal margins allow for .7" on each side and .75" on top and bottom. If you have a lot of columns and need just a little more room to fit it all on one page, you could use the narrow margin option which uses .25" margins on the left and right.

I generally use the scaling option to do this instead.

No Scaling / Fit Sheet on One Page / Fit All Columns on One Page / Fit All Rows on One Page / Custom Scaling

I use this option often when I have a situation where my columns are just a little bit too much to fit on the page or my rows go just a little bit beyond the page.

If you choose "Fit All Columns on One Page" that will make sure that all of your columns fit across the top of one page.

You might still have multiple pages because of the number of rows, but at least everything will fit across one page.

Of course, depending on how many columns you have, this might not be a good choice. Excel will make it fit, but it will do so by decreasing your font size. If you have too many columns you're trying to fit on one page your font size may become so small you can't read it.

So be sure to look at your preview before you print. (And use Landscape Orientation first if you can.)

Fit All Rows on One Page is good for if you have maybe one or two rows too many to naturally fit on the page.

Fit Sheet on One Page is a combination of fitting all columns and all rows onto one page. Again, Excel will do it if you ask it to, but with a large set of data you won't be able to read it, so be careful making this choice.

I usually end up going with Custom Scaling. If you click on that option it opens the Page Setup dialogue box to the Page tab where you can go to the Scaling section and choose to Fit To X pages by Y pages. So maybe I have a report that is five pages long right now with only one row on that last page. I can use scaling to make this 1 page wide by 4 pages long and that will bring that last row up onto my fourth page and give me a cleaner print out than if I just left it as is.

Same with if I have a report that is currently fifteen pages long because the last column extends to the next page so I have ten pages with most of my information spread across two pages wide and five pages long but then I have another five pages with just that last column. I can set this to 2 pages wide by 5 pages long and bring that last column onto the second page.

(If you need it, play around with the setting and you'll see how it can help.)

Page Setup

The Page Setup link at the very bottom gives you access to even more options through the Page Setup dialogue box. We just talked about custom scaling. This is another way to reach that setting. You can also:

1. Center Horizontally or Vertically

On the Margins tab there are two check boxes that let you center what you're printing either horizontally or vertically or both. I will often choose to center a smaller data table horizontally. If I don't do that, it tends to look off balance.

2. Header/Footer

If you want to set up a header and/or a footer for your printed document, you can do so here. The dropdown boxes that say (none) include a number of pre-formatted headers and footers for you to use.

You can see here options for including the page number, worksheet name, and workbook name, for example. Each one shows an example of the actual text that will be included.

Not visible above, because the buttons are hidden behind the dropdown, are options for customizing the header and footer.

3. Sheet

The sheet tab has a couple of useful options, but I'm going to show you a different way to set these options because I find it easier to set them when I'm in the worksheet itself.

* * *

Page Layout Tab

If you exit out of the print option and go back to your worksheet, you'll see that one of the tabs you have available to use is called Page Layout. There are certain attributes that I set up here before I print my documents. Let's walk through them.

(First, though, note that you can change margins, orientation, and size here just as easily as in the print preview screen.)

1. Print Area

If you only want to print a portion of a worksheet, you can set that portion as your print area by highlighting it, and then clicking on the arrow next to Print Area and choosing Set Print Area.

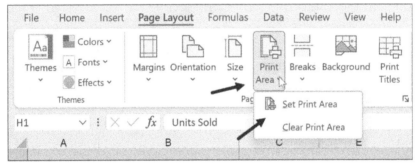

Only do it this way (as opposed to highlighting the section and choosing Print Selection) if it's a permanent setting.

Once you set your print area it will remain set until you clear it. You can add more data to your worksheet but it will never print until you change your print area, clear the setting, or deliberately override it when you choose to print.

I use this when I have a worksheet that has either a lot of extra information I don't want to print or where the formatting extends beyond my data and Excel keeps trying to print all those empty but formatted cells.

2. Breaks

You can set where a page break occurs in your worksheet. So say you have a worksheet that takes up four pages and you want to make sure that rows 1 through 10 are on a page together and then rows 11 through 20 are on a page together even though that's not how things would naturally fall. You can set a page break to force that to happen.

To insert a break, click on the cell where you want to insert the page break and then click on the dropdown for Breaks and choose Insert Page Break. You'll see a line appear on the worksheet to indicate where the page break is.

You can also use that dropdown to Reset All Page Breaks or remove a specific page break.

Personally, I find page breaks a challenge to work with, so I usually try to get what I need some other way.

3. Print Titles

This one is incredibly valuable. When you click on it, you'll see that it brings up the Page Setup box and takes you to the Sheet tab.

The first valuable thing you can do here is set the rows you want to repeat at the top of the page.

Say you have a worksheet with a thousand rows of data in it that will print on a hundred pages. How do you know what's in each column on each page? You need a header row. And you need that header row to repeat at the top of each and every page.

"Rows to repeat at top" is where you specify what row(s) is your header row. Click in that box and then select the row number(s) in your worksheet that you want to have repeat at the top of each page and Excel will write the cell notation for you. (This is why I do this in the worksheet itself instead of from the Print screen.)

The second valuable thing you can do here is set a column(s) you want to repeat on the left-hand side of each page. I need this one less often, but I do still sometimes use it.

Say, for example, that you had a list of students, one per row, and their test scores across fifty tests, and that when you printed that information it printed across two pages. Without listing the student's name in the left-hand column on every page, you wouldn't know whose scores you were looking at after the first page. But you can set that name column to repeat on each page.

To do so, click in the box that says "Columns to repeat at left", and then select the column(s) you want to repeat. Excel will once more write the cell notation you need for you in that field.

If you feel comfortable enough with cell notation you could do this from the print screen, but I never do.

You can repeat more than one row or column on each page, but if you do that, be careful that you don't end up selecting so many rows or columns to repeat that you basically just print the same thing over and over and over again. (Think of this as the printer equivalent of freeze panes if that helps.)

Okay. That's it. Let's wrap this up with a quick conclusion and then you're ready to dive in with using Excel.

Conclusion

As I explained at the beginning, this book was not meant to be comprehensive. Pick up one of the comprehensive books on Microsoft Excel and you'll see that it's two inches thick with small type.

Excel is insanely powerful, but most people don't need all of that. What I gave you here in this book is 95% of what you'll need day-to-day.

You can fill in the gaps as you go along using Excel's help function or online searches, or you can continue on with me in one of two directions if you want. (Or both, I won't mind.)

The next book in this series, *Intermediate Excel 365*, covers more advanced topics like pivot tables, charts, and conditional formatting that can be very valuable when analyzing data.

The other option is *102 Useful Excel 365 Functions.* That one covers exactly what you think it would: how to work with formulas and functions in Microsoft Excel. I've tried in that book to call out the functions I think are most useful. And I've mentioned a number of functions in passing that relate to those functions or are alternate versions of those functions.

For example, I talk about TEXTJOIN in there which allows you to join text strings. But I also cover the older functions that would let you do this, CONCATENATE and CONCAT.

But you don't have to stick with me and buy another book on these topics, because Excel has excellent help available. (The advantage my books give is they focus in specific areas and keep out the noise, so they provide a path to follow. But if you don't need the path, then you don't need a book. Anyway.)

You can open Help in Excel using F1. Or, as of now–this has changed over time–help is available by going to the Help tab at the top of the screen and then clicking on Help from there.

Either option in current versions of Excel will open a task pane on the right-hand side of the workspace that has a search bar as well as a number of help topics available.

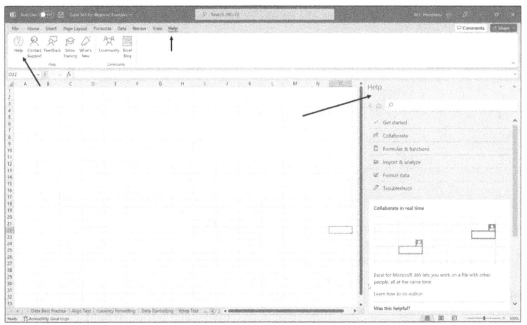

I often find it easier to click on Tell Me More which is available when you hover over specific options, like here with Format Painter.

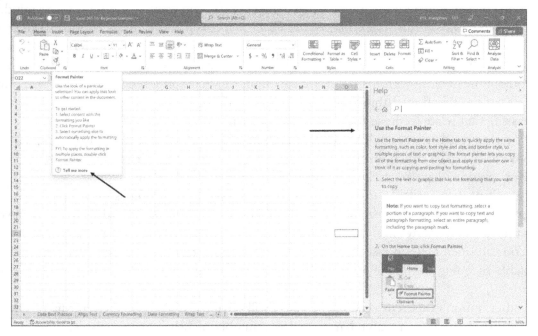

That always goes straight to the help topic for that particular option.

I will also often do a web search and then click on the link that goes to support.microsoft.com. So I might say, "microsoft excel copy formatting" and then click on the link that shows that it came from microsoft.

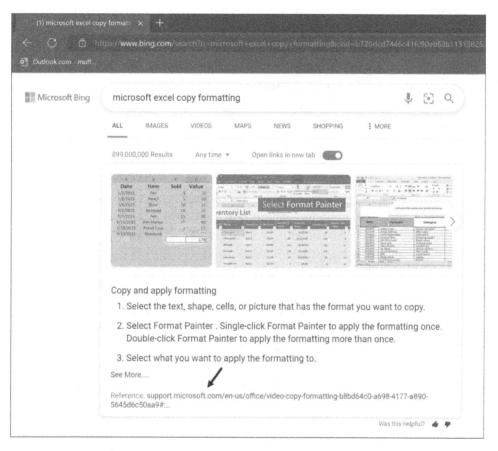

I've noticed in the last six months or so that at least the search engines I'm using give a fairly detailed preview of search results these days so that I don't even have to click through to a website sometimes to see the information I need. (Which is kind of crap for anyone who relies on ad revenue they generate from their website (which I don't), but that's the world for you. Always evolving, sometimes not in favor of the people who provide the value.)

Anyway. The Microsoft built-in help and website are both very good for when you need to know *how* to do something. "How do I copy an entry?", "How do I paste an entry?", "How does X function work?", etc.

For questions about "is this possible" they're less helpful. For that you either need to find someone who made a blog post or video doing what you want to do, or you need to wade into a tech forum somewhere and ask the experts how to do it.

You're always welcome to reach out to me with a question, too. Just know that if you start asking me to do your work for you, I'll quote you my (very expensive) consulting rates. I'm happy to clarify something or point you in the right direction, but "please build this complex calculation for me" is a step beyond that.

I will help with reasonable questions because I want you to understand this stuff, but also please respect that I can't do your work for you.

Also, know that there is no question that I will mock you for asking. I once had to train 90-year-old ladies on how to use a computer system so I know that people can be perfectly intelligent and simply struggle because something is new to them.

I try to keep in mind when I write these books what it's like to be new to Excel, but I sometimes miss something. For example, to click on the X in the top right corner to close things. Or to click on OK to be done with a dialogue box. These are things that are ingrained in me from decades of working with computers that I sometimes forget that other people don't know.

So ask what you need to ask because if I failed to teach you, that's on me.

Okay, that's it. I hope you now understand how powerful Excel can be. Don't be afraid to make mistakes. Ctrl + Z and Esc are you two best friends to get out of trouble. When all else fails, close the file without saving and come back to it.

If you're working with data for work maybe check out *How To Gather and Use Data for Business Analysis*, which is based on my lessons learned from working on data projects in a corporate setting. It talks about how to get data that you can effectively use for analysis.

If you want to understand how to apply basic math in Excel to budgeting then check out the *Juggling Your Finances: Basic Excel Guide*. It walks through Excel from the perspective of using addition, subtraction, multiplication, and division to calculate your basic financial status. (And is a companion to *Budgeting for Beginners* which explains how to use that information to improve your finances.)

You can find links to both of those at https://mlhumphrey.com/business-and-personal-finance/ and links to all of my Microsoft Office books (there are so many) at https://mlhumphrey.com/microsoft-office-all-links/.

And if there's something you need that I haven't written, let me know, I might write it. I wrote *Mail Merge for Beginners* because someone said they needed a book on that and I figured it was pretty easy for me to put it together for them.

Also if you tell me and I write it, chances are I'll send you a free ebook copy as a thank you. No guarantee I'll write it, but if I do…you get your question answered and I have another book out there that people may need. Win-win.

Okay. Good luck with it. Don't be scared. You can do this.

SHORTCUTS

The below tables contain various useful Excel shortcuts, most of which were discussed in the chapters of this book. The header row for each table shows which key to use and then the Task column tells you what that will accomplish. For example, Ctrl + N will open a new Excel file.

Ctrl +	Task
N	New File
O	Open File
S	Save File
C	Copy
V	Paste
X	Cut
Z	Undo
F	Open Find and Replace Dialogue Box to Find tab
A	Select All
P	Print
W	Close Current Workbook
B	Bold/Unbold Selected Text
I	Italicize/Remove Italics From Selected Text
U	Underline/Remove Underline From Selected Text
1	Open Format Cells Dialogue Box

Ctrl +	Task
End	Go to Last Column of Blank Worksheet OR Go to Last Column In Data Range OR Go to Next Column to the Right With Data
Home	Go to First Column of Blank Worksheet OR Go to First Column in Data Range OR Go to Next Column to the Left with Data
Down Arrow	Go to Last Row of Blank Worksheet OR Go to Last Row In Data Range OR Go to Next Row Down That Contains Data
Up Arrow	Go to First Row of Blank Worksheet OR Go to First Row In Data Range OR Go to Next Row Up That Contains Data
Right Arrow	Go to Last Column of Blank Worksheet OR Go to Last Column In Data Range OR Go to Next Column to the Right With Data
Left Arrow	Go to First Column of Blank Worksheet OR Go to First Column in Data Range OR Go to Next Column to the Left with Data

Alt +	Task
S	Refresh Pivot Table
H	Access Menu Options, Use Alt + Letter(s)/Number(s) to Select Task to Perform
Tab	Move Between Open Programs in Windows

Ctrl + Shift	Task
$	Format as Currency
#	Format as Date
!	Format as Number with Comma For Thousands
%	Format as Percent
Right Arrow	Select All Cells in Range To Right
Down Arrow	Select All Cells In Range Downward
Right and then Down Arrow	Select All Cells in Range Across and Down

Other	Task
Esc	Exit a Cell, Back Out of a Function, Close a Tool, General Escape Option
Tab	Move to the Right One Cell
Shift + Tab	Move to the Left One Cell
Windows Key + Ctrl + O	Open On-Screen Keyboard

Intermediate
Excel 365

EXCEL 365 ESSENTIALS - BOOK 2

M.L. HUMPHREY

CONTENTS

CONTENTS (CONT.)

Introduction

This book is the second in the Excel 365 Essentials series. If you're new to Excel then you're going to want to start with *Excel 365 for Beginners* because that book covers 95% of what you need to know to use Microsoft Excel on a daily basis, including the basics of entering information, formatting it, and using sorting, filtering, and basic formulas to analyze that information.

What this book does is covers topics that are more advanced than that, but still core skills that will help you use Excel on a daily basis, such as charts, pivot tables (which Excel likes to write as pivottables, but which drives me batty to write that way so I'm going to refuse to), and conditional formatting.

I'm also going to touch on the topic of pivot charts, which are charts you create from a pivot table, something I didn't do in *Intermediate Excel* or *Excel 2019 Intermediate*, the precursors to this book.

We'll also cover a few other useful but not essential topics like inserting symbols and equations, grouping data, subtotaling data, removing duplicate values, converting text to columns, fixing numbers that are stored as text, using the quick access toolbar, Excel Options, and zooming.

Most of what this book will focus on are core functions of Excel that have and will remain fairly stable over time. Excel 365 is a constantly-evolving product, but I don't expect it will evolve at any point in the near-term to make the information in this book outdated. Appearances may change a bit, but the core functionality should not. (And if it does, I'll unpublish this book because I don't want to be selling you information you can't use.)

This book does not cover formulas and functions at all, because the third book in the series, *102 Useful Excel 365 Functions*, is completely devoted to formulas and functions.

Okay. With that all said, let's get started. First things first, let's do a quick recap of the terminology that was introduced in *Excel 365 for Beginners* and then we can dive in with our first big topic, conditional formatting.

Basic Terminology Recap

Most of these terms were already defined in detail in *Excel 365 for Beginners*, so this is just to refresh your recollection.

Workbook

A workbook is what Excel likes to call an Excel file.

Worksheet

Excel defines a worksheet as the primary document you use in Excel to store and work with your data. A worksheet is organized into Columns and Rows that form Cells. A workbook can contain multiple worksheets.

Columns

Excel uses columns and rows to display information. Columns run across the top of the worksheet and, unless you've done something funky with your settings, are identified using letters of the alphabet.

The first column in a worksheet will always be Column A. And the number of columns in your worksheet will remain the same, regardless of how many columns you delete, add, or move around. Think of columns as location information that is actually separate from the data in the worksheet.

Rows

Rows run down the side of each worksheet and are numbered starting at 1 and up to a very high number. Row numbers are also locational information. The first row will always be numbered 1, the second row will always be numbered 2, and so on and so forth. There will also always be a fixed number of rows in each worksheet regardless of how many rows of data you delete, add, or move around.

Cells

Cells are where the row and column data comes together. Cells are identified using the letter for the column and the number for the row that intersect to form that cell. For example, Cell A1 is the cell that is in the first column and first row of the worksheet.

Click

If I tell you to click on something, that means to use your mouse (or trackpad) to move the cursor on the screen over to a specific location and left-click or right-click on the option. If you left-click, this selects the item. If you right-click, this generally displays a dropdown list of options to choose from. If I don't tell you which to do, left- or right-click, then left-click.

Left-click/Right-click

If you look at your mouse you generally have two flat buttons to press. One is on the left side, one is on the right. If I say left-click that means to press down on the button on the left. If I say right-click that means press down on the button on the right.

Select

If I tell you to "select" cells, that means to highlight them. You can either left-click and drag to select a range of cells or hold down the Ctrl key as you click on individual cells. To select an entire column, click on the letter for the column. To select an entire row, click on the number for the row.

Data

Data is the information you enter into your worksheet.

Data Table

I may also sometimes refer to a data table or table of data. This is just a combination of cells that contain data in them.

Arrow

If I tell you to arrow to somewhere or to arrow right, left, up, or down, this just means use the arrow keys to navigate to a new cell.

Cursor Functions

The cursor is what moves around when you move your mouse or use the trackpad. In Excel the cursor changes its appearance depending on what functions you can perform.

Tab

I am going to talk a lot about Tabs, which are the options you have to choose from at the top of the workspace. The default tab names are File, Home, Insert, Page Layout, Formulas, Data, Review, View, and Help. But there are certain times when additional tabs will appear, for example, when you create a pivot table or a chart.

(This should not be confused with the Tab key which can be used to move across cells.)

Dropdown Menus

A dropdown menu is a listing of available choices that you can see when you right-click in certain places such as the main workspace or on a worksheet name. You will also see them when you click on an arrow next to or below an option in the top menu.

Dialogue Boxes

Dialogue boxes are pop-up boxes that contain additional choices.

Scroll Bars

When you have more information than will show in a screen, dialogue box, or dropdown menu, you will see scroll bars on the right side or bottom that allow you to navigate to see the rest of the information.

Formula Bar

The formula bar is the long white bar at the top of the main workspace directly below the top menu options that lets you see the actual contents of a cell, not just the displayed value.

Cell Notation

Cells are referred to by their column and row position. So Cell A1 is the cell that's the intersection of the first column and first row in the worksheet.

When written in Excel you just use A1, you do not need to include the word cell. A colon (:) can be used to reference a range of cells. A comma (,) can be used to separate cell references.

When in doubt about how to define a cell range, click into a cell, type =, and then go and select the cells you want to reference. Excel will describe your selection in the formula bar using cell notation.

Paste Special Values

Paste Special Values is a way of pasting copied values that keeps the calculation results or the cell values but removes any formulas or formatting.

Task Pane

On occasion Excel will open a task pane, which is different from a dialogue box because it is part of the workspace. These will normally appear on the right-hand side in Excel for tasks such as working with pivot tables or charts or using the built-in Help function. (They often appear on the left-hand side in Word.)

They can be closed by clicking on the X in the top right corner.

Conditional Formatting

What is conditional formatting and why might you want to use it?

Conditional formatting is a way to take a data set and apply special formatting to certain results. It makes it much easier to see patterns as well as sort and filter your data.

I often will use conditional formatting in conjunction with a two-variable analysis grid. For example, I might build a grid with number of hours worked across the top and hourly pay rate down the side to see which combinations of hours and pay let me reach my income goal.

Let's say you need to make $500 a week. (I know, I wish that were how the world still worked, but just stay with me here.) Here's what I would put together for something like that:

	A	B	C	D	E	F	G	H
1			Hours Per Week					
2			15	20	25	30	35	40
3		$ 15.00	$ 225.00	$ 300.00	$ 375.00	$ 450.00	$ 525.00	$ 600.00
4	Pay Rate	$ 20.00	$ 300.00	$ 400.00	$ 500.00	$ 600.00	$ 700.00	$ 800.00
5		$ 25.00	$ 375.00	$ 500.00	$ 625.00	$ 750.00	$ 875.00	$1,000.00
6		$ 30.00	$ 450.00	$ 600.00	$ 750.00	$ 900.00	$1,050.00	$1,200.00
7								

I've applied conditional formatting to Cells C3 through H6 so that I can quickly see which combinations of hours per week and pay get me to that goal. 35 or 40 hours per week gets me there for all of the pay rates in the table. But if I can only work 20 hours a week, then I need to be paid $25 an hour or more.

Another place I use this is in my budgeting spreadsheet. There I have my bank account balance set with conditional formatting so that if I ever drop below the minimum balance for free checking, I can immediately see that and fix it before I end up paying an unexpected monthly account fee.

And I use this for the table where I list my revenue, ad spend, and profit from writing each month. I have it set so that each of those fields is shaded from light to dark so that I can easily see the months when I earned the most or least, the months when I spent the most or least on ads, and the months when I was most or least profitable.

That lets me spot trends across the months without looking at eight years' worth of numbers. I don't need to get hung up on the difference between $453.22 and $525.21 when I'm trying to look at trends.

I have another place where I don't even show the numbers at all. I have it set up to display colored bars instead. That lets me easily see how seasonal my results are. (Some products, like winter coats, sell better at certain times of year than others, right? The same thing can happen with different types of books.)

It can be useful to understand those patterns in your own business so that you plan accordingly. I always feel really good in January because that's a strong sales month for my books, but then I feel despair in July, which is not. Having conditional formatting to highlight the annual patterns in my sales reminds me that "this too shall pass", both the good months and the bad ones.

For a more traditional business, you could use conditional formatting to flag customer payments that are more than thirty days overdue. Or to highlight your largest sales transactions. Or flag any expense over $X which should have required pre-approval.

The possibilities are endless.

Another really great thing about conditional formatting is that you can combine it with filtering. So you could flag any customer payments that are overdue and then filter thousands of rows of customer data to only show those entries.

Now that you understand what conditional formatting is and how it works, let's walk through the various options you have in Excel.

First things first, to apply conditional formatting, select the cell range you want to use, and then go to the Styles section of the Home tab and click on the arrow for the Conditional Formatting option to show your available choices:

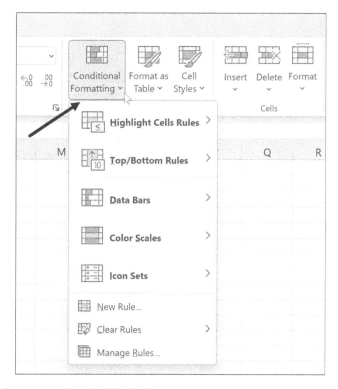

Your other option is to use the Quick Analysis button. To use this, highlight your cell range. You should then see a little icon appear in the bottom right corner of the selected range. Click on that and you'll see the Quick Analysis options.

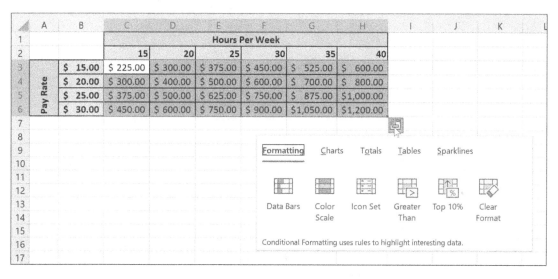

The Formatting tab is the one to use for conditional formatting. Move your mouse over those options and it will show you a preview on your data of what that will look like. The available options are going to depend on the nature of your selected data.

For text entries your options will be Text, Duplicate, Unique, Equal To, and Clear. For entries that contain text and numbers or numbers only, your options will be Data Bars, Colors, Icon Sets, Greater, Top 10%, and Clear.

Quick Analysis comes with its own preset styles that it's going to apply. If you like those styles, then it's a good option. I, at least for the greater than option and the way I use it, always have to change it from the default.

So I'm going to focus from here on out on how to apply conditional formatting using the top menu option, but do know that the quick analysis option exists and may be a quicker choice if you're willing to work with the default settings.

If you ever accidentally end up opening that quick analysis option when you didn't want to (which I have done off and on for years now), use the Esc key to close it. Your cells will remain selected but you won't have to choose one of those options.

Okay. Let's now walk through the conditional formatting dropdown menu from top to bottom.

Highlight Cells Rules

The highlight cells rules are what I used for the example above. What this section does is allows you to apply formatting to cells that meet certain criteria.

Here you can see the set of choices available via the dropdown menu:

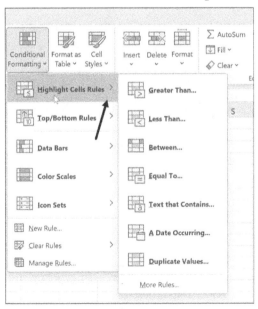

You can choose from Greater Than, Less Than, Between, Equal To, Text That Contains, A Date Occurring, and Duplicate Values. There's also a More Rules option at the bottom that will open the New Formatting Rule dialogue box.

The option I used above was Greater Than (with an edit to make it Greater Than or Equal To), so let's click on that. It brings up the Greater Than dialogue box and immediately colors your selected range of cells based on the default criteria it comes up with and the default format:

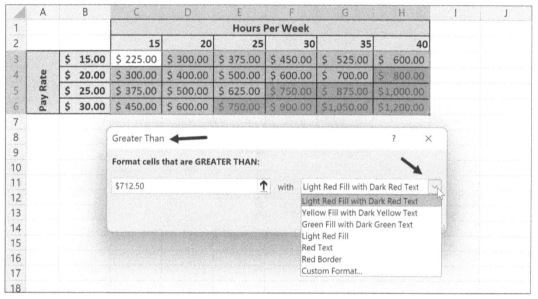

You can see here it went with greater than $712.50 and the default format is always going to be (or at least has been for decades) Light Red Fill with Dark Red Text.

Not what we want. Click into the box with the value and type in a new value. And then from the dropdown for the format you can either select one of the other options, I used Green Fill with Dark Green text above, or you can go to Custom Format and apply any formatting you want.

For a quick and dirty analysis I would likely type 499.99 into that box, choose the green formatting option, and be done. That's close enough to $500 or more and the fastest way to get my result.

But if it really matters that you have conditional formatting for $500 or more, then the default choices in that dropdown menu under Highlight Cells Rules aren't going to work.

You'll need to use the More Rules option at the bottom of the dropdown menu to have more choices. That, as I mentioned above, opens the New Formatting Rule dialogue box. By opening it through the Highlight Cells Rules dropdown it opens directly onto the "Format Only Cells That Contain" view:

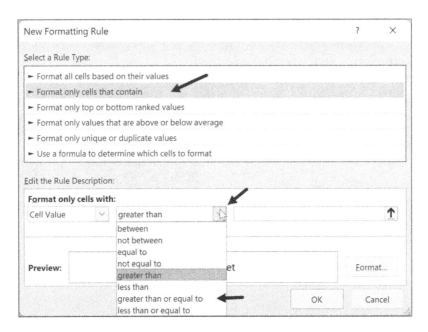

From there you can use the dropdown menu in that dialogue box to choose the "greater than or equal to" option and enter your specific value

But this way of applying a rule doesn't come with preset formatting to choose from like the options available through the Highlight Cells Rules dropdown.

To apply formatting, click on Format to open the Format Cells dialogue box.

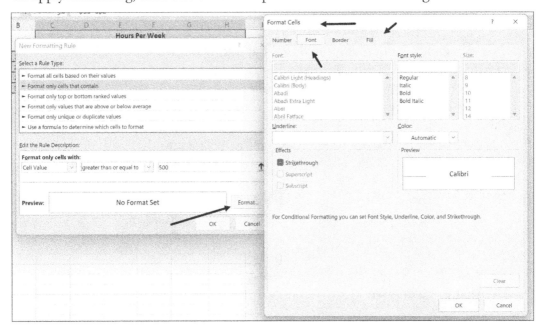

It opens onto the Font tab. That's where you can set the font color and any bolding or underline. But if you want to add a fill like the examples above use, then you'll also need to go to the Fill tab and choose a fill color from there. You cannot edit font or font size but most everything else is available to you.

When you're done click OK.

(Another option if you like Excel's default formats that we'll discuss later is to use one of the default options above, like Greater Than, apply one of the Excel formats, like the green text/green fill one, and then choose to Manage Rules and change the Greater Than option to the Greater Than or Equal To option at that point. That's how I did it. But we're not there yet.)

So. To summarize. Highlight Cells Rules for numbers come with a handful of default choices that you can access through that secondary dropdown menu. If you go that route you also have a handful of pre-defined formats you can apply.

But if you want more options, you need to use the More Rules choice and then you'll have to customize the formatting yourself.

Now let's talk about those bottom three options, Text That Contains, A Date Occurring, and Duplicate Values. I want to start with Duplicate Values because that can still be a numbers one.

Here I've selected Duplicate Values for this range of cells and left it with the red text/red fill formatting:

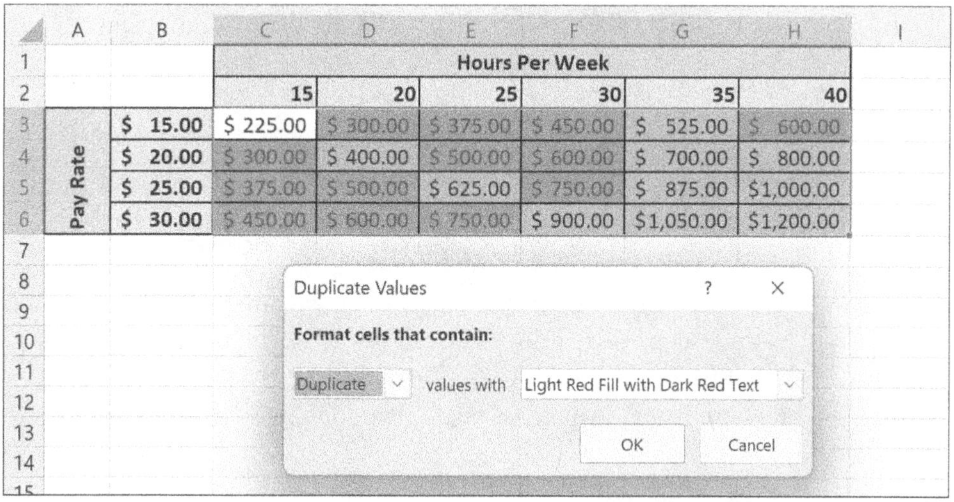

	A	B	C	D	E	F	G	H	I
1					Hours Per Week				
2			15	20	25	30	35	40	
3		$ 15.00	$ 225.00	$ 300.00	$ 375.00	$ 450.00	$ 525.00	$ 600.00	
4	Pay Rate	$ 20.00	$ 300.00	$ 400.00	$ 500.00	$ 600.00	$ 700.00	$ 800.00	
5		$ 25.00	$ 375.00	$ 500.00	$ 625.00	$ 750.00	$ 875.00	$1,000.00	
6		$ 30.00	$ 450.00	$ 600.00	$ 750.00	$ 900.00	$1,050.00	$1,200.00	

Duplicate Values dialog box:

Format cells that contain:

Duplicate ⌄ values with   Light Red Fill with Dark Red Text ⌄

OK   Cancel

(Note that you can actually also use this choice to get Unique values by changing the dropdown in the Duplicate Values dialogue box.)

I want to point out one issue to you that makes this one not have a lot of value to me. And that's that it flags all duplicate values with the exact same formatting. So here we have duplicates of $300, $375, $450, $500, $600, and $750. But as far as the formatting is concerned, they're all treated the same.

Which if you did not want any duplicates at all in your data would probably be fine. As long as any cell is formatted with red, you know you still have duplicates.

But what if I wanted to look at my duplicates and figure out which one to keep? This is not a good data set for that, but let's say I had two entries for Students A, B, C, and D in a data table. This conditional formatting option will tell me I have duplicate entries for each of those students, but it doesn't let me easily isolate Student A's duplicate entries. Maybe Student A has three. How do I know that without doing more work? (I'd have to filter by Student A, I couldn't filter by format. And in a table like the one above, that's not an option, so I'd have to use Find to see how many entries I had for Student A.)

Okay. That's the duplicate value option, it may have some limited uses, just keep in mind its limitations.

What about the Text That Contains option? That one works fine, no big surprises.

I used it in the example below to flag all transactions in the Australian Amazon store in this report and it did just fine with it:

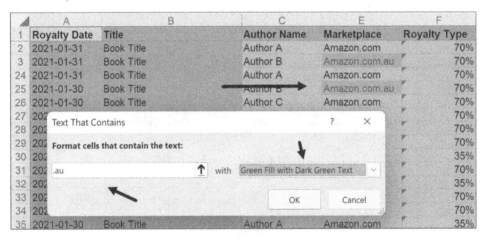

Note here that I'm still in that dialogue box but Excel is showing me what it will do to my data if I click OK. So if you put in criteria and realize that doing so flags entries you don't want to include, you can change it before you click OK. (Or Cancel.)

For example, if I had used "au" instead of ".au" that could have potentially captured other entries I didn't want.

Finally, let's look at the date one:

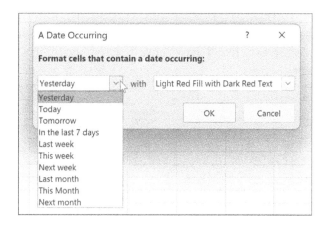

The choices are yesterday, today, tomorrow, last seven days, last week, this week, next week, last month, this month, and next month. I personally don't find this tremendously useful because I can't specify dates or criteria.

If you need one of those, great. But if you need some other set of dates to be flagged, conditional formatting using the Highlight Cells Rules option does not at this point in time give you that level of control. So, for example, "more than 30 days ago" is not an option. Nor is "between this date and that".

Also, the More Rules option doesn't give any additional choices. (This is a place they could make some useful improvements, hint, hint, so maybe that will change over time.)

Okay, next we have the Top/Bottom Rules.

Top/Bottom Rules

Here are the available quick options for that one:

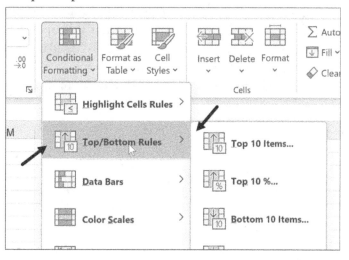

They are labeled Top 10 Items, Top 10%, Bottom 10 Items, Bottom 10%, Above Average, and Below Average. But, when you click on the ten items or ten percent options, you can edit the number in the dialogue box like I have here for the top ten percent option, which I changed to the top twenty percent:

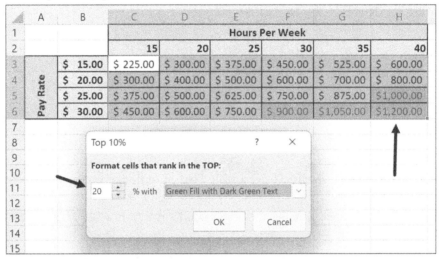

As for formatting, you have the same dropdown menu options as for the Highlight Cells Rules, including the Custom Format option at the bottom of the list.

There is also a More Rules option in the Top/Bottom Rules secondary dropdown menu which will open the New Formatting Rule dialogue box to the "Format only top or bottom ranked values" option, but it doesn't provide any additional options that aren't already listed.

Data Bars

Data bars is the one I mentioned above that I use in lieu of numbers so that I can see seasonal trends in my revenue, ad spend, and profit numbers. What this option does by default is it places a bar in each cell where the size of the bar in the cell is based upon the relative value of the amount in that cell compared to the other cells in the range.

That sounds horribly complicated, but it's not. Let's look at a few examples:

	A	B	C
1	Example 1	Example 2	Example 3
2	1	10	1
3	2	20	100
4	3	30	1000
5	4	40	2500
6	5	50	10000

Here I have three different columns of data. I have applied data bars to each column individually. (That's important, because that means that Column A's values are only being compared to the other values in Column A. Same for Columns B and C.)

Note the values in Column A are 1, 2, 3, 4, and 5. And that the values in Column B are 10, 20, 30, 40, and 50.

The relative relationships between the five values in each of those columns are identical even though the numbers themselves are different. Five is five times one, fifty is five times ten. Same relative relationship. And that's true for all five numbers.

Which is why the data bars you see in those cells are the same. The data bar in Row 2 is one-fifth the size of the data bar in Row 6 for those two columns.

But in Column C the data bars do not work like that, because the numbers I've provided there have a different relationship to one another. 1 is one-ten-thousandth of the final entry 10,000. That's why you can't even see its data bar. 2,500 is one-fourth of 10,000 which is why its data bar takes up one-fourth of its cell.

By default, when working with data bars, the largest value (Y) will have a data bar that takes up the entire cell. Every other value (X) will have a data bar that takes up X/Y portion of its cell. That's why in Columns A and B the data bars are the same size for each row despite the difference in the numeric values, and why each bar is 1/5 bigger than the bar in the row above.

The data bar menu choices are very basic:

You can basically choose one of six colors in either a solid version (as I did above) or in a gradient version. The gradient shows within each cell. So each data bar shades from darker to lighter, however big that data bar is. Like so:

	A	B	C
1	Example 1	Example 2	Example 3
2	1	10	1
3	2	20	100
4	3	30	1000
5	4	40	2500
6	5	50	10000

Which means that choosing gradient here is just an aesthetic choice. The shading does not give additional information about relative value.

Where things can get interesting with data bars is if you click on that More Rules option and bring up the New Formatting Rule dialogue box. By default, data bars are applied as I described above where it looks at the actual values in the cells and then applies bars based on their relation to one another. But you can change that.

Here, for example, for the data bars in Column B I've set a specific range that is not based on the values in those cells. Now the data bars are applied based upon where a value falls between 0 and 100. That means for each cell the data bar size is determined by the value in that cell (X) divided by 100.

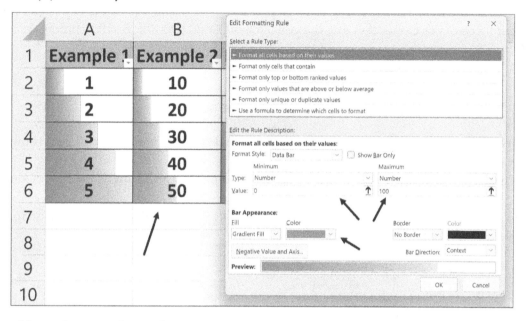

Now 50, our largest value, only generates a data bar that's half the size of the cell.

You can also see that I used the Color dropdown menu to choose a custom color other than one of the six default choices.

The other thing I want to point out to you is that little checkbox for "Show Bar Only". If you don't want to be distracted by the actual values, you can check that box and then you will not see the values in those cells. Like so:

Just be careful on that one. Because, as I showed you at the beginning, data bars for 1, 2, 3, 4, and 5 are going to look identical to the data bars for 10, 20, 30, 40, and 50. So you lose that type of nuance when you hide the values behind the data bars.

Say, for example, these two columns represented sales performance for two sales reps. You'd think that Sales Rep A and Sales Rep B are performing the same, and in terms of percent increase per month they are, but you'd miss the fact that Rep B sells ten times as much as Rep A every month.

Okay. On to Color Scales.

Color Scales

Color scales is one I use a lot. It's the one I use to shade my revenue, ad spend, and profit and loss values per month.

What they do is color a cell a shade of a color or along a continuum of colors based upon the relative value in that cell compared to the values in the rest of the selected cells.

So, much like data bars except color-based. And, like data bars, the secondary menu for this one is color choices:

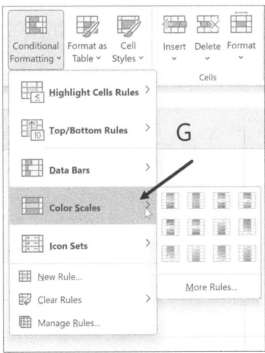

In this case you can choose green-yellow-red, red-yellow-green, green-white-red, red-white-green, blue-white-red, red-white-blue, white-red, red-white, green-white, white-green, green-yellow, and yellow-green.

I almost always use the More Rules option to choose a different color since red, green, and yellow tend to have set meanings of "bad", "good", and "okay". So I'll often use the color dropdown menu and change it so that my color for the lowest value is the lightest color in one of the provided color columns and the color for my highest value is one of the darkest colors in that same column. Like so:

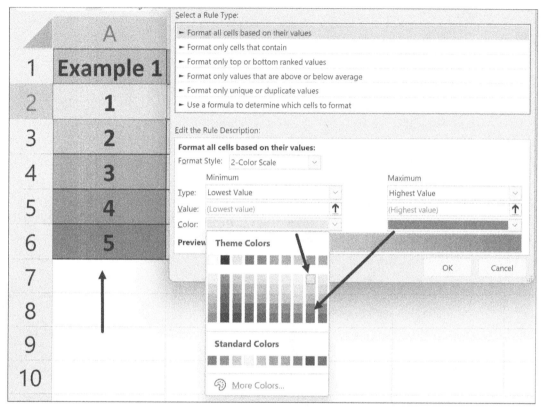

Be careful on this one what colors you choose and what that implies. For example, if I go from gray to orange to brown, which of those colors is "good"? Which is "bad"?

If all you want is to distinguish values from one another, that's fine. But if you're trying to see the "best" results or the "worst" results, take that into consideration when choosing your colors.

Make sure the color you use supports what you're trying to display. At least in the United States, for example, you don't want to shade your "good" values red since red is generally considered "bad". Especially if the other end of the shading spectrum is green which is usually considered "good."

Also, if using a color like red or green, you may want to use multiple colors. Let's say -100 is good and 100 is bad but if it's all shades of red it makes it all look "bad" to one degree or another. Same with all green, it makes it all look "good" to one degree or another.

Two more things to point out here. We've been dealing with set values, but you can also have Excel apply color scales (or data bars) based upon percent, percentile, or a formula that you provide.

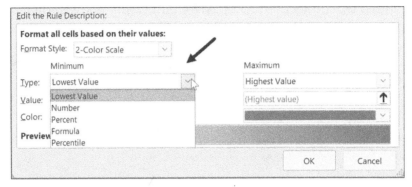

You also have the choice to customize to either a two-color scale or three-color scale by changing the Format Style dropdown.

Finally, if you do have color scales that use a really dark color and you want your values to show in the cell, consider formatting those cells using white text to make the entries more visible.

(You could do this by adding a second conditional formatting rule to that cell range that applies white text to cells with values in that upper range using a custom format and the Highlight Cells Rules. Or if the data is relatively stable, just format those cells with white text manually.)

Okay, next up, Icon Sets.

Icon Sets

Icon sets are much like color scales or data bars, except they show various icons next to the values. Here's the dropdown menu:

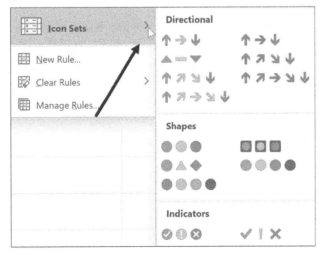

Here are some examples of those in action:

	A	B	C
1	Example 1	Example 2	Example 3
2	⬇ 1	⬤ 10	⬛ 1
3	⬇ 2	⬤ 20	⬛ 100
4	➡ 3	⬤ 30	⬛ 1000
5	⬆ 4	⬤ 40	⬛ 2500
6	⬆ 5	⬤ 50	⬛ 10000

As you can see there are choices that break your data into thirds, fourths, or even fifths, some of which also use color-coding. If you use these icons on your data, Excel will let you then filter your results by icon using the Filter By Color option:

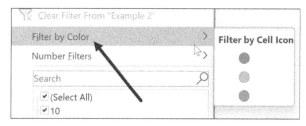

(This is also available if you're using color scales, but not for data bars.)

You can use the More Rules option to bring up the New Formatting Rule dialogue box and customize your icon sets. You can either use one of the same icon sets already shown or combine different elements of an icon set using the dropdown menu:

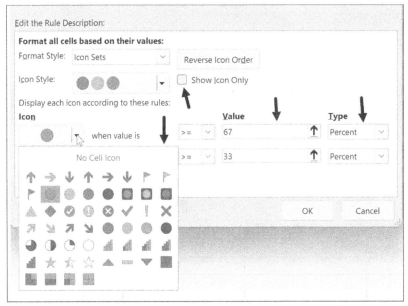

And you can set parameters as percent of the range, number, percentile, or as a formula. Here I've combined icons from three different icon sets and used absolute number values to apply the icons:

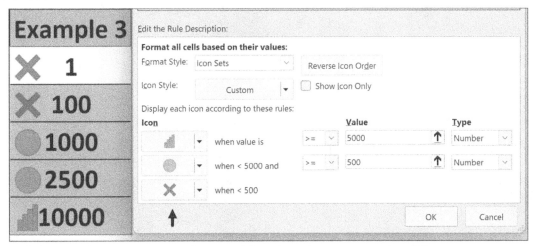

(Proof that just because you can do something doesn't mean you should.)

New Rule

If you just want to jump straight in to customizing a rule and don't want Excel to start you off with any sort of help, you can choose New Rule from the Conditional Formatting dropdown menu in the Styles section of the Home tab.

This will open the New Formatting Rule dialogue box set to the top option, "Format all cells based on their values" and then you can navigate from there.

In general, I wouldn't recommend this. Because as you've seen with the More Rules option on each of the secondary dropdown menus, going to one of those first starts you off on the right screen when you open the New Formatting Rule dialogue box.

In my opinion it's better to know the type of conditional formatting you want to apply and click on the More Rules option from that secondary dropdown menu instead.

The only exception to this might be the final option there, "Use a formula to determine which cells to format". Because if you're applying basic formatting to your cells using a formula (and not applying data bars, color scales, or icons), that may only be possible through this option and there's no quick shortcut to get there.

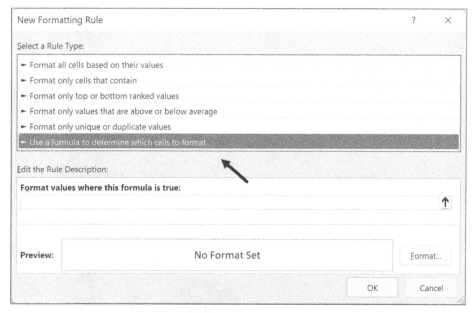

Using Formulas

Okay, so let's talk about using a formula. First, know that the help screen for conditional formatting has a very useful video on this if you want to reinforce what I say here or see another example.

To write a formula for conditional formatting, the formula must return a true or false value and start with an equals sign (which indicates that it's a formula).

For example, let's say that I want to flag those results in Column C where the value in Column B is greater. What you do is write your formula so that it returns a TRUE or FALSE value based upon the first cell in your selected range.

Here, for example, my selected cell range begins with Cell C2:

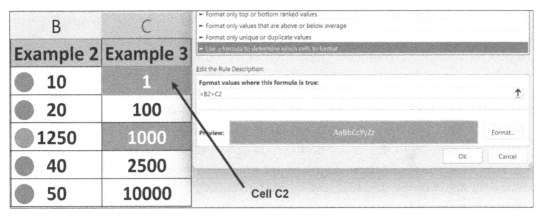

B	C	
Example 2	Example 3	
⬤ 10	1	
⬤ 20	100	
⬤ 1250	1000	
⬤ 40	2500	
⬤ 50	10000	Cell C2

Which means the formula I write in the formula field in my New Formatting Rule dialogue box has to be written for that cell. (I've selected Cells C2 through C6 to apply the formatting, but the cell I write the formula for is Cell C2.)

The formula I wrote is

$$=B2>C2$$

That says, this is a formula (=), look at B2, is it greater than C2? If so, return a value of TRUE, which means format the cell. If not, return a value of FALSE and don't format the cell.

I had it apply a bright green fill and white text. But note that you can also use formulas for data bars, color scales, and icon sets.

The key with formulas is to write them so that they return a TRUE or FALSE result and to write them as if writing a formula for the top cell in the selected range.

Also, you can't reference values in an external workbook although you can reference a value in another worksheet.

Copy Conditional Formatting To New Data

There are a few more topics to cover, but before I forget this and because it's especially useful with dealing with formulas and conditional formatting, if you want to copy conditional formatting from one cell to another, you can use the Format Painter in the Clipboard section of the Home tab.

I just did this a moment ago and it worked like a charm, so hopefully the same is true for you. Click on the cell with the conditional formatting you want to copy, then click on the Format Painter image in the Clipboard, and then click on the cell(s) where you want to transfer that conditional formatting.

I was able to take the formula-based formatting we just created and copy that to Cell F8 with no issues using this approach.

Edit Rules

I will admit that I have been cheating a bit with some of the screenshots you've seen in this section. Because I couldn't show you the conditional formatting applied and the settings I'd applied at the same time using the New Formatting Rule dialogue box. I had to apply the formatting and then go edit the rule to get the dialogue box settings visible next to the formatted cells.

So how do you edit an existing conditional formatting rule? Go to the Conditional Formatting dropdown menu and choose Manage Rules from the bottom of the dropdown menu.

That will open the Conditional Formatting Rules Manager which will default to showing the rules applied to your current selection:

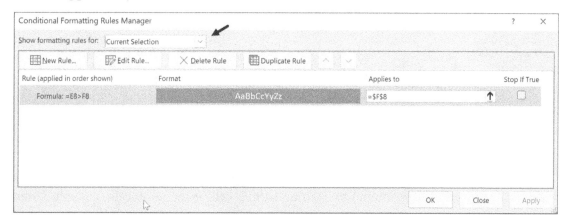

You can change that dropdown to the current worksheet or to any other worksheet in your workbook.

To edit an existing rule, click on the row for that rule and then click on Edit Rule. This will bring up the familiar-by-now dialogue box, but the top of the dialogue box will say that it's the Edit Formatting Rule dialogue box.

Make the changes you want to make and then click on OK. This will take you back to the Conditional Formatting Rules Manager dialogue box where you can either click OK or Apply to make your change. OK will close the dialogue box. Apply will apply the change but keep the dialogue box open.

I will sometimes edit my conditional formatting rules to extend the cell reference range by clicking into the box that lists the referenced cells and editing it. It's probably not the best method to use. But if you do it, do not use the arrow keys while in that box. It will start editing your cell reference range. You need to either click directly where you want to make your edit or backspace to delete the text until you get to that spot.

You can also use the arrow with a bar under it at the end of the listed cell range to select your cell range directly in the worksheet.

I used to have to do this because I would add more entries at the bottom of an existing set of data and the conditional formatting would not carry through to the new entries, but when I was writing this chapter it looks like maybe Excel now extends formatting automatically for you.

Delete Rule or Clear Formatting

If you want to delete a single conditional formatting rule, you can do so through the Manage Rules option in the Conditional Formatting dropdown menu. Click on Manage Rules, find the rule you want to delete, select it, and then click Delete Rule.

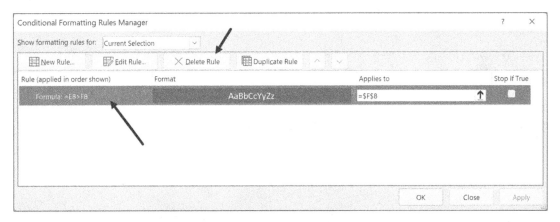

If you want to clear all conditional formatting from a cell or range of cells, though, I think that Quick Analysis option we discussed at the start is faster. Select your cell(s), click on the Quick Analysis icon in the bottom right corner, and then click on the Clear Format option.

There is also a menu option to clear rules from cells. Go to the Conditional Formatting dropdown menu, go down to Clear Rules, and then choose either Clear Rules from Selected Cells or Clear Rules from Entire Worksheet.

(We're going to cover conditional formatting of pivot tables in the pivot table section, but there's an option for that there as well.)

Find Conditional Formatting

If you use the Manage Rules option and choose to look at the current worksheet, that's going to show you all of the rules in that worksheet and which cells they apply to.

But according to Excel, you can also use the Find option to find conditional formatting.

Go to the Editing section of the Home tab, click on the dropdown arrow for Find & Select, and then choose Conditional Formatting from there:

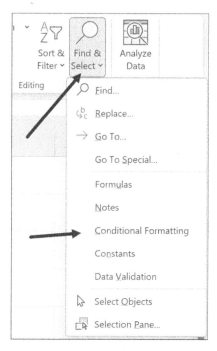

What that does is selects every cell in the worksheet that has conditional formatting applied. They're shaded gray and if you choose to remove conditional formatting from selected cells it will remove it from all of the cells in that worksheet that have conditional formatting applied.

If you want to just find a specific type of conditional formatting, click on a cell that has that type of formatting applied, and then go to the Find & Select option and choose Go To Special. In the dialogue box that appears, click on Conditional Formats, and then choose Same under Data Validation. That will highlight all of the cells that have that specific conditional formatting.

I did have one situation where it did not work where I had used the Format Painter to transfer a formula-based conditional format to a cell that was not in the same column, but otherwise I was able to get it to work.

Multiple Rules

One final thought. It is possible, as I alluded to before when talking about formatting cells with white text if the fill color on that cell is dark, to apply more than one type of conditional formatting to the same cell or range of cells.

Be careful if you do this that the formatting doesn't conflict, because one format may overwrite the other.

There is a "Stop if True" checkbox you can click for a rule to make sure that if there are multiple rules that if one is met no more conditional formatting is applied.

Also, you can change the order of the rules, by using the Manage Rules option to see all rules and then moving a rule above or below the others to get them to apply in the "correct" order. I find that I sometimes just have to experiment a bit to get the result I want.

And since I haven't said it yet in this book, remember that Ctrl + Z, Undo, is your friend. If you do something that looks bad, undo it, and try again.

Insert Symbols

That was a lot to cover, so let's step back and discuss a few much simpler things you can do in Excel. I'll start with how to insert a symbol into a cell.

This isn't going to come up often, but let's say you're using text in your worksheet and find yourself needing to insert the copyright symbol, ©.

The easiest way to do that, assuming you haven't changed your settings to prevent it, is to just type (c) in the cell. When you then hit the space bar to move forward that will convert into the copyright symbol.

Excel has a number of these shortcuts pre-programmed. You can see them if you go to the File tab and then click on Options at the bottom of the screen to open the Excel Options dialogue box. Go to the Proofing section on the left-hand side and then click on AutoCorrect Options to open the AutoCorrect Options dialogue box:

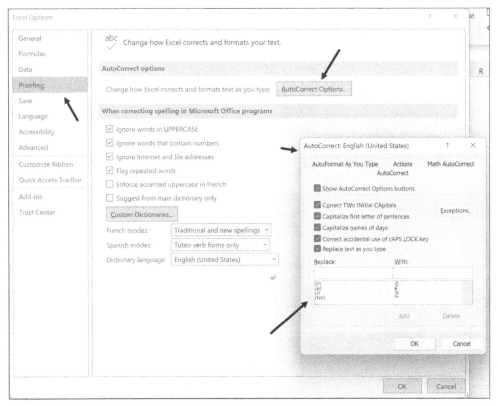

It's a little hard to see in that screenshot, but there are shortcuts listed for copyright, Euro, registered trademark, and trademark. If you click over to the Math AutoCorrect tab you'll see that there are many more text to symbol options listed there.

If you don't like one of the autocorrect options you can delete it. For example, I did a lot of regulatory work at one point in time and was far more likely to be referring to 3110(c) than I was to need the copyright symbol. So one of the first things I would do when I upgraded to a new version of Word or Excel was track that one down and delete it.

You can also add a shortcut to that list if there's a symbol you use often. In the AutoCorrect Options dialogue box, type the shortcut text you want to use in the Replace field, and then paste in the symbol you want in the With field. Click Add and then OK.

(I'll show you in a moment how to insert a symbol without using a shortcut so that you can insert that symbol and copy it for use in creating your shortcut.)

Just think it through before you create a shortcut. I have a program where I mainly do formatting and have shortcuts set up for applying formatting to my text using Shift + 1, Shift + 2, and Shift + 3. They're great to use, because they're right there, but each time I need an exclamation mark, an at sign, or a pound sign, I have a problem. It's worth it to me in that program because I need the formats more than I need those three symbols, but every once in a while it catches me out.

To insert a symbol without using a shortcut, click into the location where you want to insert that symbol—so a blank cell or within the text that's already in a cell. Go to the Insert tab and at the far right end there should be an image for Symbols with a dropdown arrow. Click on that and choose Symbol from the dropdown menu.

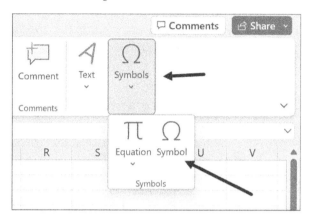

That will open the Symbol dialogue box:

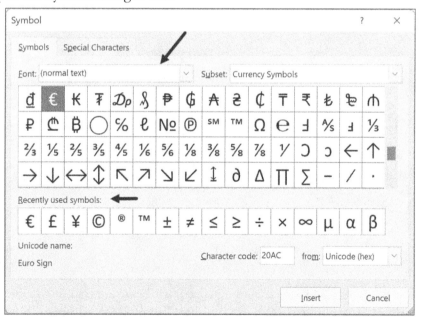

A few key things to point out here. At the top is a dropdown menu for Font and Subset. In the screenshot above the font is (normal text) and the subset is Currency Symbols.

Below that are four rows of symbols related to that font and subset.

You can either change the font or subset using the dropdown menus or you can use the scroll bar on the right-hand side of those symbols to move through all of your symbols.

Below the symbols related to the font and subset is a row of "recently used symbols".

I haven't used any symbols in Excel yet, so this is Excel's default list: some currency symbols, some copyright and trademark symbols, and then some mathematical symbols.

The math symbols you see are text, not something to use to perform mathematical calculations. You use an asterisk for multiplication in an Excel formula, not an x, for example.

Note also that there is another tab you can click on at the top of the dialogue box for Special Characters. These are mostly writing-related. So various types of dashes, hyphens, spaces, quotes, etc.

If you see the symbol you want, double-click on it to insert it in your cell. If that's all you needed, click Close or the X in the top right corner to close the dialogue box. If you need another symbol, go find it and insert it.

If the symbol you want is not visible, then you'll need to use the scroll bar on the side or use the Font or Subset dropdown menus to get to the font you want.

Often the Wingdings fonts include images so if that's the sort of thing you need, look there first:

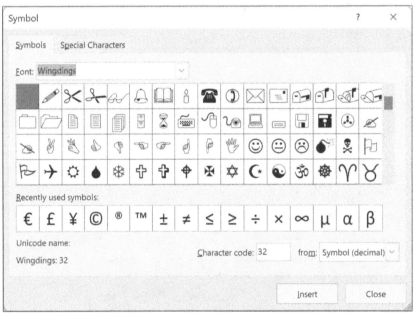

I have some custom fonts that also include images. Just be aware that if you use a font other users don't have they may not be able to see that "symbol" as an image. Also, if you use Wingdings or another font like that, be very careful about changing your font after you do so.

Here, for example, in Cell A1 I have the Euro symbol inserted using the default (normal text) menu that was available when I opened the Symbols dialogue box. Next to that is a yin yang symbol I inserted from the Wingdings font and then a stylistic little symbol I also inserted from there as well.

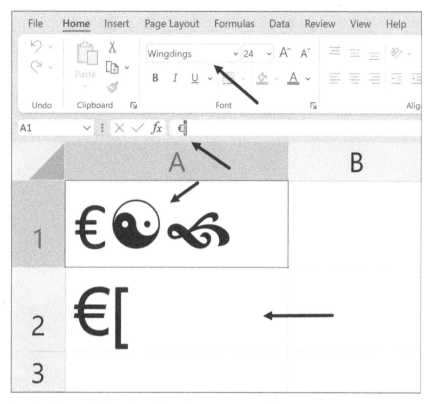

You can see in the formula bar that the yin yang symbol is actually a left bracket ([ ) and that the stylistic symbol has no associated character. It takes up a space in that formula bar, but there's nothing to see there.

I copied the contents of Cell A1 to Cell A2 and applied the Arial font to the contents. You can see that the Euro symbol is still a Euro symbol, although it has changed to reflect the applied font. But because we're no longer using the Wingdings font in Cell A2, the yin yang symbol became a left bracket and the stylistic symbol is gone. (It will come back, though if I change the font for that cell to Wingdings. Same with the yin yang symbol. But if I do that, the Euro symbol changes to a zero in a circle.)

Most symbols are tied in to the chosen font. So if you use them, have your font established before you start inserting them, just to be safe. The ones that are shown under the (normal text) section probably have an equivalent version in most fonts, but I'd still double-check them after changing the font.

Once inserted into your worksheet a symbol can be formatted color- and size-wise like any other text.

Insert Equations

You may have noticed that in that same dropdown menu for symbols there was also an option for Equation:

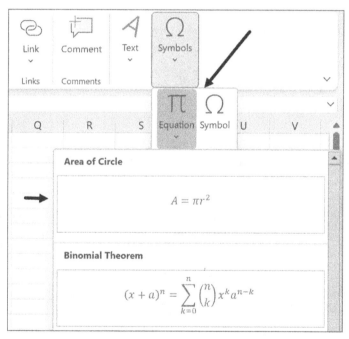

Click on that option and you'll see some pre-formatted equations such as the two above for area of a circle and binomial theorem.

If you click on one of these options, it will insert as a text box. It is not inserting the equation into a cell in your worksheet. It inserts on top of the worksheet and can be moved around within the worksheet by clicking and dragging when your cursor looks like four arrows, one pointing in each direction.

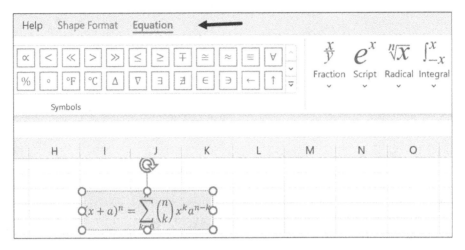

Above you can see that I inserted the binomial theorem equation and that it's sitting on top of my cells, it's not part of any of them. This is a visual presentation of a formula not to help you build a function that uses that formula.

When you insert an equation into your worksheet, Excel will display two new tab options, Shape Format and Equation. These will be visible at any time that you have the equation selected and will not be visible at other times.

I could use the Equation tab options to insert additional symbols to help build out the formula from here.

You can't see the full section, but on the right-hand side are more options grouped by category (Fraction, Script, Radical, Integral, etc.) where there are dropdown menus and you can select common notation for each of those categories.

On the left-hand side of the Equation tab are three options for how to format the equation: Professional, Linear, and Normal Text. The default format is Professional which uses italics for letters like n unlike the Normal Text option which does not. The Linear option writes the entire formula on a single line. So (x+a) to the nth power becomes (x+a)^n, for example.

The Shape Format tab is where you can change the color and style of the text of the equation or the border around the text. (Although for the text the normal text formatting options on the Home tab will also work as long as you select the text first.)

I'm not going to dive in any deeper on this, because I don't think many people will need it, I just wanted to mention it because it was there and you might have been curious.

I'll just close with a reminder that Excel treats these equations not as text, but as shapes. They will not behave like normal cells and text do.

Insert Illustrations

I don't want to cover this one in detail either, but I feel I have to at least mention it because more people are using illustrations in Excel and if you come across one like I did the other day, you need to know how to deal with them.

In that same Insert tab, on the left-hand side is an option for Illustrations. If you click on the dropdown arrow you'll see a number of choices, including Pictures, Shapes, Icons, 3D Models, SmartArt, and Screenshots.

Here I've clicked on the dropdown arrow for Shapes and you can see the beginning of what is a very large dropdown menu of shapes that can be inserted into an Excel worksheet:

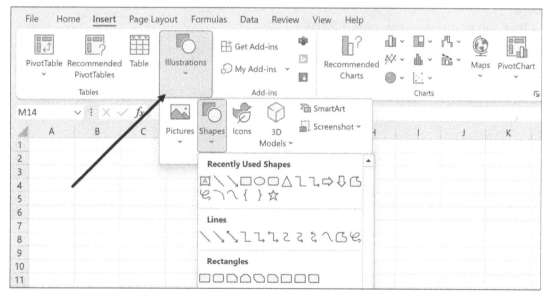

For Pictures, Icons, and 3D Models, when you make your selection and click on Insert it will automatically insert on top of the worksheet.

For Shapes, click on one of those options and then click and drag on the worksheet to create the shape.

For SmartArt, after you choose your SmartArt it will insert a template on your worksheet along with a dialogue box where you can input the values you want to use.

All of these are inserted on top of the worksheet, not embedded in an individual cell in the worksheet. You can click and drag them around (when the cursor has arrows pointing in four directions).

You can also resize them by clicking on them and then clicking and dragging from one of the white circles in the corners or around the perimeter. Be careful about scale because if you click from one of the sides then only the height or only the width will adjust, but not both.

You can also resize using the special Format tab which will appear for that object. (The names are slightly different for each tab, but they all have Format in them and will appear to the right of the Help tab when you click on the object.) Size is at the far right side on each tab. Input the numeric values you want there.

That Format tab is also where you can specify colors, borders, etc. and where you can dictate which of multiple objects is in front or in back if they happen to overlap.

I could spend a good forty pages on this and do cover SmartArt and objects in far more detail in the PowerPoint books, but most of you will not need it in Excel. So all I'm going to tell you here is that if you see text in a worksheet that doesn't seem to be part of a cell, it's likely from a shape someone has inserted into that worksheet. And if you need to remove it (like I recently did with Amazon's attribution tracking workbook), click on the object and use Delete.

Okay. On to our next big topic, Charts.

Charts – Basics and Types

Charts are a great way to visualize data. Sometimes numbers can be overwhelming, but a quick picture based on those numbers makes trends and patterns very clear.

Data Format

First things first, you need to format your data so that Excel can use it to create a chart.

(We'll talk about pivot tables and pivot charts later. If you work with those the pivot table basically already does this for you and then Excel knows how to build charts off of it, but I wanted to cover charts first before we have that conversation.)

For most chart types you want data labels across the top and data labels down the side, but no grand totals or sub-totals or sub-headers. Like this:

	January-2020	February-2020	April-2020	May-2020	June-2020	July-2020	August-2020	Total
Author A	$23.60	$74.26	$262.40	$296.36	$266.15	$250.00	$322.00	$1,494.77
Author B	$17.13	$6.88	$95.68	$3.44	$6.88	$5.59	$121.00	$256.60
Author C	$8.44	$6.01	$61.76	$8.98	$5.34	$1.47	$681.81	$773.80
Author D	$8.63	$0.52	$13.86	$22.08	$50.85	$128.46	$61.22	$285.62
Author E	$3.38	$0.07	$2.74	$3.47	$16.05	$11.24	$42.12	$79.07
Author F	$1.69	$0.06	$1.29	$1.33	$3.78	$7.14	$40.84	$56.12

(I usually do not include any sort of label in that top left corner, but just now when I left one there it still worked. Note this is randomly-generated data not real sales data.)

Which data label goes across the top versus down the side will impact the default chart that Excel tries to build when you choose your chart type, but there's an option to flip those if it's not how you want it in the chart, so don't worry too much about that.

If you do happen to have grand totals or labels like I do here with the Total Column, that's okay, but you'll want to select only the cells with the data and labels you want to include in your chart.

It is important that you format the data in the table you're going to use before you create your chart. I will often create charts that include a data table below the chart and when I do that the formatting of those values is directly sourced from the original data table.

So, for example, when I'm going to include a data table below my chart, I format my currency values to not have any decimal places, because it takes up too much space and that level of detail is not necessary.

Create a Chart

To create a chart, select the data you want to use for the chart and then go to the Charts section of the Insert tab and click on the dropdown for the chart type you want.

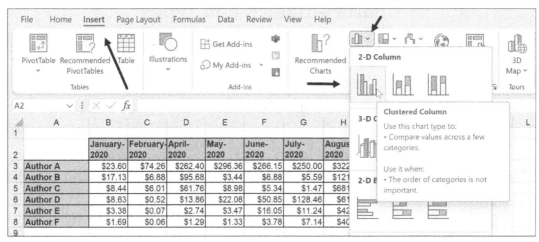

From there you'll see a list of available choices. If you hold your mouse over each one, Excel will tell you more about that specific type of chart (as you can see above for Clustered Column).

It will also create and show you the chart, but not actually insert it. If you move your mouse, the chart will disappear.

When you find the chart option you want, simply click on it and that chart will then be officially inserted into your worksheet and remain there after you move your mouse away. Charts work like equations and illustrations so are inserted on top of your worksheet, not as part of a cell. Like this:

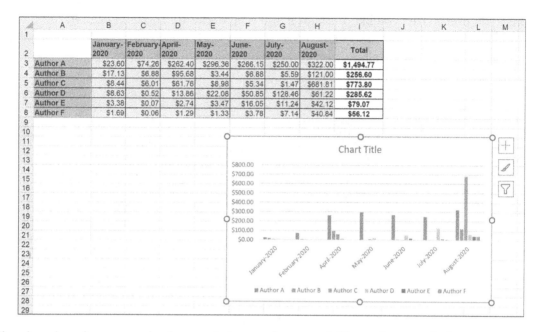

	January-2020	February-2020	April-2020	May-2020	June-2020	July-2020	August-2020	Total
Author A	$23.60	$74.26	$262.40	$296.36	$266.15	$250.00	$322.00	$1,494.77
Author B	$17.13	$6.88	$95.68	$3.44	$6.88	$5.59	$121.00	$256.60
Author C	$8.44	$6.01	$61.76	$8.98	$5.34	$1.47	$681.81	$773.80
Author D	$8.63	$0.52	$13.86	$22.08	$50.85	$128.46	$61.22	$285.62
Author E	$3.38	$0.07	$2.74	$3.47	$16.05	$11.24	$42.12	$79.07
Author F	$1.69	$0.06	$1.29	$1.33	$3.78	$7.14	$40.84	$56.12

The chart is going to stay in that worksheet unless you deliberately move it, but it's on top of the cells, not embedded in them, so you can left-click and drag to move it around in the workspace without the cells being impacted.

Another option for inserting a chart is to select your data, go to the Insert tab, and then click on Recommended Charts instead. This will open the Insert Chart dialogue box and will show some recommended charts based on your data.

You can also click over to All Charts and click through there to see how your data will look with each chart type like I've done here:

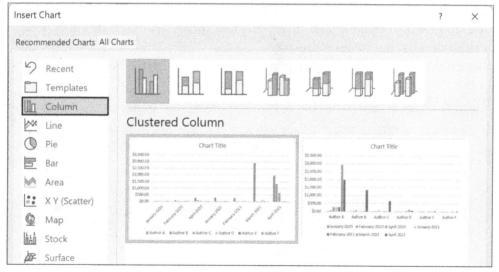

Once you find a chart you like, click on it and then click OK and it will insert.

Another option for inserting a chart is to use the Quick Analysis option. Select your data and then click on the quick analysis icon in the bottom right corner and go to Charts and you'll see some basic options there:

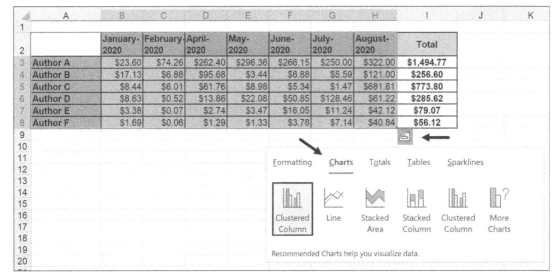

Click on any of those chart options and a chart of that type will immediately be inserted into your worksheet. Clicking on More Charts opens the Insert Chart dialogue box.

* * *

It is possible to create a chart using data that is not touching.

For example, I will sometimes have a chart like the one above that also has a totals column at the end, and want to create a chart using just that totals column. But I also need the first column to know what the values represent.

In that case, use Ctrl to select your two cell ranges, like I have here with Column A and Column I:

	January-2020	February-2020	April-2020	May-2020	June-2020	July-2020	August-2020	Total
Author A	$23.60	$74.26	$262.40	$296.36	$266.15	$250.00	$322.00	$1,494.77
Author B	$17.13	$6.88	$95.68	$3.44	$6.88	$5.59	$121.00	$256.60
Author C	$8.44	$6.01	$61.76	$8.98	$5.34	$1.47	$681.81	$773.80
Author D	$8.63	$0.52	$13.86	$22.08	$50.85	$128.46	$61.22	$285.62
Author E	$3.38	$0.07	$2.74	$3.47	$16.05	$11.24	$42.12	$79.07
Author F	$1.69	$0.06	$1.29	$1.33	$3.78	$7.14	$40.84	$56.12

Selected Data

Just make sure that your selected ranges are the same size. I've selected Cell A2 here even though it has no data in it because I have that Total label in Cell I2 that I want to include. After that it's the same process of going to the Insert tab and making a choice. (I couldn't see the Quick Analysis option when the data I selected was not contiguous, but maybe that will change in the future.)

Which Chart

That was how to insert charts, but a big part of working with charts is figuring out which one to use. There are a few things to consider when looking at your data and making this choice. We'll walk through the type of questions you can ask yourself first and then we'll dig in and look at examples of each of the chart types mentioned.

So ask yourself…

Is there a time component to the data? For example, are you looking at sales across the months of a year?

I will, for example, use charts to look at sales for 13 months for each author name, series name, and title I publish to see if those sales are steady, increasing, or decreasing and to also compare to the same time period one year before.

For that sort of scenario, something like a bar or column chart or even a line chart is a good option. Each of those lets you visually see the changes across time periods.

Bar and column charts are better for when you have multiple variables you want to chart, like my analysis of the performance of multiple titles over the course of a year. Line charts work better with a single variable. (Although, there is a type of chart related to line charts, the area chart, that you can use for multiple variables, but at that point you're not working with a straight line, you're working with a shaded area. We'll get back to this.)

Are you instead looking to see what share of the whole each component represents? For example, at year-end I want to see what percentage of my total sales each series represented for that year. It's a snapshot of that year, I'm not looking at trends over time.

In that case something like a pie chart or doughnut chart is a good choice.

Are you trying to find a relationship between different variables? For example, how does the value of X impact the value of Y?

A scatter plot is a good choice for that one. (Excel calls them scatter charts.) You can also use a bubble chart.

Are you trying to see the distribution of a series of results. So, what's the average outcome given the data you have? In that case, a histogram can be a good choice.

There are a number of other chart types that Excel offers, but those are the ones I'm going to cover in this book. If you're curious or you need a different chart type, you can see all of them in the All Charts tab of the Insert Chart dialogue box:

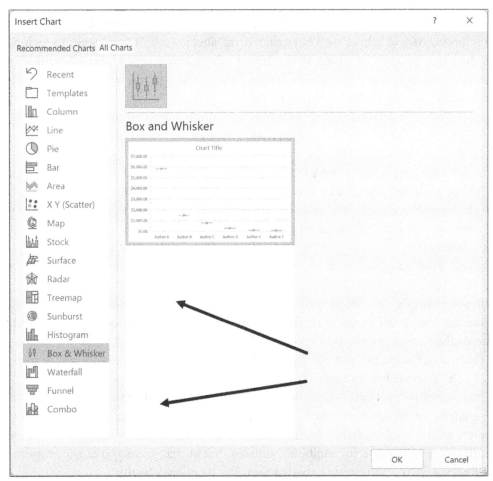

Click through to see how each one will look with your data. Some of the options require a third data component or a specific format. When that's the case they won't show a preview but will instead tell you what kind of data they need. (See Stock as a good example of this.)

If you use one of those other chart types, this is a good place to open Excel's Help related to that chart and read it so you know any quirks the chart type might have. Hopefully when we're done with this discussion you'll have a solid foundation for how to insert and format any chart, but the key issue for each chart type is generally going to be making sure that you've formatted your data properly.

Okay, then. Let's now discuss our chosen chart types in more detail.

Column and Bar Charts

Column and bar charts are basically the same thing. The main difference is whether the bars are vertical (columns) or horizontal (bars.)

In the Insert Chart dialogue box they are currently listed separately, but in the Charts section of the Insert tab they are currently combined under the top leftmost choice. Here are your options:

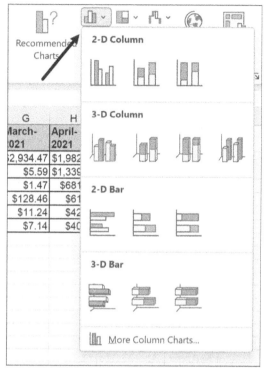

That More Column Charts choice does not in fact give you more choices, it just takes you to the Insert Chart dialogue box and gives you the same options you can see here.

The 3D options work the same as the 2D options, it's just a matter of whether you want three dimensionality or not. Since they're basically the same, I'm just going to cover your 2D choices in that first and third row.

Hold your mouse over the top of each of the three 2D choices for column or bar charts in that dropdown and you'll see that they are named clustered, stacked, and 100% stacked, respectively.

The icons for each one try to give a feel for what they look like, but we'll look at actual examples below.

Clustered column or bar charts take the results for each variable and place them side-by-side for each time period or category. For example, in the charts below we have author income for each month for six authors with a column or bar for each author for each time period, where the size of the column or bar is based on the dollar-value of the sales for that author for that time period relative to all dollar values in the data set.

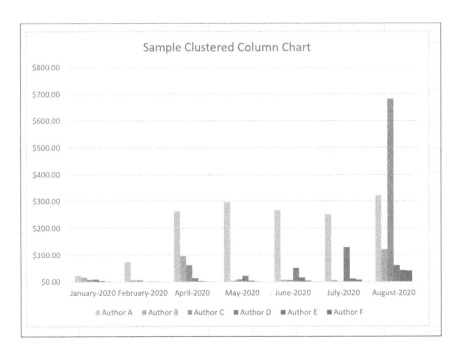

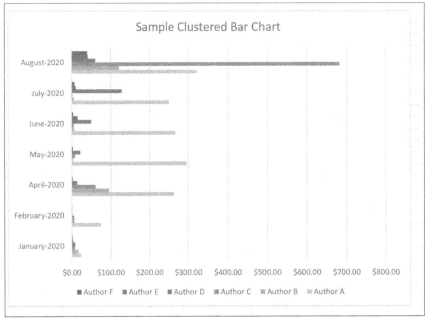

Clustered column charts can get very busy very fast so they're not the best choice when you have a large number of variables if you're also looking at a large number of time periods or categories.

Stacked column or bar charts have one column or bar per time period or category. The overall size of the column or bar for each period or category is based on the total for all variables for the period and relative to the totals for the other periods or categories. There are separate colored or shaded sections of each column or bar for each variable to show the share of the total for that variable.

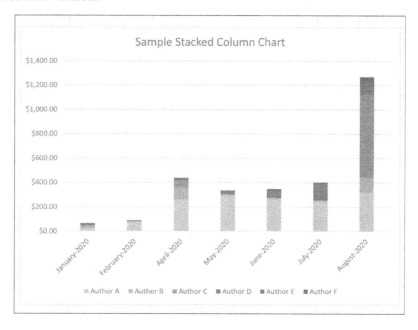

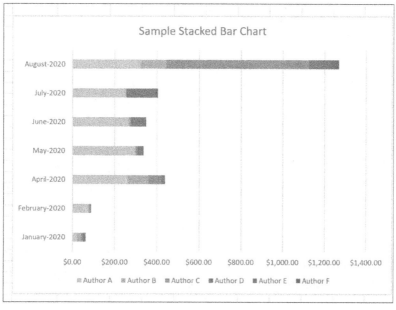

It's basically taking the individual columns or bars from a clustered chart and stacking them on top of each other.

Stacked charts are good for seeing trends over time for total performance. We can see here, for example, that August 2020 was much better than the prior months. And that January/February 2020 were much lower than the other months.

But stacked charts make it harder to see trends for the individual components that make up that whole. I can still see how Author A was dominant in most months and how Author C did really well in August 2020, but the clustered chart is better for seeing those individual-level trends.

The last bar or column chart type is the 100% stacked chart. The size of the column or bar for each time period or category is always the same, because it's always 100% of the total for that period or category.

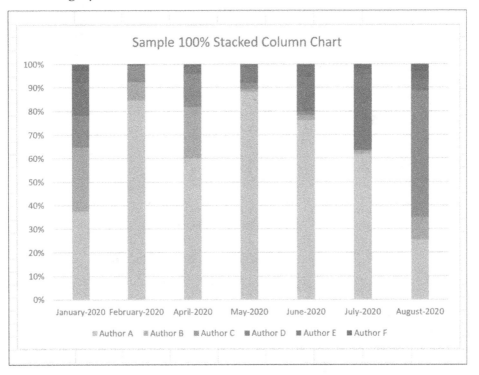

Each bar or column will be colored or shaded in sections to show the percent of the whole for each variable.

With a 100% stacked chart you lose the relative difference in actual results between time periods. Above you can see change in percentage of the whole better—we can really see that Author A dominated in all time periods—but you can't see that the first time period only had sales of $63 and the last time period had sales of $1269.

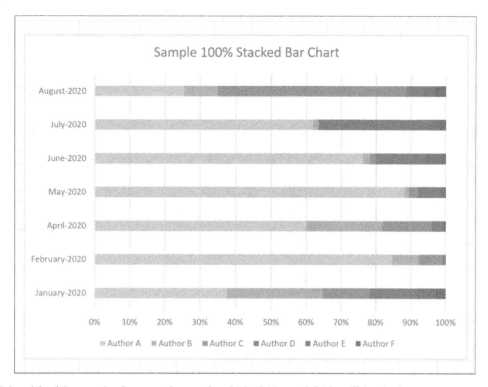

The risk with this one is that a column for $10, $40, and $50 will look the same as a column for $10,000, $40,000, and $50,000. So, if the actual amount earned in a period matters, don't rely on the 100% stacked chart for your analysis.

(One final note here, if there is a component that's a significant outlier, it can sometimes help to remove that component from the analysis so that you can better see the detail for the others. I will often drop my top-selling author or series name from my analysis to better see the results for my other authors and series.)

Pie or Doughnut Chart

As mentioned above, a pie or doughnut chart is good for a snapshot analysis where you want to see how much each variable represents of the whole. These choices are available on the left-hand side, bottom row in the Charts section of the Insert tab. Here are your choices:

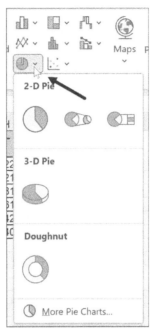

Once again, the More Pie Charts option does not actually give you more choices and I'm skipping the 3D option which has a 2D counterpart.

The data for a pie or doughnut chart is a set of labels and then a set of values, so just two columns.

Here's a basic pie chart and doughnut chart of the same data:

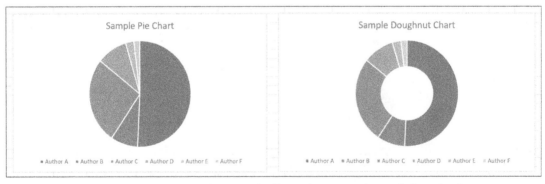

As you can see, the doughnut chart is just a hollowed-out version of the pie chart.

Both clearly show that for this data Authors A and C dominated the total share with Author A representing about half of all sales.

Those are the two main options and the ones I recommend using, but pie charts has two more options available, pie of pie and bar of pie.

These can be used to call out smaller values so that they're better visualized. BUT, if a reader is not used to seeing a chart like that, it can lead to some real confusion, in my opinion.

Let's look at the pie of pie chart for this same data to see what I'm talking about:

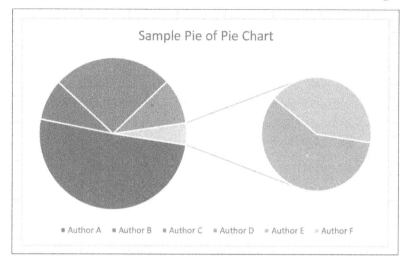

If I look at this chart without knowing how it works, I think that Author A is a big chunk of things, but then I turn to Author E in the other pie chart.

And what this is really doing is saying, "See that light blue slice of the left-hand pie? The *smallest* slice? Well that's actually two authors combined. And if we look at just those two authors in a separate pie chart, Author E has a bigger share of that small blue slice than Author F."

That right-hand pie chart that is so visible only represents 5% of the total sales. But because it gets called out this way it feels instinctively like it's a bigger share of things.

That's why if I am ever going to use one of these, I prefer the bar of pie chart, which looks like this:

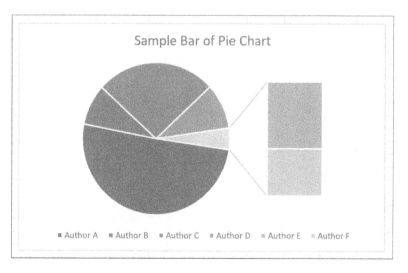

At least using a bar chart for the second chart makes it clear these are not apples to apples.

It still for me calls too much attention to those smallest values. If that slice were thirty different variables so that none of them dominated the bar chart on the right-hand side (and it's really a column, isn't it?) that might work.

But as is, with this data, I'm not a fan of using either of those charts to present this data. I'm sure they exist because there are circumstances where they make sense to use, but just be careful. Evaluate where a reader's eye might go and how they might interpret the image and whether that properly conveys the data. If it doesn't, don't use it.

Okay, now on to line and area charts.

Line and Area Charts

Line and area charts are the first chart type shown in the second row of choices in the Charts section of the Insert tab.

Once more we have 2D and 3D choices. And once more the More Choices option doesn't really give you more choices. The Insert Charts dialogue box has the choices you see here split between Line and Area charts.

Be sure here, and really with any data that has a time component to it, that your data is sorted in order. It can't be randomly listed in your data table.

I want to start by looking at the first option there which is the basic Line chart:

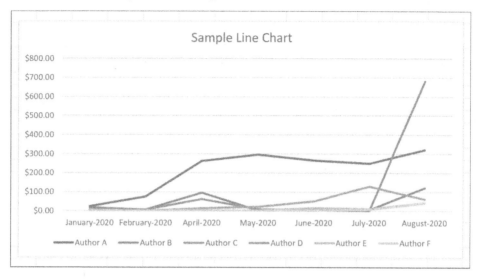

You can see here that very clear spike from Author C in August 2020. And you can see how Author A went up at the start and then plateaued at a level above the rest for most of the period.

Line charts are good for seeing a linear trend across time periods or categories. But they are not good for situations where you only have one or two data points. If I had a new author start selling in August 2020 there'd be no line to draw.

Here I've dropped Author C to better see the trend for the other authors and also changed the chart type to Line With Markers:

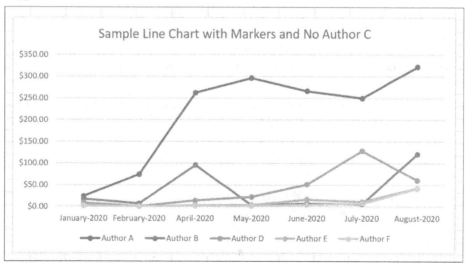

The line chart with markers option is the fourth listed choice. (It used to be that in older versions of Excel this lined up nicely so it was the first option on the second row, but that's no longer the case. Just think of it as the first of the options that shows markers, those dots on the line that represent specific data points.)

Using a line chart that includes markers for each data point can sometimes be helpful because it better shows where there's an actual data point versus where it's just a line connecting two points. The more markers between two points, the more faith you can have that the data actually followed that path.

Here, for example, is the data we've seen already for Authors A, B, and C for each month from January to August 2020 in the left-hand chart. In the right-hand chart we just have the data for January and for August.

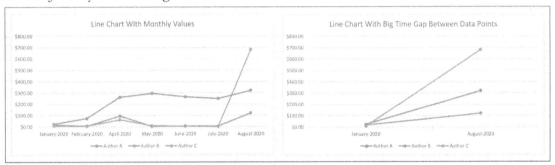

For Author A, I have more faith that the change in earnings from January to August followed a steady pattern given the number of results in the first chart because there are six data points charting that rise versus just one in the second chart.

We can also see here how the second chart with just a beginning and an ending observation hides how Author C basically didn't perform at all until the final time period.

Basically, the more data, the better, and markers can be an indicator of how much data there was.

Those are the two line charts I recommend because they are what people traditionally expect of line charts. Each line is showing the values for that line and is separate from the other lines.

The other line chart options shown there are stacked and 100% stacked line charts. They act like the stacked and 100% stacked bar and column charts, meaning the lines are building upon one another to reach a total value for the period or to reach 100% for each period. But it's just not intuitive to most users that that's what they're seeing, so I don't recommend using them.

Here's the stacked line chart for this data, for example:

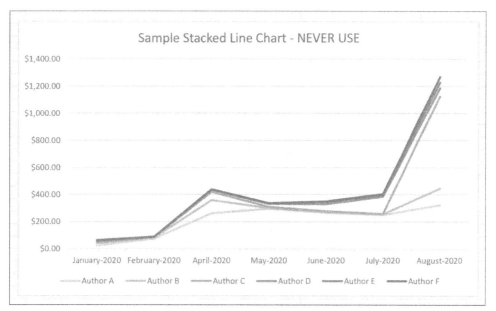

See what I mean? You just automatically assume that those lines are the results for each Author because that's how we're used to interpreting lines on charts. Or at least *I* do.

Area charts fix this issue. You've probably seen one or two over the last couple years, because they're used often with epidemiological data.

Here are the two area charts I recommend using applied to this data. The first is the Stacked Area chart:

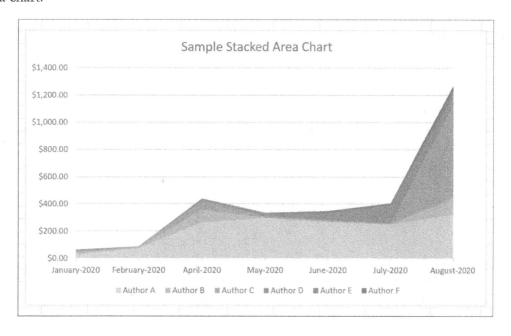

See how filling in the space between the lines gives the overall image cohesion? You can more readily understand that the various filled-in areas are adding up to something instead of representing separate results when the spaces between the lines are filled in.

The second is the 100% stacked area chart:

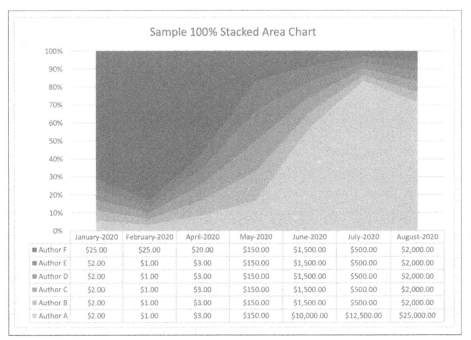

	January-2020	February-2020	April-2020	May-2020	June-2020	July-2020	August-2020
■ Author F	$25.00	$25.00	$20.00	$150.00	$1,500.00	$500.00	$2,000.00
■ Author E	$2.00	$1.00	$3.00	$150.00	$1,500.00	$500.00	$2,000.00
■ Author D	$2.00	$1.00	$3.00	$150.00	$1,500.00	$500.00	$2,000.00
■ Author C	$2.00	$1.00	$3.00	$150.00	$1,500.00	$500.00	$2,000.00
■ Author B	$2.00	$1.00	$3.00	$150.00	$1,500.00	$500.00	$2,000.00
■ Author A	$2.00	$1.00	$3.00	$150.00	$10,000.00	$12,500.00	$25,000.00

Be careful with the 100% stacked option, because it can give a misleading impression of the overall share of the results across time as you can see with the data I created for use in this one.

If you just look at the chart without the data, you would think that Author F and Author A just switched places. One was dominant early and then the other took over, but they basically had equal shares overall.

Which is true percentage-wise. Early on Author F was doing 2.5 times what all the other authors were doing combined. And at the end Author A was doing the same.

But what you'd completely miss from this chart (without the data table included) is that Author F made a grand total of $4,220 for the period covered by the chart and Author A made $47,656. Author A made *ten times* more than Author F, but that's completely hidden when you present the data using a 100% stacked area chart.

As a matter of fact, Author F who looks so great in this chart only earned $64 more than Authors B, C, D, and E.

Not obvious from what we see here because it's showing % share for each time period. The problem is that the use of a shaded area that crosses time periods makes the data feel connected when it's really not. At least not in that way.

The 100% stacked bar and column charts don't have this issue because each column or bar is discrete so they do a better job of reminding a viewer that the percentages are for that time period or category only.

Hope that makes sense. Basically, if you have wide swings in your actual results between time periods, do not use the 100% Stacked Area chart. It's misleading.

Okay, then. On to scatter plots.

Scatter and Bubble Plots

Scatter plots take two inputs and plot them on a grid to make a data point. A scatter plot can connect those data points to see if there's some sort of relationship between the two inputs, but it doesn't have to.

The scatter plot dropdown is the last one, on the bottom row, next to pie charts.

There are five options:

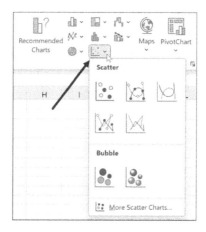

The first one just plots the points. The other options allow you to add either a smoothed line or a straight line that connects the points. The line can either show markers for the data points or not.

Here is a small data table with the data points plotted but not connected.

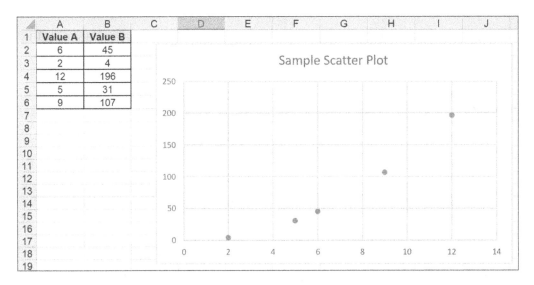

You can see that there's probably a relationship there, right? When one value goes up, so does the other. It's not perfectly linear, but it's there. (I created it so I know it's there.)

Now, here's the tricky thing with scatter plots. If I add a line connecting my data points Excel will draw that line by connecting the first point to the second point to the third point and on and on.

Here I used the smooth line option with markers:

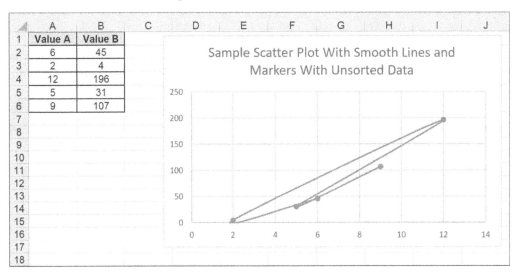

That's a hot mess, isn't it? Why?

Because while there is a relationship between Value A and Value B, it's one that's independent of the order in which the observations were made.

If I sort my data by value, now we see it:

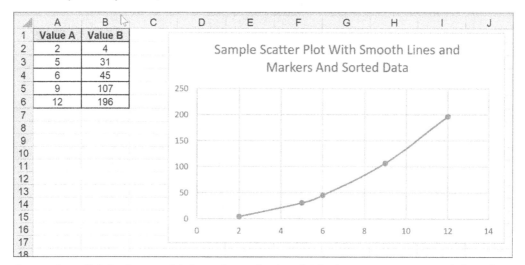

The data points didn't change. It's just the order in which they were connected that changed.

Whether you should sort the data in your plot like I just did or not is going to depend on what the data is and why it was in that order.

You can also plot multiple sets of data in the same scatter plot. The first column of data will drive the values on the x axis (the bottom) and then any other columns of data will be plotted against the y axis (the side).

Here, for example, I have three columns of data (Columns B, C, and D) plotted against the values in Column A.

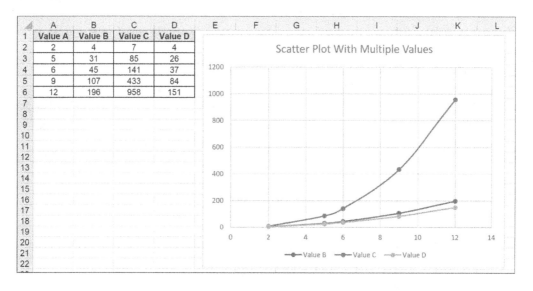

You don't have to use lines when you do this, the data points for each column will have their own color, but I recommend it. It makes it easier to see which points belong to each column.

Above you can see that there is a relationship between the values in Column A and the values in Columns B, C, and D, but that that relationship is not the same. Here I've edited the values for Column C so there is no clear linear, quadratic, or binomial relationship:

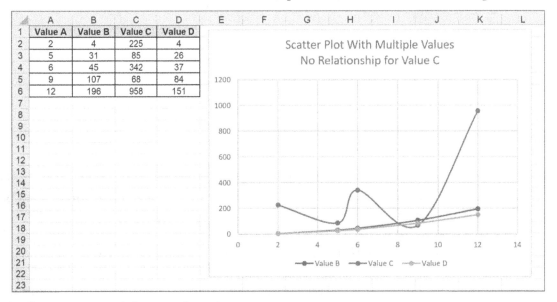

The line goes up and down and not in any apparent pattern.

In the same dropdown as scatter plots, you can also see bubble plots. A bubble plot takes two points and plots them against each other and then it takes one more piece of information and uses that to determine the size of the data point so you end up with three pieces of information shown for each data point.

Often you'll see this with country GDP, for example. So the original plot is spending versus population but then the size of the bubble is the overall "wealth" of the country. Or percent of population that adopted some health measure versus an outcome for that measure with the size of each data point showing per capita income. That sort of thing.

Here is a basic example, using the same data as our original scatter plot, but now with a number of observations column added to dictate the bubble size.

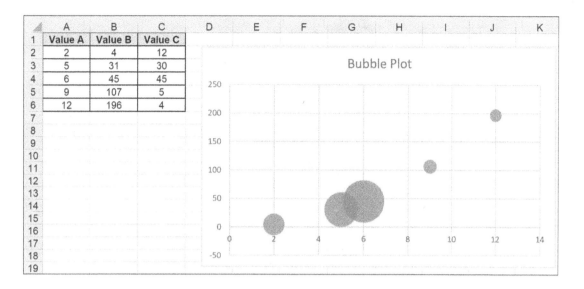

	A	B	C
1	Value A	Value B	Value C
2	2	4	12
3	5	31	30
4	6	45	45
5	9	107	5
6	12	196	4

This lets us see that the majority of the data is centered around two values for A, 5 and 6, which makes me less confident that the apparent pattern in this data exists since the data that is on the far left and on the far right is much less robust. (One outlier data point can sometimes skew your data in weird ways.) But there's still a handful of observations for each data point so it probably does exist. The bubble chart just lets me know to be more cautious with values for A that are further away from 5 or 6.

Okay. That was scatter and bubble plots. I used to use them a lot in physics class and economics, but one I actually use for my writing is the histogram. So let's talk about that one next.

Histogram

The histogram chart was a recent addition to Excel. It lets you take your data and create buckets of observations that are close in value and then plots a count of how many observations are in each bucket.

So instead of treating 31, 32, 33, and 34 as separate values, it might group those all into a 30 to 40 bucket. This can be nice because it removes the noise in your data and lets you better see any patterns.

The histogram option is in the middle of the chart choices and requires one column of values. Here I've created a histogram from randomly generated values between 0 and 100.

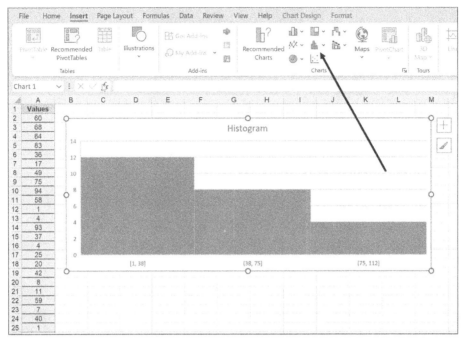

The histogram by default is going to look at the values that you give it and come up with the buckets it places those values into. In this case it used three buckets, 1 to 38, 38 to 75, and 75 to 112.

The height of each bar is based on the number of values that fall into that bucket. You can see that right now the 1 to 38 bucket contains the most values with 12 observations.

You can manually choose how many buckets to use and how wide they are in the formatting task pane (which we'll discuss in detail shortly.) For a histogram this is under Horizontal Axis, Axis Options, and then the Axis Options section. Here I've changed the number of bins (buckets) to ten and capped the histogram between 0 and 100.

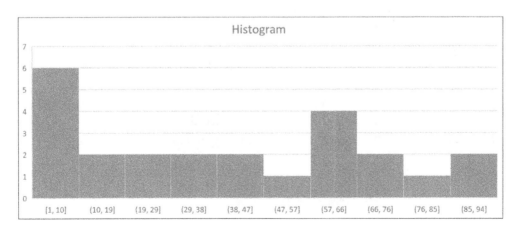

As you can see it definitely impacts where we think most results will fall. Also, interestingly enough because I know how this data was created, we clearly don't have enough data points yet to see the true pattern in this data.

I added more observations and plotted again:

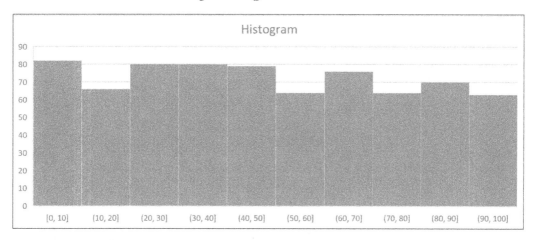

This is far closer to the true data pattern behind these values but still not quite there. Which is a reminder to always exercise caution in interpreting data when there aren't enough observations yet.

Okay, that was the last of the chart types I wanted to cover in more detail. We'll cover pivot charts when we cover pivot tables. They'll use these same chart types, the main difference is basically where the data is coming from.

For now, though, let's talk about all the bells and whistles you can add to a chart and how to edit charts to make them look exactly how you want. (Some of which I've been doing behind the scenes already.)

Charts – Editing and Formatting

If you look back at the screenshots I showed you in the last section you will notice that the charts have descriptive titles that tell you what type of chart it is. And that some of the charts are different sizes or shapes and that they don't use the default color palette.

That's because I edited them. There are a large number of edits you can make to charts.

Let me start with those basic things I did in the last section and then we'll go through more systematically.

Resize a Chart

To resize a chart, click on the chart. You will then see big circles appear at each corner and in the middle of each side of the chart. Like this:

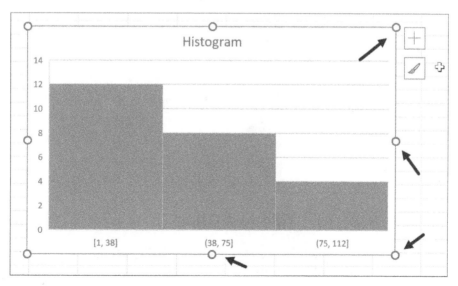

Left-click on one of those circles and drag to change the size of your chart.

To resize both the top and side at once, click and drag from one of the corners. If you do so at an angle, the chart should resize proportionately. All of the elements within the chart space should also resize to fit the new dimensions.

I find resizing charts essential when I include data tables with my charts like I did in one of the examples above. And I usually use this click and drag method because I'm a visual person so I want to resize to what "looks right".

But you can also go to the Format tab that appears for your chart when you click on it and on the far right-hand side you'll see a Size section where you can type in a new value for height, width, or both. Just click into each box and type your new value.

That expansion arrow in the corner of the Size section will open the task pane for Format Chart Area where you can also enter specific values. Clicking on Lock Aspect Ratio will make sure that any change you make to one value (height or width) will also be reflected in the other value (width or height) so that the proportion of width to height remains the same.

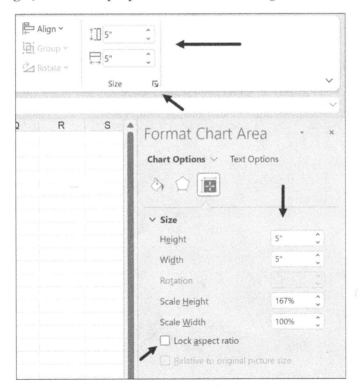

Move a Chart

You can also move a chart from where Excel places it. Left-click on the chart and drag to move it to a new location in your workspace. Be careful when you click on the chart that you click somewhere on the chart that doesn't have a chart element, like the title. Because if you click on a chart element you may end up moving the element around instead of the chart.

Charts can also be copied or cut and pasted using the Ctrl shortcuts (Ctrl + C, Ctrl + X, Ctrl + V) or the menu options. This is how I normally move them.

If you right-click and choose Move Chart from the dropdown menu it will show you a dialogue box that will let you move the chart to a different worksheet or a new worksheet. If you choose to move to a new worksheet it will be one that has no cells in it. And you can't undo that move or cut the chart from that worksheet, so the only way to put the chart back in its original location is to right-click and choose to move it again and then select the original worksheet as the location.

The Move Chart option can also be found in the Location section of the Chart Design tab.

When you move a chart to a new worksheet, workbook, or other Office document, your data does not move, only the chart does. (Which is usually what you want, but something to be aware of regardless.) Depending on how you pasted the chart it may still be impacted by any changes to that source data.

Change the Chart Title

To change the title of your chart, click on the name of the chart. Click again on the name to see your cursor blinking amidst the text. Select the text for the current name and then type in what you want to use. (If you want to replace the entire title, Ctrl + A will highlight the current title which will be replaced when you start typing.)

Move Elements Within a Chart

You can move the elements in a chart by clicking on them and then left-clicking and dragging or clicking on a circle in one of the corners to change the shape or size. If an element in a chart can be moved or have its size/shape changed, it will show that frame with circles.

Change A Field Name Used in the Legend

The best bet is to do this in the actual data table that is the source of the data used in the chart. But if that's not possible, use the Select Data option in the Chart Design tab. In the Select Data Source dialogue box, click on the field name, then click on Edit. In the Edit Series or Axis Labels dialogue box that appears, type in the new name in the Series Name or Axis Label Range field.

* * *

M.L. Humphrey

Chart Design Tab Options

Okay. Those were the quick basics that I almost always need. Now let's be more systematic about this and walk through the editing options in the Chart Design tab (which can be found to the right of the Help tab when you click on a chart).

Let's start with those options there on the right-hand side, Switch Row/Column, Select Data, and Change Chart Type.

Switch Row/Column

This is the one that makes it irrelevant which data you put across the top or down the side in your data table for a standard bar/column chart or line graph. Because if you find when you create your chart that the wrong variable is along the bottom or the wrong variable is shown in the main chart space, you can flip them using this.

If you use the Insert Chart dialogue box to insert your charts you probably will never even need to do this, because that way of inserting charts shows you both choices:

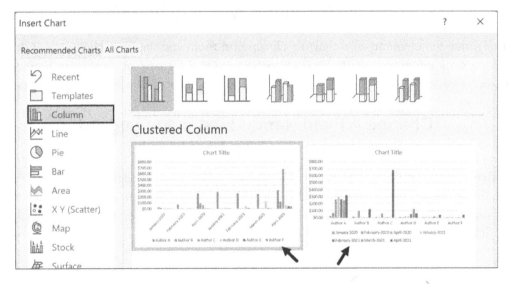

It may be a little hard to see, but the two clustered column choices in the screenshot above have different X axis values. One is showing months on the X axis and then plotting the data by author name for each of those months. The other is showing author names on the X axis and then plotting the data by month for each author name.

Clicking that Switch Row/Column button basically moves you between those two choices.

It's only available when there is data to switch (all of the chart types we discussed except for histograms have it available) and it sometimes won't make any sense to use it (for pie and doughnut charts for example).

Select Data

The Select Data option opens the Select Data Source dialogue box.

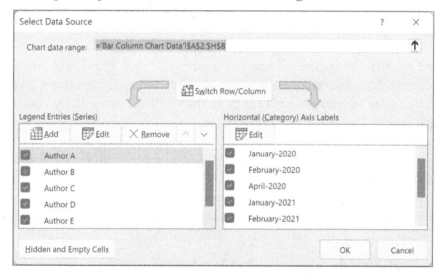

You can do a number of things here.

First, you can switch row/column by clicking on that option in the center of the dialogue box.

Second, you can uncheck the boxes for any of the inputs to the x- or y-axis to exclude them from the chart. This is where I would go to drop Author A, for example, if Author A's data was dominating a chart and I couldn't adequately see the other results.

Third, as mentioned above, you can click on Edit and edit the name for each series of data if you can't edit that name in the data table that's the source for the chart.

And, fourth, you can change the range of the data that's being used by clicking into the Chart Data Range field and changing the cell notation to your new data range.

I prefer to change my data range in the data table itself, however, so let me walk you through how to do that real quick.

First step is to click onto the chart that's using that data table. That will highlight the cells in your data table that are being used by that chart.

Here I have a data table that shows sales for Authors A through F, but if you look at the data table only the data for Authors A through E is highlighted.

	A	B	C	D	E	F	G	H	I
1									
2		January-2020	February-2020	April-2020	May-2020	June-2020	July-2020	August-2020	Total
3	Author A	$23.60	$74.26	$262.40	$296.36	$266.15	$250.00	$322.00	$1,494.77
4	Author B	$17.13	$6.88	$95.68	$3.44	$6.88	$5.59	$121.00	$256.60
5	Author C	$8.44	$6.01	$61.76	$8.98	$5.34	$1.47	$681.81	$773.80
6	Author D	$8.63	$0.52	$13.86	$22.08	$50.85	$128.46	$61.22	$285.62
7	Author E	$3.38	$0.07	$2.74	$3.47	$16.05	$11.24	$42.12	$79.07
8	Author F	$1.69	$0.06	$1.29	$1.33	$3.78	$7.14	$40.8	$56.12
9									

The cells that are being used are shaded differently and there is a colored line around them indicating which part of the chart those cells populate.

To expand the chart to include Author F, I need to left-click and drag in the bottom right corner of either the Author E cell or the last sales entry for Author E (see arrows in image above).

That will bring the selection down to include the row for Author F. Doing either the cell that contains Author E or that last cell with sales data should select the entire next row, including the author name and author sales data for Author F. (If it doesn't, you'll have to do them both separately. I want to say that I have to do that for my line graph of sales, ad spend, and profit, for example.)

When your mouse is appropriately positioned, the cursor should be an angled line with arrows on each end. It's a little hard to see, but here's a screenshot of what that looks like:

	A	B	C	D	E
3	Author A	$23.60	$74.26	$262.40	$296.36
4	Author B	$17.13	$6.88	$95.68	$3.44
5	Author C	$8.44	$6.01	$61.76	$8.98
6	Author D	$8.63	$0.52	$13.86	$22.08
7	Author E	$3.38	$0.07	$2.74	$3.47
8	Author F	$1.69	$0.06	$1.29	$1.33
9					

Once your mouse looks like that, just left-click and drag to select the rest of the data you need. (Note that you can also drag upward if you want to use less data in your chart, but usually I'm adding more data using this method.)

Okay. So to recap: click on the chart, find the edge of the current data range, left-click and drag to make it include my other cells.

But, as mentioned, you can also do so by editing the text in the Select Data dialogue box.

Change Chart Type

To change the chart type for an existing chart, click on the chart, and then click on this option. It brings up the Change Chart dialogue box which is identical to the Insert Chart dialogue box. Click on the new chart type you want and then choose OK.

* * *

Okay, now let's move on to the formatting options on the left-hand side of the Chart Design tab:

Chart Styles

I'm going to continue working right to left because that final option (Add Chart Element) is going to be a doozy.

Chart Styles are pre-formatted styles that you can apply to your chart. They will vary based upon what kind of chart you use. Click on the downpointing arrow in the bottom right corner (noted in the screenshot above) to expand the selections list and see all available options at once, like here where there are fourteen possible column chart styles available:

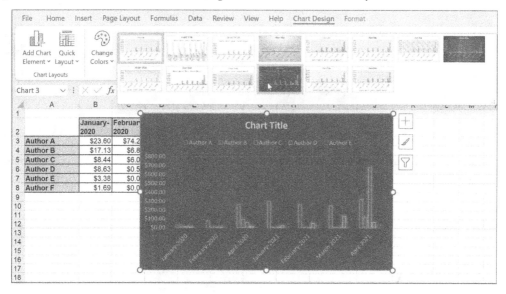

You can also just use the up and down arrows on the right-hand side to see more options (if there are any).

Hold your mouse over each option to see it applied to your chart.

Above I'm looking at one with a black background and different outline and fill color used for each column.

For me personally these styles never are what I want. But they can be a good way to get close to what you want and then tweak from there.

Change Colors

The change colors dropdown allows you to change from Excel's default color scheme, which for me has blue, orange, gray, and yellow for the first four choices, to one of the color schemes shown in the dropdown.

I actually did this for the charts in the last section because I wanted to make sure that a black and white image of that chart in the print books would still have clear differences between the different variables in each chart.

The monochromatic options all work for that. I went with a blue choice so that the ebooks would still have color in them, but I could have chosen monochromatic palettes 3, 7, or 10 if I wanted to only use shades of gray and black.

As with Chart Styles, you can hold your mouse over each choice and see what it will look like before you make your selection by clicking on it.

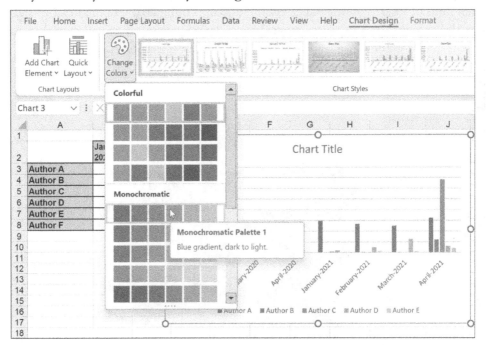

Quick Layout

The quick layout dropdown is another one that shows different potential layouts for your data and will vary based on chart type. It doesn't include different formatting like the Chart Styles do, but is more about including different chart elements.

You can hold your mouse over each one to see it applied and see what it's supposed to include:

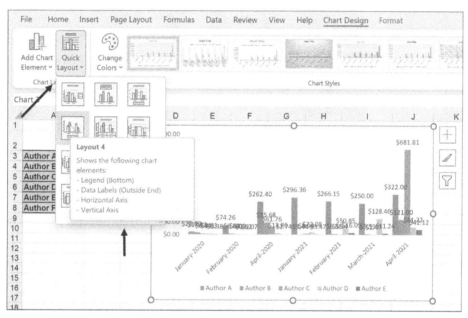

Even when the option is ugly, like this one above, it can give you an idea of which chart elements you may want in your own chart.

Click on the option if you want to keep it.

Be careful if you want to use both Quick Layout and Chart Style because they may overwrite one another. Quick Layout will keep the colors of a Chart Style but may change other elements. Chart Style can sometimes appear to completely replace a Quick Layout, but not always. So the best bet is to see where you end up at the end and use Ctrl + Z if needed to undo.

Or you can get ideas from both of them and then add your own chart elements and formatting, which we'll discuss now, starting with the chart elements.

Add Chart Element

This is where I do most of my chart editing. I almost always want a data table under the chart which means I also remove the chart legend. And I also like to use trendlines sometimes.

To see the list of available Chart Elements, click on the dropdown arrow next to Add Chart Element.

The available options vary by chart type since not all chart types can use all of the chart elements listed. Grayed-out elements are not available for that chart type, like here where Lines and Up/Down Bars are not available options.

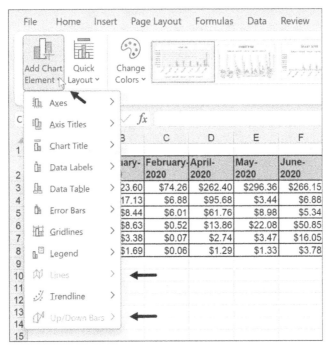

Each element will have a secondary dropdown with the choices for that element. Hold your mouse over the element name to see the available options and then hold your mouse over each choice to see it applied temporarily to your chart. Click on the choice to apply it permanently.

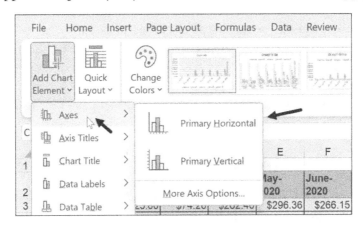

Here you can see the choices for Axes, Primary Horizontal and Primary Vertical.

Clicking on the More [X] Options choice at the bottom of the dropdown opens the task pane for formatting that element, which is where the most options are available.

Now let's walk through each option and what it does:

Axes

Axes allows you to add or remove the data point labels on each axis. For example, I sometimes will share a line chart of sales data on my blog but I don't feel the need to share the dollar values involved or sometimes even the months covered by that data, so I remove those labels from my chart.

Here I have removed the $ values from the y-axis and months from the x-axis but the overall trends across periods are still clear.

(If this were a chart I was going to share with others I'd need to change the title so others would know what is being plotted here. Something like "Author Revenues Over Time.")

Axis Titles

Axis titles are the text that tells you what each axis contains. You can add or remove them through this menu option.

By default they are not applied. Adding one creates a text box with the text "Axis Title". You then need to edit that text to whatever descriptor you want to use. See below for an example of a chart with an axis title (Months Covered).

Chart Title

The chart title option lets you add, move, or remove a chart title.

There is one present by default that is centered above the chart. You can also place the chart title in a centered overlay position where it's in the center but on the contents of the chart. Like so:

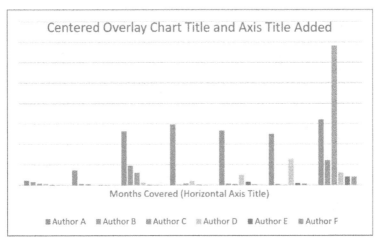

See how the horizontal gridlines run behind the text? With the Above Chart option, they'd all be below the title.

Data Labels

Data labels show the specific value for each data point. They are not present by default.

With most charts you can hold your mouse over any column, bar, data point, pie slice, etc. to see the actual specific value for that data point, even when it's not visible on the chart itself.

But sometimes you want the values showing on the chart. I find this particularly necessary with pie charts which are showing a percentage share because I also want to know the dollar value for that data point.

Here is a pie chart with data labels using the Outside End option:

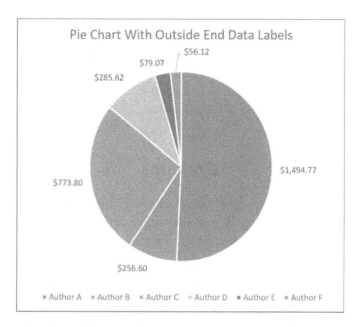

Sometimes two data labels will be too close together and you can't read them because they're on top of each other. That happened in the image above with the $79.07 and $56.12 at the top of the pie chart.

To fix that, click on the data label you want to move and then left-click and drag to move it to a better position. Excel will add a line from the data label to the element it's associated with so you can still see which label belongs to which element in the chart. (You can see that above with the $56.12.)

Data Table

This is one I use often. It places a table below the chart of all of the values that were used to create the chart. I always choose the "with legend keys" choice because that lets me get rid of the legend. If you use that option, the data table can serve both purposes.

When I add one of these, I almost always need to increase the height of the table to show all of the data. Depending on how much data you're including, the data table can at times be bigger than the chart itself.

Also, it's important when using a data table to think about the format of your data in the source data table. I often will format that data in the source table to remove the cents portion of my values so they take up less room.

Error Bars

Error bars lets you add bars to your chart that show standard error, standard deviation, or percentage error in your data. You can also customize the error bars in the task pane to show what a X% error range would be for that data point. If you're curious about how Excel calculates the values, see the Help text for error bars. This is one I recommend you only use if you know what you're doing.

Gridlines

Gridlines are those lines that run behind the chart space that let you more easily track from a data point to its value along an axis. If you want more lines than you're seeing on the chart, you can add minor lines. The default is usually major horizontal lines.

Legend

The legend is what tells you which color in the chart goes with which variable. You can add or remove a legend using this option and you can also choose whether the legend is displayed on the top, bottom, left, or right of the chart.

I definitely recommend having one if you don't have a data table with legends included and there's more than one primary variable shown in the chart. (When in doubt preview it and see if it helps.) Legends are generally included by default in chart types that need them.

Lines

The lines option allows you to add high-low lines or drop lines to a line chart. High-low lines basically connect the highest and lowest value for a time period or observation. Drop lines go from the highest value down to the axis. If you need them you probably know how to use them.

Trendline

A trendline looks at your values and estimates an overall line that shows the direction of those values. This is one I like to use often for things like profit and loss or revenue.

If you have multiple lines in a chart, you have to add one trendline per line. It will by default be a dotted line in the same color as the line it's related to.

Be careful choosing which type of trendline to add. Your choices are linear, exponential, linear forecast, and moving average.

In this chart below I have four trendlines, two each for Authors A and B.

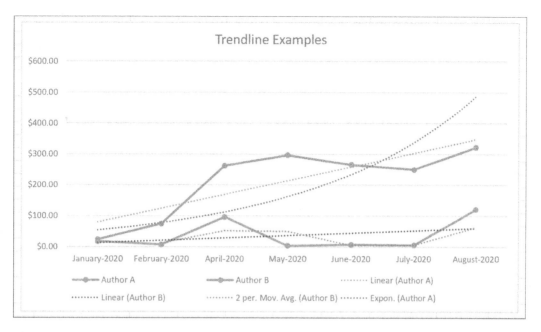

For Author A the straight dotted line that's colored blue is a linear trendline. The curved dotted line that's colored purple is an exponential line.

Of the two, the straight dotted line is the better fit, because Excel doesn't allow a logarithmic trendline choice which is what would likely best fit this data.

For Author B the dark purple dotted line is the linear trendline and the red dotted line that goes up and down is the moving average trendline.

While the linear trendline is close at the beginning and end points, it has no relationship whatsoever to the points in between. This is not linear data. The moving average line doesn't help much either. Although it does better fit the results than the linear line.

Sometimes trendlines help, sometimes they don't. You have to see your data plotted first to decide.

Up/Down Bars

Up/Down Bars connect the first data series data point to the last data series data point.

These get added by default in stock charts.

* * *

Customize Formatting

Okay. So that was a discussion of the various elements you can add or remove from a chart.

Now let's talk about how to customize your formatting. We're going to start with the Format tab that's available when you click on a chart. The formatting options are located in the middle of that Format tab:

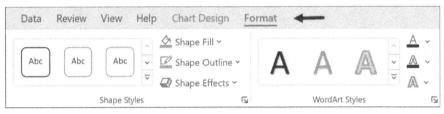

Shape Styles are preformatted styles that use different outline colors, interior colors and formats, and text colors (white or black, depending). Click on the downward pointing arrow to see all of the available styles at once. You'll mostly use these for the chart elements like columns or bars, but they can also be applied to text boxes, such as the one around a chart title.

WordArt Styles are for text and involve various text effects such as shadows, beveling, outline colors, fill colors, and patterns. (I don't recommend using them, to be honest.)

In addition, to the right side of both Shape Styles and WordArt Styles are options for fill, outline, and effects that allow you to completely customize the appearance of the shape and text elements in your chart.

To apply these formats to a chart element, you first need to select the element in the chart that you want to format.

So if I want to convert my blue column to a different color, I'd click on one example of that blue column in the chart. That should select all other instances of the blue column. They'll all be outlined and have those circles at the corners like you can see here:

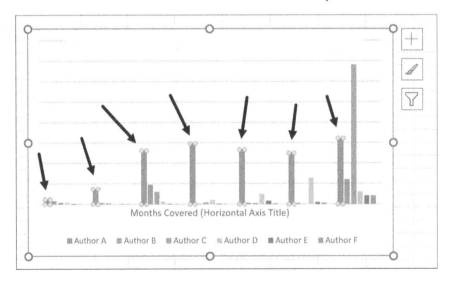

Once all instances of an element are selected, you can then click on the formatting option you want to apply. Holding your mouse over an option will temporarily apply it. Click to permanently apply it.

In this case, if I wanted to apply a different color to that column I could use the Shape Fill dropdown menu to choose a new color.

Or here, for example, I'm holding my mouse over a Shape Style that uses a white fill color with a green outline and you can see it applied to those five columns in the background.

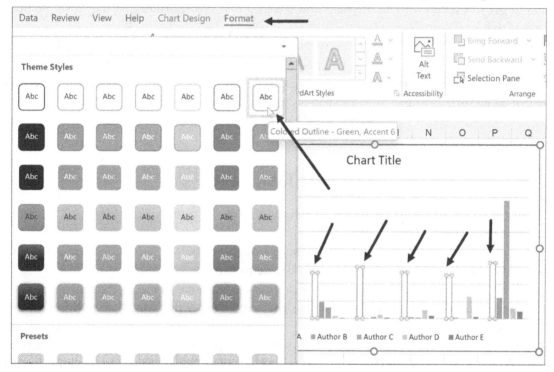

A few more tips on using these options.

With pie and doughnut charts, make sure that you only select one slice or section. It's very easy to select them all at once for some reason, so check which slices are outlined before you apply a format. Usually, I have to click on the slice or section I want to format twice to make sure it's the only one selected.

Use Shape Fill to change the color of columns, bars, pie wedges, etc. Use Shape Outline to change the color of lines.

You can use both shape fill and shape outline on columns, bars, etc. to give a border color around a shape that is different from the interior, like we saw above with the green outline and white fill.

If the fill color is not white, the border may not be obvious. You can adjust the line weight using the Weight option in the Shape Outline dropdown menu. (Unlike with borders, you don't have to adjust the weight first before applying the color. As long as the elements are still selected, you can adjust the line weight at any point in time.)

In addition to color changes and line weight, the dropdowns for fill, outline, and effects allow a number of other formatting choices like adding a gradient or texture, using a picture, adding edges and shadows, etc.

Feel free to explore them. Just be sure if you go down that path that you're not overwhelming the data in the chart with weird formatting. There can be a tendency for newer users to get so excited with all the bells and whistles that Excel offers that they lose the point of what they're doing.

A chart is meant to effectively convey information about complex data in a simple and intuitive manner. If the formatting you add to a chart is not helping do that, don't use it.

That's why I'm not going to go into more detail here on these formatting options, because you can do all sorts of things to your shapes and text in your chart, but you probably shouldn't.

* * *

Chart Task Pane

We've touched on the chart task pane with respect to charts a few times now, but I wanted to address it specifically.

The chart task pane is definitely the most thorough option for formatting a chart. And if you want to, you can start with it when you decide to format.

(I don't use it by default because I don't think it's as intuitive to use as the Format tab.)

To open the task pane, right-click on your chart and choose the Format [X] option towards the bottom of the dropdown menu.

What option is listed will vary depending on where you are on the chart when you right-click. For example, I had various choices like Format Data Series, Format Gridlines, Format Plot Area, Format Chart Area, etc.

Any of those will open the chart task pane on the right-hand side of your worksheet.

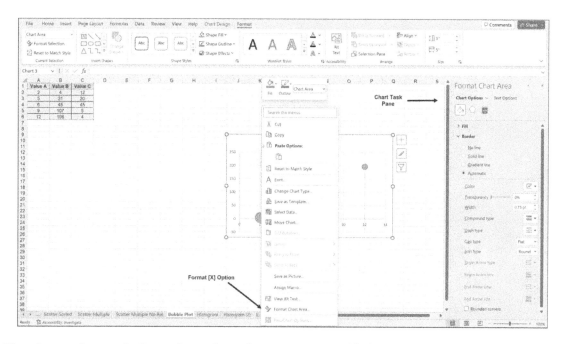

The chart task pane is dynamic so the task pane you see will depend on where you were in the chart when you opened it. You can change what you're seeing using the dropdown arrow next to that top options header, which in this case is Chart Options:

Above, for example, we have the option to change it to edit settings related to the chart area, chart title, horizontal axis, legend, plot area, etc.

Each task pane has icons at the top that you can click on to see various options. Hold your mouse over the icon to see what it covers. Here, for example, the middle icon is for effects:

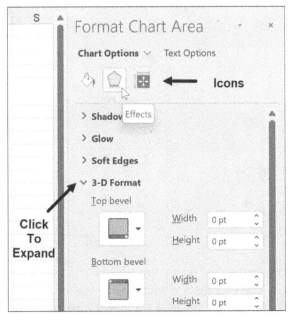

When you click on one of those icons, the pane will show various categories of settings. So above you can see Shadow, Glow, Soft Edges, and 3-D Format. Click on the arrow to the left of each category to expand it and see the settings for that category like I have above for 3-D Format.

The chart task pane is the only way I know where you can "explode" a pie chart. If you explode a pie chart you take the individual slices and move them outward from the center so that there's more space between them.

To do this, click on the pie chart portion of the pie chart and then right-click and choose Format Data Series to open the task pane. Change the task pane settings until you are in Series Options and have clicked on the third icon which is also Series Options. Pie explosion is the setting at the bottom. Use the slider or change the percentage to "explode" the pie until there's enough space between the slices for what you wanted.

This is a pie chart with a 10% explosion setting:

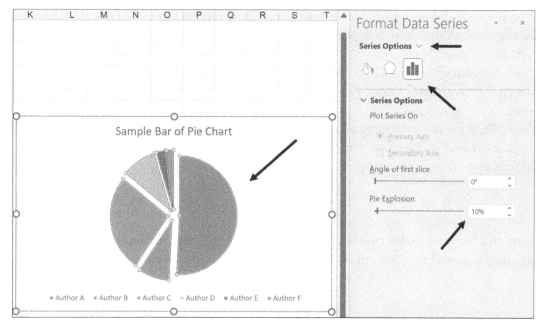

This is also where I go to change the pie chart labels to % values. This can be done in the Label Options section. (Label Options, Label Options, uncheck the box for Value and check the box for Percentage.)

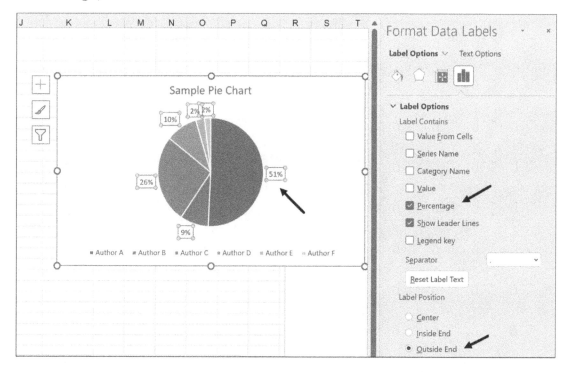

In this case, I did have to add labels using the Chart Design tab first. That could just be my unfamiliarity with the chart task pane, but it seems to only provide options for elements that are already in your chart.

Also, for histograms the chart task pane is the only way I know to customize the bins. As mentioned above, that's under Horizontal Axis, Axis Options, and then the Axis Options section.

Basically, if there's something you want to do with a chart that you think should be possible and you can't find it elsewhere, it's probably somewhere in the chart task pane. (Also, try the Help function which is pretty robust for charts.)

* * *

Alright, that was the basics of charts. Let's take a bit of a breather and cover grouping and subtotaling data and then we can dive in on our next big topic, pivot tables.

Group Data

Okay, let's cover a simpler topic now, grouping data. In *Excel 365 for Beginners* I covered how to hide or unhide columns and rows. (Select them, right-click, choose Hide from the dropdown menu. To unhide, select on either side of the hidden rows or columns, right-click, choose Unhide.)

But that's a more permanent option than what I like to use sometimes. I have worksheets I've created where there are columns that I routinely want next to one another when I'm adding data, but that I don't want next to each other all the time.

Like here with my advertising tracking worksheet:

Title	ASIN	Author	Series	Advertiser
A19 Beginner	B08Y852VDZ	M.L. Humphrey	Access Essentials 2019	Amazon CPC
Office 2019 Beginner	B095Q278NW	M.L. Humphrey	Office Essentials	Amazon CPC
Apub for Ads	B09RNBB9JF	M.L. Humphrey	Affinity Publisher	Amazon CPC
E19 Charts	B08WN7RMBQ	M.L. Humphrey	Easy Excel Essentials 201	Amazon CPC
Mail Merge for Beginners	B07QQ2T6GX	M.L. Humphrey	Mail Merge Essentials	Amazon CPC
Tables	B07QNZWJTP	M.L. Humphrey	Easy Word Essentials	Amazon CPC
Charts	B07DGHM1LM	M.L. Humphrey	Easy Excel Essentials	Amazon CPC

Column E is the title of the book I was advertising. Columns F, G, and H are information I want about that book, but not information I have to input myself. (I used VLOOKUP to populate those columns.) Column I is who I advertised with.

You can't see it, but Column J is how much I spent and then there are click and performance measurements after that.

When I'm inputting my advertising data, I don't want to see Columns F, G, and H. But at other times I do want them visible. So I need a solution that lets me toggle back and forth between having them hidden and not hidden. That's what grouping does. I can group my columns and then I just have to click on the minus sign for that group to hide those columns or the plus sign to see them.

Let's walk through how to do this now. I have moved a sample of that data into a new worksheet with Title in Column A, ASIN, Author, and Series in Columns B, C, and D, and then Advertiser in Column E.

To be able to group Columns B, C, and D, I have to select them first. (So click on the letter for Column B or for Column D and then left-click and drag to select all three.) Next, I go to the Outline section at the end of the Data tab and click on Group.

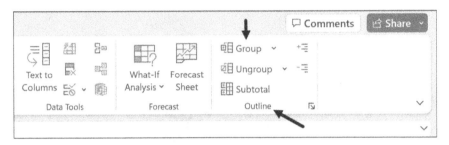

When you group a set of rows or columns you will see a gray area above the columns or to the left of the rows which will initially have a line with a minus sign at the end that spans the grouped columns or rows. Like this:

A	B	C	D	E	F
1 Title	ASIN	Author	Series	Advertiser	
2 Apub for Ads	B09RNBB9JF	M.L. Humphrey	Affinity Publisher	Amazon CPC	
3 E19 Charts	B08WN7RMBQ	M.L. Humphrey	Easy Excel Essentials 2019	Amazon CPC	
4 Mail Merge for Beginners	B07QQ2T6GX	M.L. Humphrey	Mail Merge Essentials	Amazon CPC	
5 Tables	B07QNZWJTP	M.L. Humphrey	Easy Word Essentials	Amazon CPC	
6 Charts	B07DGHM1LM	M.L. Humphrey	Easy Excel Essentials	Amazon CPC	

When the grouped columns or rows are visible you'll see that minus sign at the end. Click on it to collapse the group and hide the columns or rows.

When you do that you'll see a plus sign in that gray area above where the columns were and they'll be hidden. Note how this goes from Column A to Column E:

A	E
1 Title	Advertiser
2 Apub for Ads	Amazon CPC
3 E19 Charts	Amazon CPC
4 Mail Merge for Beginners	Amazon CPC
5 Tables	Amazon CPC
6 Charts	Amazon CPC

Simply click on that plus sign to show those columns or rows once more. (There are also options in the Outline section of the Data tab to Show Detail or Hide Detail, which are to the right of Group and Ungroup, but by default it shouldn't be necessary to use them, because you have the plus and minus signs to use. If you ever get rid of those, though, that is another way to show or hide your grouped columns or rows.)

To remove grouping from a worksheet, go back to the Outline section of the Data tab and choose Clear Outline from the Ungroup dropdown menu. This will remove all groups in that worksheet as long as you didn't have one specific group selected.

If you select only one set of grouped columns or rows, Clear Outline will just remove that grouping.

Ungroup also works to remove grouping. You have to select all cells in the worksheet or those grouped rows or columns first, then click on Ungroup, and then when the dialogue box appears choose either rows or columns, and then click OK.

You cannot undo Ungrouping. Ctrl + Z does not work to reverse that, so if you accidentally ungroup your worksheet and didn't mean to, you'll need to build it back manually.

One final note, you can only group columns or rows that are next to one another. So if you can't select them using left-click and drag or the Shift key, Excel won't let you group them. You'll get an error message when you try to.

Subtotal Data

In that same Outline section of the Data tab there is also an option to Subtotal, which takes a data table and performs a calculation each time there is a change in the value in the designated column. So, a sum of revenue for each change in customer name, for example.

The first step when subtotaling your data is to sort it properly. If you want to subtotal by each change in X column, then you need to sort X column so that all like values are grouped together. (I'll show you in a minute what happens if you don't do that.)

The next step is to select your data, go to the Outline section of the Data tab, and click on Subtotal.

This will bring up the Subtotal dialogue box. Here you can see the data we're going to use for this sample as well as the dialogue box:

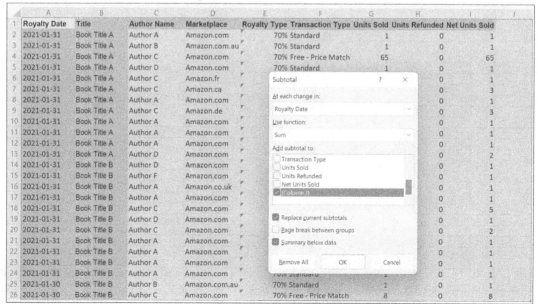

The dialogue box will be pre-populated with default suggestions, but you can change them.

The first choice is what column is driving your subtotals. In this case I'm going to change that to Title. The data is split between two titles, Title A and Title B.

The next choice is what calculation you want Excel to perform. The default is to sum the values in a column, but you can also choose to count the values, average them, return the minimum value, return the maximum value, calculate the product of the values, count the numbers, or calculate different types of variance or standard deviation.

I'm going to leave that as sum.

The next choice is which columns you want to perform those calculations for. You only get that one choice, sum, average, etc. but you can perform it for multiple columns. Just check the boxes for each one you want.

I'm going to do Units Sold, Units Refunded, and Net Units Sold.

Check "replace current subtotals" when you're editing a data table that already has them.

If you want the results to print out on separate pages for each change in the variable, check the box for "page break between groups". And if you want a grand total value as well, make sure the box for "summary below data" is checked.

By default it will replace any existing subtotals and provide a summary. I chose to also have the page break between groups just to show you how that appears in your workspace. Here we go:

Royalty Date	Title	Author Name	Marketplace	Royalty Type	Transaction Type	Units Sold	Units Refunded	Net Units Sold
2021-01-31	Book Title A	Author A	Amazon.com	70%	Standard	1	0	1
2021-01-31	Book Title A	Author B	Amazon.com.au	70%	Standard	1	0	1
2021-01-31	Book Title A	Author C	Amazon.com	70%	Free - Price Match	65	0	65
2021-01-31	Book Title A	Author D	Amazon.com	70%	Standard	1	0	1
2021-01-31	Book Title A	Author C	Amazon.fr	70%	Free - Price Match	1	0	1
2021-01-31	Book Title A	Author C	Amazon.ca	70%	Free - Price Match	3	0	3
2021-01-31	Book Title A	Author A	Amazon.com	70%	Standard	1	0	1
2021-01-31	Book Title A	Author C	Amazon.de	70%	Free - Price Match	3	0	3
2021-01-31	Book Title A	Author A	Amazon.com	35%	Standard	1	0	1
2021-01-31	Book Title A	Author A	Amazon.com	70%	Standard	1	0	1
2021-01-31	Book Title A	Author A	Amazon.com	70%	Standard	1	0	1
2021-01-31	Book Title A	Author D	Amazon.com	70%	Standard	2	0	2
	Book Title A Total					81	0	81
2021-01-31	Book Title B	Author D	Amazon.com	70%	Standard	1	0	1
2021-01-31	Book Title B	Author F	Amazon.com	35%	Free - Price Match	1	0	1
2021-01-31	Book Title B	Author A	Amazon.co.uk	70%	Standard	1	0	1
2021-01-31	Book Title B	Author A	Amazon.com	35%	Standard	1	0	1
2021-01-31	Book Title B	Author C	Amazon.com	35%	Free - Price Match	5	0	5
2021-01-31	Book Title B	Author D	Amazon.com	70%	Standard	1	0	1
2021-01-31	Book Title B	Author C	Amazon.com	70%	Standard	2	0	2
2021-01-31	Book Title B	Author A	Amazon.com	70%	Standard	1	0	1
2021-01-31	Book Title B	Author A	Amazon.com	70%	Standard	1	0	1
2021-01-31	Book Title B	Author A	Amazon.com	70%	Standard	1	0	1
2021-01-31	Book Title B	Author A	Amazon.com	70%	Standard	1	0	1
2021-01-30	Book Title B	Author B	Amazon.com.au	70%	Standard	1	0	1
2021-01-30	Book Title B	Author C	Amazon.com	70%	Free - Price Match	8	0	8
	Book Title B Total					25	0	25
	Grand Total					106	0	106

Look at Row 14 where there is a subtotal for Book Title A. And then Row 28 is the subtotal for Book Title B. And Row 29 is the total for both. On the left-hand side are grouping lines that let you collapse either the details for Book Title A or the details for Book Title B (under group 2) or that let you collapse everything and just show the grand total row (under group 1).

That line you can see under Row 14 is the page break, but you'd have to go to print preview to actually see the data separated out onto a separate page.

As you can see, subtotal also groups data. But you can remove the grouping by using the Clear Outline option under Ungroup. That will leave the subtotals but remove the grouping and ability to collapse the various levels of the data table.

To remove subtotals, go back to Subtotal and when the Subtotal dialogue box opens, click on the Remove All button at the bottom left corner of the dialogue box.

Now let me show you what happens if you don't sort your data first. I'm going to do exactly the same thing, but for Author Name. There are five author names in this data. Let's see if we get five groups:

	Royalty Date	Title	Author Name	Marketplace	Royalty Type	Transaction Type	Units Sold	Units Refunded	Net Units Sold
3			Author A Total				1	0	1
5			Author B Total				1	0	1
7			Author C Total				65	0	65
9			Author D Total				1	0	1
12			Author C Total				4	0	4
14			Author A Total				1	0	1
16			Author C Total				3	0	3
20			Author A Total				3	0	3
23			Author D Total				3	0	3
25			Author F Total				1	0	1
28			Author A Total				2	0	2
30			Author C Total				5	0	5
32			Author D Total				1	0	1
34			Author C Total				2	0	2
39			Author A Total				4	0	4
41			Author B Total				1	0	1
43			Author C Total				8	0	8
44									
45									
46									
47			Grand Total				106	0	106

No.

I clicked on the 2 on the left-hand side to collapse everything one level and hide each row of detail so that we were only seeing the subtotal rows. As you can see, there are far more than five groups.

If you look closer you'll see that most of the authors have more than one subtotal. Author A, for example, has five subtotals as noted in the image above.

That's because the data was not sorted. And Excel doesn't know better. What it's doing is going down that column and every time the value changes, it subtotals. So when the data changed from Author A to Author B, subtotal. From Author B to Author C, subtotal. And so on and so on down the list. If there were two rows for an author that were next to each other those were grouped and subtotaled together, but otherwise, no.

What else to tell you?

I mentioned that I clicked on the 2 to collapse everything to hide the detail. To bring it back for all rows, I can click on the 3. You can also click on individual plus or minus signs to expand or collapse a particular subset of entries.

Click on the 1 to just show the grand total row.

I had an issue just now where clicking on the 1 hid everything, even the grand total row. I believe this was caused by including blank rows from below the data table when I subtotaled. (I just used Ctrl + A to select all cells in the worksheet.) Going back and more carefully choosing only rows with data in them fixed the issue.

(Don't be afraid to make mistakes in Excel. If you think something should work, go back and try again. Sometimes little quirky things like that will mess you up but what you want to do will in fact be possible.)

If you ever have data that has more grouping levels than that, just think of the 1 as the highest level of grouping and the others as more granular levels of grouping. Let the gray lines in the grouping section guide you. For example, here you can see that Rows 36 and 37 are grouped and will disappear if I click on that minus sign there.

	A	B	C	D	E	F
33	2021-01-31	Book Title B	Author C	Amazon.com		70% Standard
34			Author C Total			
35	2021-01-31	Book Title B	Author A	Amazon.com		70% Standard
36	2021-01-31	Book Title B	Author A	Amazon.com		70% Standard
37	2021-01-31	Book Title B	Author A	Amazon.com		70% Standard
38	2021-01-31	Book Title B	Author A	Amazon.com		70% Standard
39			Author A Total			
40	2021-01-30	Book Title B	Author B	Amazon.com.au		70% Standard
41			Author B Total			
42	2021-01-30	Book Title B	Author C	Amazon.com		70% Free - Price Match
43			Author C Total			
44			Grand Total			

One final note about subtotals. If you select only the data but not the header row, Excel will show an error message dialogue box and ask if you want to include that header row in your selection. Click on Yes to proceed with that row included. Click on No if you don't want to. If you click on No it will treat the first row of values you did select as a header row. Cancel or closing the dialogue box will take you back to the worksheet without subtotaling.

Pivot Tables – Insert and Build

Introduction

First off, Excel writes pivot table as PivotTable, but I don't like that so I'm not going to do it. I did for the Excel 2019 books, but for this one I've decided not to. They let you search for pivot tables in the help screen just fine, so that's what we're going with.

Pivot tables are fantastic. I learned about them when I was in college and provided support to an Econ researcher who needed me to summarize some data. (He looked at me with horror when I confessed I didn't know what they were, but in my defense this was back in the day when I didn't even have a personal computer and the internet was not a place where I learned things.)

Once I learned about them, I was convinced that they are one of the most valuable tools in Excel. There is no better way to take a table of data and quickly summarize it.

In the beginner book and here I've occasionally used an anonymized version of one of my sales reports from Amazon. The one I'm using has 631 rows that include information for seven different author names with sales in ten different Amazon stores and three different sales types.

I could use filtering to see results for a single author, store, or transaction type. Or even combinations of those three. Or I could sort and then subtotal by one category. But pivot tables are just better. Let me show you.

Insert

Here are the first few rows of the data we're working with:

	A	B	C	D	E	F	G
1	Royalty Dat▾	Author Name ▾	Marketplace ▾	Transaction Ty▾	Net Units So▾	Royalty ▾	Currency ▾
2	2021-01-31	Author A	Amazon.com	Standard	1	5.70	USD
3	2021-01-31	Author B	Amazon.com.au	Standard	1	5.03	AUD
4	2021-01-31	Author C	Amazon.com	Free - Price Match	65	0.00	USD
5	2021-01-31	Author D	Amazon.com	Standard	1	2.76	USD
6	2021-01-31	Author C	Amazon.fr	Free - Price Match	1	0.00	EUR
7	2021-01-31	Author C	Amazon.ca	Free - Price Match	3	0.00	CAD
8	2021-01-31	Author A	Amazon.com	Standard	1	5.83	USD
9	2021-01-31	Author C	Amazon.de	Free - Price Match	3	0.00	EUR

Because my worksheet is set up with the header information in the first row and then only rows of data after that, I can just select the whole worksheet. (Ctrl + A or click in the top left corner where that dark gray triangle is.)

You can work with data that starts elsewhere in your document, but what you do need to have is data that has a clear header row, no subtotals or grand totals, and ideally no breaks in columns or rows within the data. Also, no merged cells.

So get your data formatted properly and select it.

Next step is to go to the Insert tab and click on the image for PivotTable in the Tables section. Be sure to click on the image and not the dropdown arrow.

(The image is the same as the From Table/Range option in the dropdown, so if you click on the dropdown arrow accidentally (like I often do) you can just select that option.)

Your other choice there is to use an external data source, something we are not going to cover here. Working with external data increases the risk of something breaking along the way.

The PivotTable From Table Or Range dialogue box will appear.

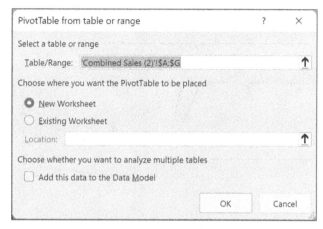

It will show your selected data and then give you the option of putting the table in a new worksheet or an existing worksheet.

I generally do not recommend putting a pivot table in the same worksheet as any other data so I almost always go with new worksheet.

I will on occasion put the pivot table in the same worksheet as my data when I know it's a one-off and that all of my data is already in place.

The reason not to put a pivot table in a worksheet with other data is because pivot tables are dynamic. They will change size and shape based upon what data is feeding into them.

So if I, for example, create a pivot table with author names in it and then add my own analysis text below that or to the right side, and later decide to add marketplace to the pivot table, I will have a problem. Because the pivot table will need to expand to include that new information but won't be able to because of my text. (Excel does at least tell you this is an issue before overwriting the text and gives you the chance to cancel doing so, but it's best to never have to worry about it in the first place.)

If you really do want that pivot table in your same worksheet as your data, then be sure to put it to the right or below any of your other data in that worksheet to avoid problems. Whatever cell you choose for placing the pivot table, Excel will build from that spot over and down.

Okay. So I'm leaving those settings alone because I already selected my data and want to put the table in a new worksheet, which means I can just click OK.

Excel will then open a new worksheet that has a blank pivot table in the main workspace and a PivotTable Fields task pane on the right-hand side.

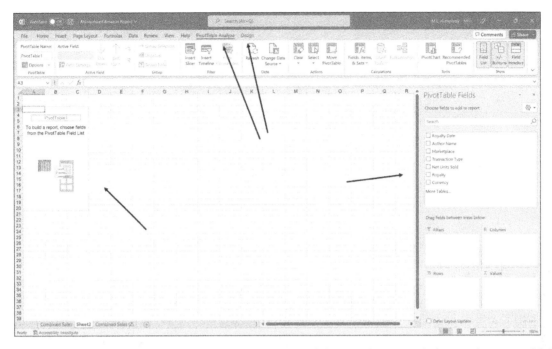

There are also PivotTable Analyze and Design tabs visible at the top of the workspace which we will cover in detail later. They will only be visible when you are working with the pivot table. Click on it to see them if you click away.

Build

You have two options for building your pivot table. You can check the boxes for the fields you want to include in your pivot table in the top of the task pane and let Excel place the fields for you where it thinks they make the most sense.

Or, and this is the method I use, you can place the fields yourself at the bottom of the task pane by left-clicking on each field name in the top section and dragging it down to one of the Filters, Columns, Rows, or Values boxes.

Here, for example, I have dragged Author Name into the Rows box and Net Units Sold into the Values box:

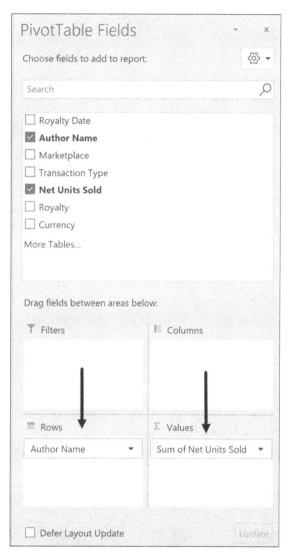

When I clicked and dragged those fields down, Excel automatically checked the box next to each field name in the top section.

That gives me a pivot table that has all of my author names listed on the left-hand side in rows and then, because I don't have anything in the Columns box, it leaves me with one single column next to that where the total number of units for each author is shown. Like so:

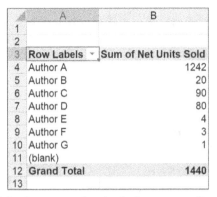

(Excel will automatically decide the type of calculation to perform on any field you put in the Values box. In this case, sum. But if you want to change that you can. We'll discuss how to do so later.)

So there we go. Less than a minute to summarize 600+ rows of data. And I can see all of it in one glance without having to filter or sort or add formulas.

That was the most basic of pivot tables. Now, let's start making more complex pivot tables.

I want to look at amount earned per author, but the problem is that this report includes different currencies, so I can't just sum up the Royalty column for each author because while maybe Euros and Dollars are about the same right now, something like Japanese Yen will throw everything out the window.

What I need is to list the amount earned in each currency for each author.

To do this, I can add Currency to my Columns box and put Royalty into the Values section.

This is what I now have in the pivot table task pane:

And this is what that pivot table looks like:

	A	B	C	D	E	F	G	H	I	J	K
1											
2											
3	Sum of Royalty	Column Labels ▾									
4	Row Labels ▾	AUD	CAD	EUR	GBP	INR	MXN	USD	(blank)	Grand Total	
5	Author A	12.35	108.12	13.03	337.01		40.25	5839.71		6350.47	
6	Author B	15.09			28.42			22.79		66.3	
7	Author C		0	0	0	0		8.98		8.98	
8	Author D	3.79			7.43			293.38		304.6	
9	Author E			2.56				14.71		17.27	
10	Author F							0		0	
11	Author G				0.35					0.35	
12	(blank)										
13	Grand Total	31.23	108.12	15.59	373.21	0	40.25	6179.57		6747.97	
14											

(We'll cover formatting later.)

Now let's build a pivot table that uses the Filter section to filter the entire pivot table based upon a field value. Here I've created a pivot table that has Author Name in Rows, Net Units Sold and Royalty in Values, and Transaction Type and Marketplace in Filters.

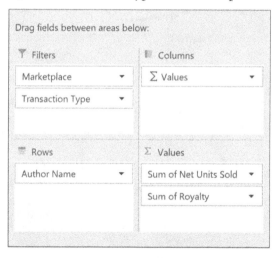

This is how that looks by default:

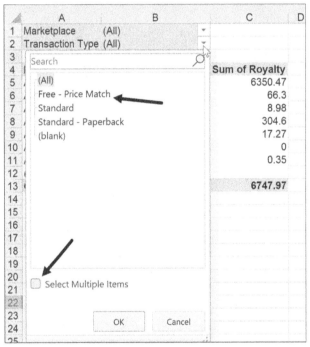

But we put in filters for a reason, so let's go to the Transaction Type filter and click on the dropdown arrow:

I want to remove Free – Price Match from that list. To do so, I click on Select Multiple Items down there at the bottom of the dropdown. That's going to put checked boxes by each of the values up top and I can then uncheck Free – Price Match.

(If there are a lot of choices and you only want one, click the checkbox next to Select Multiple Items, and then click the box next to All to unselect all. You can then check the one or two you want. It's easier than unchecking each one individually.)

After you remove some of the values, that All in parens next to the field name will change to either Multiple Items or the one value you've chosen if you chose just one.

Here is that table with Marketplace limited to just one value, Amazon.com, and Transaction Type limited to all but Free – Price Match:

	A	B	C
1	Marketplace	Amazon.com	
2	Transaction Type	(Multiple Items)	
3			
4	Row Labels	Sum of Net Units Sold	Sum of Royalty
5	Author A	1129	5839.71
6	Author B	6	22.79
7	Author C	3	8.98
8	Author D	76	293.38
9	Author E	3	14.71
10	Grand Total	1217	6179.57
11			

To see which fields that Multiple Items is showing (or not showing), you can click on the filter symbol:

	A	B	C
1	Marketplace	(All)	
2	Transaction Type	(Multiple Items)	

Search

- ■ (All)
- ☐ Free - Price Match
- ✔ Standard
- ✔ Standard - Paperback
- ✔ (blank)

Sum of Royalty: 6350.47, 66.3, 8.98, 304.6, 17.27, 0.35, 6747.97

Click

Checked Fields Have Data Showing

✔ Select Multiple Items

OK   Cancel

Now let's create an even more-complex pivot table that uses multiple fields for both Rows and Columns.

To do this, I went back to my original data table that's feeding this pivot table and added columns with month and year data and then refreshed the pivot table. (We'll cover Refresh later.)

For this new pivot table, I placed both year and month in Columns, both Author Name and Currency in Rows, and Royalty in Values:

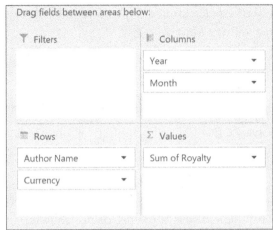

When you have more than one field in Columns or Rows, order matters. In this case I wanted Year to be the highest-level with months below that and then Author to be the highest level with currency below that.

Here's what that looks like:

Sum of Royalty	Column Labels											
	2021				2021 Total	(blank)	(blank) Total	2020			2020 Total	Grand Total
Row Labels	January	February	March	April		(blank)		January	February	April		
⊟Author A	350.56	342.83	3174.69	2091.06	5959.14			28.45	96.21	266.67	391.33	6350.47
AUD	9.96				9.96				2.39		2.39	12.35
CAD	27.14	5.75	47.49	23.85	104.23				3.89		3.89	108.12
EUR	1.66		4.2		5.86				7.17		7.17	13.03
GBP	15.44	30.68	188.53	84.74	319.39			4.85	8.5	4.27	17.62	337.01
MXN		40.25			40.25							40.25
USD	296.36	266.15	2934.47	1982.47	5479.45			23.6	74.26	262.4	360.26	5839.71
⊟Author B	40.61	9.64	9.17		59.42				6.88		6.88	66.3
AUD	15.09				15.09							15.09
GBP	22.08	2.76	3.58		28.42							28.42
USD	3.44	6.88	5.59		15.91				6.88		6.88	22.79
⊟Author C	8.98				8.98			0			0	8.98
CAD	0				0							0
EUR	0				0			0			0	0
GBP	0				0							0
INR	0				0							0
USD	8.98				8.98							8.98
⊟Author D	22.43	54.64	128.46	68.3	273.83			8.63	8.28	13.86	30.77	304.6
AUD		3.79			3.79							3.79
GBP	0.35			7.08	7.43							7.43
USD	22.08	50.85	128.46	61.22	262.61			8.63	8.28	13.86	30.77	293.38
⊟Author E	6.03		11.24		17.27							17.27
EUR	2.56				2.56							2.56
USD	3.47		11.24		14.71							14.71
⊟Author F	0				0							0
USD	0				0							0
⊟Author G	0.35				0.35							0.35
GBP	0.35				0.35							0.35
⊟(blank)												
(blank)												
Grand Total	428.96	407.11	3323.56	2159.36	6318.99			37.08	111.37	280.53	428.98	6747.97

See that each author is listed first with their transactions broken down by currency and that each year of sales is listed first with the transactions by month listed under that.

It looks very complex but what it's showing is how much was earned each month of each year in each currency for each author.

By placing Author above Currency in the Rows section, the data is ordered with each currency listed for each author. If I had instead placed Currency first, it would be listed with each author for each currency. Like this:

	A	B	C	D	E	F
1						
2						
3						
4	Sum of Royalty	Column Labels ▾				
5		⊟2021				2021 Total
6	Row Labels ▾	January	February	March	April	
7	⊟AUD	25.05	3.79			28.84
8	Author A	9.96				9.96
9	Author B	15.09				15.09
10	Author D		3.79			3.79
11	⊟CAD	27.14	5.75	47.49	23.85	104.23
12	Author A	27.14	5.75	47.49	23.85	104.23
13	Author C	0				0
14	⊟EUR	4.22		4.2		8.42
15	Author A	1.66		4.2		5.86
16	Author C	0				0
17	Author E	2.56				2.56
18	⊟GBP	38.22	33.44	192.11	91.82	355.59

See how now the data shows for each currency and then any author who had sales in that currency is listed below that?

Same thing happens in the Rows section.

I put year first and then month so that you have all monthly values listed under each year. If I'd reversed that order you'd have all yearly values listed under each month. So the table would start with January and then show both 2020 and 2021 values for January before then doing the same for February and then March.

Okay. So that's how to build pivot tables. Basically, make sure your data is formatted well for use with a pivot table, select it, insert a pivot table, and then click and drag the fields you want to use into place.

If you have more than one field in Rows or Columns, the order matters. The one listed first is the primary category.

You can put more than one field into the Values section, too, but I don't recommend doing so if the Columns and Rows sections are complex. Basically, step back when you're done and ask yourself if there's so much information in the table that it's too hard to follow. If there is, simplify and maybe use more than one pivot table. Or make some of those fields into filters. (Or add Slicers, which we'll discuss soon.)

Okay. That was the basics of how to insert and build pivot tables, but there's a lot more to this topic. Let's now cover some common tricks for working with a pivot table. Things I did in this chapter that I didn't want to stop to discuss at the time.

Pivot Tables – Work With

In the last chapter there were a number of basic tasks related to pivot tables that I performed but didn't cover or that I wanted to explain. They come up often enough that I wanted to highlight them in their own chapter. But later we'll more systematically go through the pivot table tabs and other options you have related to pivot tables to cover more obscure tasks, too.
So.

Change Calculation Type

We were very lucky in the last chapter that Excel recognized the value for Net Units Sold as a number that it could sum. Often with my data sets I receive from my vendors I am not that lucky. Excel brings in the numeric values in those workbooks as text and then defaults to *counting* the values instead of summing them up.

To fix this, click on the arrow on the right-hand side of the entry in the Values section, and choose Value Field Settings from the dropdown menu. Like here:

This will open the Value Field Settings dialogue box:

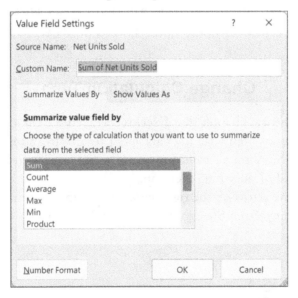

If you just want a basic calculation like sum or count it's available right there on the Summarize Values By tab.

You can make different choices for different columns of data if you have more than one field in the Values section. But be careful. Because it may not be immediately obvious that one column is a count, one is a sum of values, and one is an average.

I generally, unless my data labels and formats and other attributes make it abundantly clear, do not mix and match what I'm doing with multiple columns of data. Everything sums. Or everything takes the maximum value. Or everything takes the minimum value. Etc.

But it's a free world, you can do what you want. Just keep your audience in mind and make sure they'll quickly see what you've done.

There are two other ways to open the Value Field Settings dialogue box.

One is to click on an entry in your pivot table and go to the Active Field section of the PivotTable Analyze tab where you will see that field you selected listed. Click on Field Settings to open the Value Field Settings dialogue box and edit the settings for that field.

The other is to right-click on a value in the pivot table and then choose Value Field Settings from the bottom section of that dropdown menu.

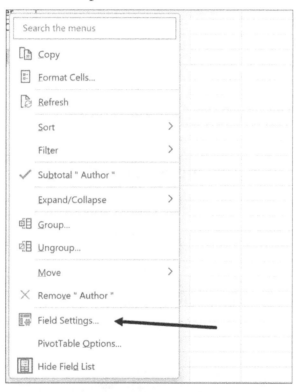

All of those options rely on using the Value Field Settings dialogue box. This is my general approach because at the same time I can format the cells.

But, that dropdown also lets you directly choose how to summarize values (sum, count, average, etc.) using the Summarize Values By option, which lists all of those choices in a dropdown menu format.

Use a Comparison Calculation

You can also do a comparison-style calculation with a field in your pivot table instead using the Show Values As tab in the Value Field Settings dialogue box or using the Show Values As dropdown menu:

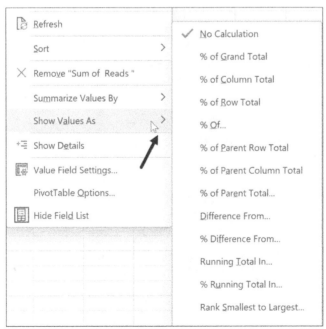

As you can see, there are a large number of choices, such as % of Grand Total, % of Column Total, % of Row Total, and many many more.

You can actually add a field a second time and have one use of the field for a calculation like sum and the other use of the field for a comparison value like % of column total. I've done that here for Net Units Sold:

	A	B	C
1			
2			
3	Row Labels	Sum of Net Units Sold	Sum of Net Units Sold2
4	Author A	1242	86.25%
5	Author B	20	1.39%
6	Author C	90	6.25%
7	Author D	80	5.56%
8	Author E	4	0.28%
9	Author F	3	0.21%
10	Author G	1	0.07%
11	(blank)		0.00%
12	**Grand Total**	**1440**	**100.00%**

We can see that Author A is 86% of the units sold for the data set. Same as taking 1242, the actual total of the net units sold for Author A, and dividing by 1440, the total net units sold for all authors.

I can show both here and it looks fine because we're only looking at one variable, net units sold. If I were to add a second variable, like royalty, that would make things a bit messy, so I'd probably want to choose one or the other, but not display both. Again, think of your audience when building any pivot table or chart. Will they understand what they're seeing?

Remove a Field From a Pivot Table

The easiest way to remove a field from a pivot table is to just uncheck the checkbox in the top of the task pane. But if you used a field more than once like I did above and you want to remove only one of the uses, that won't work.

Another option is to click on the arrow to the right of the field name, and then click Remove Field from the dropdown.

Or you can right-click on one of the values for that field in the actual pivot table and choose the "Remove [X]" option from the dropdown menu, where X is the field name.

You can also left-click and drag the field away from the bottom of the task pane.

Sort Pivot Table Data

One of the things I often like to do when dealing with pivot tables is sort my data. I usually want my most successful authors or titles or series shown at the top of the table.

To sort a pivot table, right-click in a cell in the column where you want to sort, find Sort in the dropdown menu, and then choose the type of sort you want:

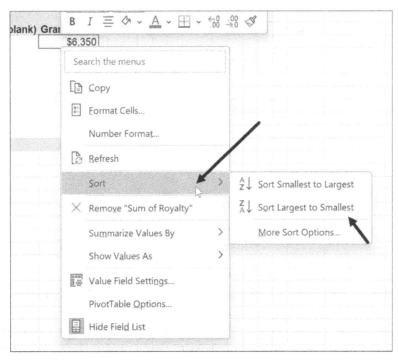

That will sort your data by the values in that selected column, in this case Column J, Grand Total:

	A	B	C	D	E	F	G	H	I	J	K
1											
2											
3	Sum of Royalty	Column Labels ▼									
4	Row Labels ▾	AUD	CAD	EUR	GBP	INR	MXN	USD	(blank)	Grand Total	
5	Author A		$12	$108	$13	$337		$40	$5,840		$6,350
6	Author D		$4			$7			$293		$305
7	Author B		$15			$28			$23		$66
8	Author E				$3				$15		$17
9	Author C			$0	$0	$0	$0		$9		$9
10	Author G					$0					$0
11	(blank)										
12	Author F								$0		$0
13	Grand Total		$31	$108	$16	$373	$0	$40	$6,180		$6,748
14											

Now I have my largest values at the top and my smallest at the bottom.

Hide Entries in A Pivot Table

You can also hide certain entries by clicking on the arrow next to Row Labels or Column Labels and then unchecking the ones you don't want to see:

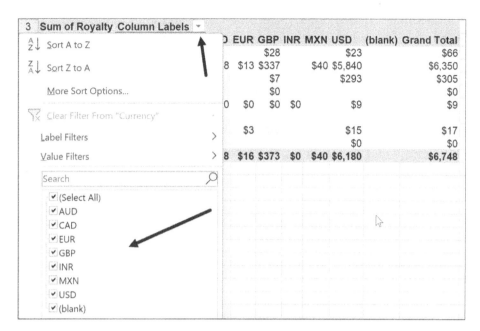

It works just like selecting or unselecting values when filtering data. I sometimes have "blank" as values in my tables and I don't need it there so I'll do this to remove it.

Here I made it so that only CAD transactions show:

Note that the arrow turned into a filter so you know that this is not a complete listing of all of your data.

Also, note how the pivot table size changed when I did that. There were only two authors with sales in Canada for that month, so not only did the number of columns go down, but so did the number of rows. Remember, pivot tables are dynamic, they adjust to display data based on your choices as to what to include or not include.

If there are two fields for columns or rows, click on a value in the pivot table for the one you want to edit first so that that's the dropdown menu that you see.

Group Values In a Row or Column in a Pivot Table

You can also group values in a row or column in a pivot table. Values you want to group *do not* have to be located next to each other. Select the values you want to group by clicking on the first one and then using Ctrl or Shift or clicking and dragging to select more.

Below I've chosen Authors C, E, and G, for example, by holding down Ctrl as I clicked on each one.

Once the values you want to group have been selected, right-click and choose Group from the dropdown menu:

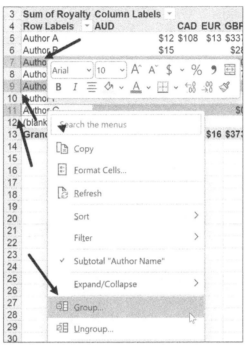

That will create a new level in that table for groups where the grouped values you selected are in one group and all other values are in their own group that only contains them and is named after them. Like so:

	Sum of Royalty	Column Labels								
	Row Labels	AUD	CAD	EUR	GBP	INR	MXN	USD	(blank)	Grand Total
5	⊟Author A		$12	$108	$13	$337		$40	$5,840		$6,350
6	Author A		$12	$108	$13	$337		$40	$5,840		$6,350
7	⊟Author B	$15			$28			$23		$66
8	Author B	$15			$28			$23		$66
9	⊟Group1		$0	$3	$0	$0		$24		$27
10	Author C		$0	$0	$0	$0		$9		$9
11	Author E			$3				$15		$17
12	Author G				$0					$0
13	⊟Author D	$4			$7			$293		$305
14	Author D	$4			$7			$293		$305
15	⊟Author F							$0		$0
16	Author F							$0		$0
17	⊟(blank)									
18	(blank)									
19	Grand Total		$31	$108	$16	$373	$0	$40	$6,180		$6,748

Group 1 contains Authors C, E, and G and then all of the other authors (and blank) have their own group.

The PivotTable Analyze tab also has a Group section where you can either group entries or ungroup them. You'll need to select your items first before you can use it.

Rename Group

When you click on a group name you should also see that name in your formula bar. You can edit the name by going to the formula bar and typing in what you want to use for that group:

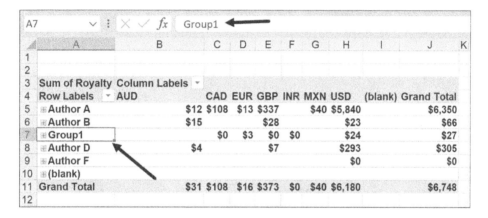

Collapse Groups

You can collapse the groups, like I have in the screenshot above, by right-clicking on a group name, going to Expand/Collapse in the dropdown menu, and choosing Collapse Entire Field.

		Search the menus		$337	$40	$5,840	$6,350
7	**Author**			$28		$23	$66
8	Autho	Copy		$28		$23	$66
9	**Group1**			$0	$0	$24	$27
10	Autho	Format Cells...		$0	$0	$9	$9
11	Autho					$15	$17
12	Autho	Refresh		$0			$0
13	**Author**			$7		$293	$305
14	Autho	Sort	>	$7		$293	$305
15	**Author**					$0	$0
16	Autho	Filter	>			$0	$0
17	**(blank)**	✓ Subtotal "Author Name2"					
18	(blank						
19	**Grand To**	Expand/Collapse	>	+⊒ Expand			$6,748
20							
21		Group...		-⊒ Collapse			
22							
23		Ungroup...		+⊒ Expand Entire Field			

To collapse just one group at a time click on the minus sign next to the group name.

Expand Groups

To once again see the details for each group, right-click on a group name and then choose Expand Entire Field from the Expand/Collapse secondary dropdown.

To expand just one group, click on the plus sign next to the group name.

Clear Pivot Table

To start over, go to the Actions section of the PivotTable Analyze tab and use the Clear dropdown to select Clear All.

Remove Filters

If you have filters applied to your pivot table and you want to remove all of them, you can go to the Actions section of the PivotTable Analyze tab and choose Clear Filters from the Clear dropdown.

This will remove all filters from the pivot table, including the ones on your Column and Row Labels.

Refresh Pivot Table

If the data that is feeding into your pivot table changes, you need to refresh the pivot table.

To do so, go to the Data section of the PivotTable Analyze tab, and click on Refresh.

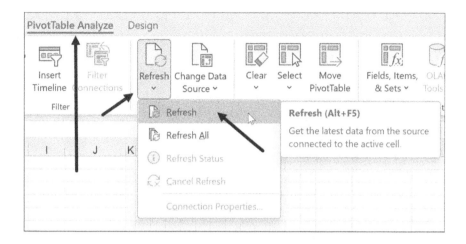

You can also use Alt + 5. (I just never remember it.)

The dropdown for Refresh has a Refresh All option which will refresh all data sources in the workbook. You can use this if you have multiple pivot tables that need refreshed.

If you change existing values in your data table or add new rows or columns into the middle of it, Refresh should work to update your pivot table or pivot table field choices.

But if you instead add data outside of the prior data range, then use the Change Data Source option right next to Refresh instead. That will bring up a dialogue box showing your current data selection. You can then change that range to include your new data.

* * *

Okay. So those are some basic common tasks I often need to perform with respect to pivot tables. Now let's talk about how to format your pivot table.

Pivot Tables – Format

In this chapter we're going to cover how to format your pivot table and the entries in that table. I'm going to start with a few formatting options that I use all the time and then we'll go through and be more systematic about your formatting options.

Value Field Settings Dialogue Box For Values Fields Formatting

As I mentioned above, I use the Value Field Settings Dialogue box to tell Excel what type of calculation to perform on my fields because it's also the best place to format the data in a pivot table.

You *can* just select fields in a pivot table and use the Home tab formatting options or right-click on selected fields and use the Number Format option in the dropdown menu. But the problem with those approaches is that they only apply formatting to those specific entries.

If you expand the data in your table at some point, the new entries will not be formatted that way. So if I start with just Author Name in my table and manually format those entries but then add Currency, all of the new entries will not be formatted.

But if you use the Value Field Settings Dialogue box to format the entries for that field, they will.

So how do you do this?

Open the Value Field Settings dialogue box and click on the option for Number Format in the bottom left corner.

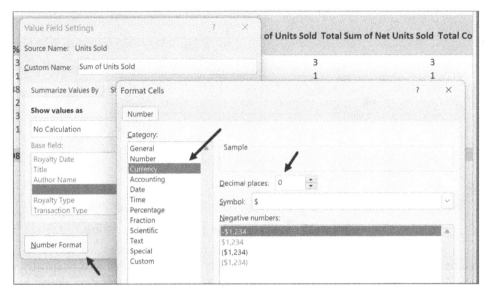

This will open the Format Cells dialogue box where you can then choose how to format the values in that field.

I usually need to do this for currency values to make them look like currency. I will often set the decimal places to zero when I do this to remove clutter from my table.

Subtotals and Grand Totals

Here is a standard complex pivot table that Excel will create by default:

Sum of Royalty	Column Labels											
	2021				2021 Total	(blank)	(blank) Total	2020			2020 Total	Grand Total
Row Labels	January	February	March	April		(blank)		January	February	April		
AUD	25.05	3.79			28.84					2.39	2.39	31.23
Author A	9.96				9.96					2.39	2.39	12.35
Author B	15.09				15.09							15.09
Author D		3.79			3.79							3.79
CAD	27.14	5.75	47.49	23.85	104.23					3.89	3.89	108.12
Author A	27.14	5.75	47.49	23.85	104.23					3.89	3.89	108.12
Author C	0				0							0
EUR	4.22		4.2		8.42			0	7.17		7.17	15.59
Author A	1.66		4.2		5.86				7.17		7.17	13.03
Author C	0				0			0			0	0
Author E	2.56				2.56							2.56
GBP	38.22	33.44	192.11	91.82	355.59			4.85	8.5	4.27	17.62	373.21
Author A	15.44	30.68	188.53	84.74	319.39			4.85	8.5	4.27	17.62	337.01
Author B	22.08	2.76	3.58		28.42							28.42
Author C	0				0							0
Author D	0.35			7.08	7.43							7.43
Author G	0.35				0.35							0.35
INR	0				0							0
Author C	0				0							0
MXN		40.25			40.25							40.25
Author A		40.25			40.25							40.25
USD	334.33	323.88	3079.76	2043.69	5781.66			32.23	89.42	276.26	397.91	6179.57
Author A	296.36	266.15	2934.47	1982.47	5479.45			23.6	74.26	262.4	360.26	5839.71
Author B	3.44	6.88	5.59		15.91				6.88		6.88	22.79
Author C	8.98				8.98							8.98
Author D	22.08	50.85	128.46	61.22	262.61			8.63	8.28	13.86	30.77	293.38
Author E	3.47		11.24		14.71							14.71
Author F	0				0							0
(blank)												
(blank)												
Grand Total	428.96	407.11	3323.56	2159.36	6318.99			37.08	111.37	280.53	428.98	6747.97

If you look across that top row you can see that Excel added subtotals for each year to the table. There's also a grand total row at the bottom.

I often generate pivot tables just to get data to work with, and when I do that I do not want all of that extraneous summary information, I just want the data. So I will often remove the subtotals and grand totals.

To edit your subtotals and grand totals, go to the Layout section of the pivot table Design tab.

The first option there is for Subtotals:

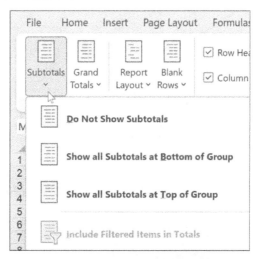

If you just want to remove your subtotals, then click on the Do Not Show Subtotals option.

The other two options you can see there let you decide where to display any subtotals for your rows. By default, at least with my settings, the subtotals show at the bottom of the group. Like here for Group 1:

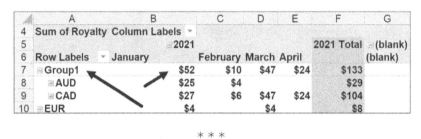

	A	B	C	D	E	F	G
4	Sum of Royalty	Column Labels ▾					
5		2021				2021 Total	(blank)
6	Row Labels ▾	January	February	March	April		(blank)
7	Group1						
8	AUD	$25	$4			$29	
9	CAD	$27	$6	$47	$24	$104	
10	Group1 Total	$52	$10	$47	$24	$133	

You can see the label for Group 1 and then the details for the group and then the Group 1 Total. But in this dropdown you can change that so that the subtotals show on the top instead. Like here where the subtotals for the group now show on the same row as the group name:

	A	B	C	D	E	F	G
4	Sum of Royalty	Column Labels ▾					
5		2021				2021 Total	(blank)
6	Row Labels ▾	January	February	March	April		(blank)
7	Group1	$52	$10	$47	$24	$133	
8	AUD	$25	$4			$29	
9	CAD	$27	$6	$47	$24	$104	
10	EUR	$4		$4		$8	

* * *

Next up is the Grand Totals dropdown:

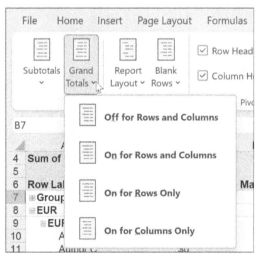

You can choose to have grand totals for rows only, columns only, both, or neither. If I plan on using the data in my pivot table for a chart (not a pivot chart, but just a basic chart), I will turn them all off. Because what I want is a header row with just data underneath.

Here is that same table from above but now with no subtotals or grand totals.

	January	February	March	April	(blank)	January	February	April
Sum of Royalty — Column Labels								
	2021				**(blank)**	**2020**		
Row Labels								
AUD								
Author A	$10						$2	
Author B	$15							
Author D		$4						
CAD								
Author A	$27	$6	$47	$24			$4	
Author C	$0							
EUR								
Author A	$2		$4				$7	
Author C	$0					$0		
Author E	$3							
GBP								
Author A	$15	$31	$189	$85		$5	$9	$4
Author B	$22	$3	$4					
Author C	$0							
Author D	$0			$7				
Author G	$0							
INR								
Author C	$0							
MXN								
Author A		$40						
USD								
Author A	$296	$266	$2,934	$1,982		$24	$74	$262
Author B	$3	$7	$6				$7	
Author C	$9							
Author D	$22	$51	$128	$61		$9	$8	$14
Author E	$3		$11					
Author F	$0							
(blank)								
(blank)								

Pivot Table Display Options

I can't use the pivot table in that image above as a data table. Right? If I copied and pasted it right now I'd have my values split across multiple rows. The currency for each entry isn't on the same line as the author name or results.

I can fix that though using the Report Layout dropdown menu:

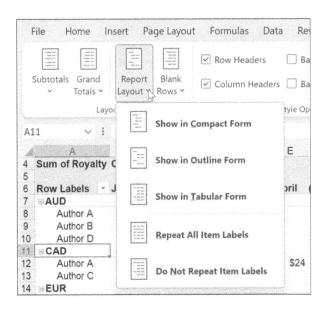

Your three main formatting options there are Compact Form, Outline Form, and Tabular Form. The thumbnail image next to each one tries to show what it would look like, but I often just apply them to see which one I want.

Below that you have the option to either Repeat All Item Labels or not.

If I'm trying to turn a pivot table into a data table, I choose Repeat All Item Labels and Tabular Form. That gives me this:

	A	B	C	D	E	F	G	H	I	J
4	Sum of Royalty		Year	Month						
5			2021	2021	2021	2021	(blank)	2020	2020	2020
6	Currency	Author Name	January	February	March	April	(blank)	January	February	April
7	AUD	Author A	$10						$2	
8	AUD	Author B	$15							
9	AUD	Author D		$4						
10	CAD	Author A	$27	$6	$47	$24			$4	
11	CAD	Author C	$0							
12	EUR	Author A	$2		$4				$7	
13	EUR	Author C	$0					$0		
14	EUR	Author E	$3							
15	GBP	Author A	$15	$31	$189	$85		$5	$9	$4
16	GBP	Author B	$22	$3	$4					
17	GBP	Author C	$0							
18	GBP	Author D	$0			$7				
19	GBP	Author G	$0							
20	INR	Author C	$0							
21	MXN	Author A		$40						
22	USD	Author A	$296	$266	$2,934	$1,982		$24	$74	$262
23	USD	Author B	$3	$7	$6				$7	
24	USD	Author C	$9							
25	USD	Author D	$22	$51	$128	$61		$9	$8	$14
26	USD	Author E	$3		$11					
27	USD	Author F	$0							
28	(blank)	(blank)								
29										

I can now select the whole worksheet, use Ctrl + C to copy and then Paste Special – Values to replace my pivot table with a data table. I will still have to change that top two rows of the table into one row that combines month and year data, but this gives me a summarized data table I can use to create an ordinary chart.

Here that is:

	A	B	C	D	E	F	G	H	I
			January-2021	February-2021	March-2021	April-2021	January-2020	February-2020	April-2020
2	Currency	Author Name							
3	AUD	Author A	9.96					2.39	
4	AUD	Author B	15.09						
5	AUD	Author D		3.79					
6	CAD	Author A	27.14	5.75	47.49	23.85		3.89	
7	CAD	Author C	0						
8	EUR	Author A	1.66		4.2			7.17	
9	EUR	Author C	0				0		
10	EUR	Author E	2.56						
11	GBP	Author A	15.44	30.68	188.53	84.74	4.85	8.5	4.27
12	GBP	Author B	22.08	2.76	3.58				

Note that there is a chapter on pivot charts later in this book if you don't want to do what I just did. Pivot charts let you build a chart directly from a pivot table. Which has the added benefit of remaining dynamic and adjusting as your data changes and you refresh your pivot table. Of course, that can also sometimes be a detriment. I often do that Paste Special – Values trick so that I lock in my values and don't inadvertently delete or change data that is flowing into my charts or calculations.

* * *

Okay. So those are the formatting options I use often with pivot tables in Excel. I format the entries in the Values section, I remove subtotals and grand totals, and I convert the table so that it can be copied and pasted-special and I have a good, working data table.

But there are many more formatting options than that. And it's time to walk through them.

Blank Rows

The final dropdown menu in the Layout section of the Design tab that we haven't covered yet is Blank Rows:

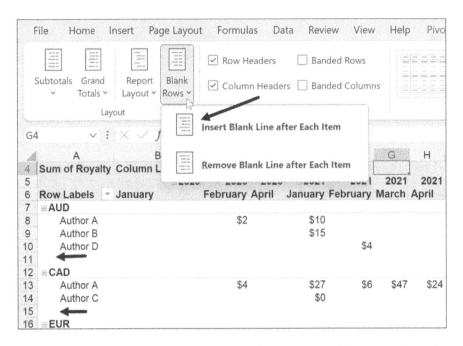

Blank Rows will let you insert a blank row after each "item". In this screenshot above an item is a group, so you can see blank rows that were inserted at Row 11 and Row 15.

I never use this one, but you might want to use it if you need a bit of visual separation between each of your top-level groups in your pivot table. It tends to break the visual of your data as you scan downward so that groups are more distinctive.

PivotTable Style Options and PivotTable Styles

Now let's look at the PivotTable Style Options and PivotTable Styles sections of the Design tab.

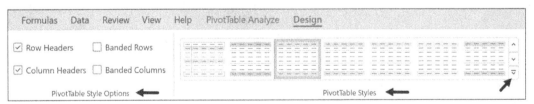

I'm going to skip to the styles first. I want to click on that down-pointing arrow with a line above it in the bottom right corner there as seen in the screenshot above. What that does is expands that section to show more styles:

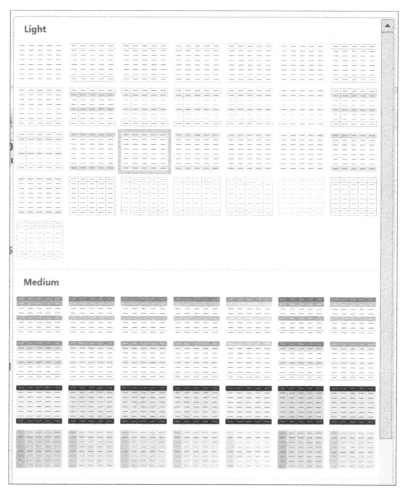

This will probably be a little hard to see in black and white print but essentially what you're seeing here are about sixty different pre-formatted pivot tables. Some have darker colored bands for the header row, some don't. Some use colored bands for subtotal rows, some don't. Some section off the first column, some don't.

There are a lot of choices. And if you scroll down you can see even more.

You can also see that the default style we've been working with so far is one of the choices in the Light section, in the third row. (As of December 2022.)

Hold your mouse over each style in the dropdown and Excel will show you in your worksheet what that style will look like. Click on the style to actually apply it.

Here I've applied Light Blue, Pivot Style Medium 6. (You can see the name when you hold your mouse over each option.)

	A	B	C	D	E	F	G	H	I	J
4	**Sum of Royalty**	Column Labels								
5		⊞2020	2020	2020	⊞2021	2021	2021	2021	⊞(blank)	Grand Total
6	Row Labels ▼	January	February	April	January	February	March	April	(blank)	
7	⊟AUD									
8	Author A		$2		$10					$12
9	Author B				$15					$15
10	Author D					$4				$4
11										
12	⊟CAD									
13	Author A		$4		$27	$6	$47	$24		$108
14	Author C				$0					$0
15										

It has a little more substance to it than the default style. Also, that extra formatting helps distinguish the values in the table.

Once you've applied a style, you can then use those checkboxes in the PivotTable Style Options section to add or remove row headers, column headers, banded rows, and banded columns formatting. The best way to see what it will do is just check and uncheck those boxes.

Custom Pivot Table Formatting

What if none of those options really give you what you want? Click on the New PivotTable Style option at the very bottom of the dropdown to bring up the New PivotTable Style dialogue box where you can customize everything to your heart's desire:

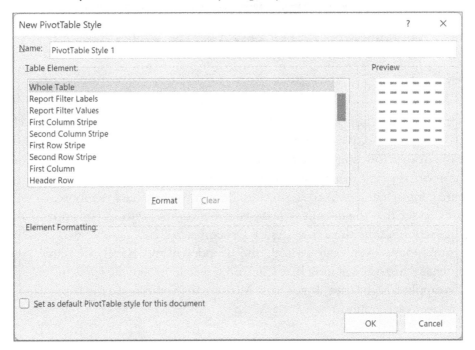

We are not going to go any further down that rabbit hole in this book. Suffice it to say it exists and if you really feel inspired it is there for you to use.

Pivot Tables – More Advanced Analysis

Okay, so I covered some very basic sorting, filtering, and grouping already which is where I spend 98% of my time when dealing with pivot tables, but there's more you can do.

So let's cover that part now. To do this, we need to go to the PivotTable Analyze tab and look at the Filter and Calculations sections.

Slicers

The first choice in the Filter section is Insert Slicer. Click on that and an Insert Slicers dialogue box will appear that lists all of your available fields.

Slicers will sit on top of your workspace and work much like the filter options, letting you pick and choose which values appear in your pivot table. Here I've chosen to show them for Month and Year:

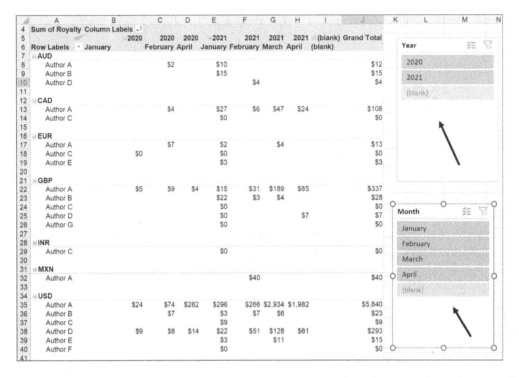

You can left-click and drag each box to move it, which I've done here to place the two slicers to the right-hand side of the pivot table.

Now that they're there I can click on those options to manipulate my pivot table. Here I've chosen to only display information for January 2020:

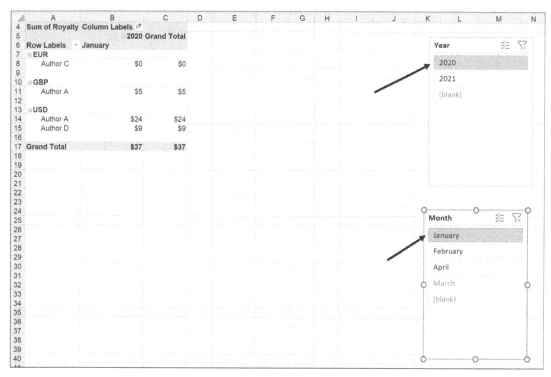

Note that the slicers stay where you've positioned them, but the pivot table, being dynamic, shrinks to only show my limited values. Keep this in mind if you feel tempted to move your slicers around when your pivot table is filtered, because as soon as I remove my filtering, that pivot table is going to go back to taking up that entire space once more.

To select January and 2020, I just clicked on them in each slicer.

But if you want to select more than one value in the slicer, you either need to use Alt + S or click on that icon with the checkmarks and lines next to them at the top of the slicer for that field. (See below. Alt + S basically turns that on.)

What you need to do at that point will depend on whether you've already selected a value or not. If all values are still selected, then as you click on a value it will be *unselected*. If you had already clicked on one value and then realized you wanted more than one, as you click on values they will be selected.

So pay attention to whether a field is shaded (like January and 2020 are in the last screenshot), or not. The shaded ones are the ones you're seeing results for.

To remove any applied filters from a slicer, use Alt + C or click on that little filter with an X on it in the top right corner of each filter. (Alt + C will only work if you select the filter first.)

Another option is the Clear Filters option in the Clear dropdown in the Actions section of the PivotTable Analyze tab that we covered previously but remember that will remove all filters in your pivot table as well as all of your slicers.

Slicers remain visible even when you're not clicked onto the pivot table. The advantage to using them over putting a field into the Filters section is that when you have multiple values selected but not all values, you'll be able to see which ones. Also, it's much more intuitive for users to just click on what they can see as opposed to try to use dropdown menus.

Timeline

Next to the slicer is another option, Insert Timeline, which is specific to fields that are dates.

I find this one very tricky to work with, because it doesn't always recognize dates in my data as dates.

For example, I've been showing you anonymized data from an Amazon report. There is a Date field in that data, but when I used that field, Excel told me it was not a date field. Okay, fine. I went back to that data and formatted it as a date. Still not a date field according to Excel. Okay…I copied and pasted special values into a new worksheet and then formatted as a date. Still not a date according to Excel.

Next, I used the DATE function to build a date. Finally, that worked. Excel saw that as a date.

But…weirdly enough, when I added the Date field to my pivot table it would only display the dates in the table as their month. Even when I tried to change the format.

Good news, though. The Timeline option let me filter the data by day of the month, year, and quarter, so even though I couldn't get that information to display in the table itself, I could filter by it.

Here's that table with the timeline set to DAYS to show the days of the month I could filter by:

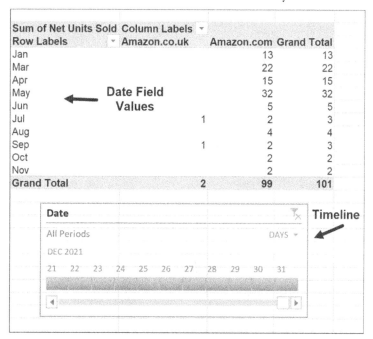

I can change the available choices in the timeline by using that dropdown there that currently says DAYS and setting it to YEARS, QUARTERS, or MONTHS.

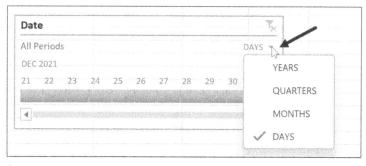

As that changes from DAYS to YEARS to QUARTERS to MONTHS, the available options also change to reflect that choice.

From what I can tell, the available choices will cover the date range from first date to last date, so especially with DAYS, even if there are no results on a particular day it will still show that date as an available option in the timeline if it's between the first and last dates in your data. For example, as you can see above in the pivot table there are not dates in December in this data, and yet the timeline shows December dates to choose from.

Click on any of those values to filter your table. Here I've changed it to YEARS and chosen 2021:

From what I can tell, it's not possible to choose date values that aren't connected, but you can click on one entry, hold down the Shift key and click on a later entry to select a date range, like I've done here for January 1 through 8, 2020:

Sum of Net Units Sold	Column Labels	
Row Labels	Amazon.com	Grand Total
Jan	13	13
Grand Total	13	13

Date

Jan 1 - 8 2020   DAYS

JAN 2020

1   2   3   4   5   6   7   8   9   10   11

Note also that there is a scroll bar below the entries in the timeline so that if there are more available entries than you can see, you can scroll right or left to see the rest of them.

To remove a filter from your timeline, click on the funnel with the X in the top corner. Or use the Clear Filters option in the PivotTable Analyze tab.

Okay, that's the timeline. Don't feel bad if it doesn't work well for you, because it never does for me.

Format Your Slicer or Timeline

First, because we haven't covered this yet, to remove a slicer or a timeline, just click on it and then use the Delete key.

If you want to format your slicer or timeline, you can do so. When you insert a slicer or timeline there will be a menu tab up top that says Slicer or Timeline that has pre-formatted style choices as well as a new style option at the bottom of that list. Here is the one for the Slicer:

More interesting to me is the right-hand side of that tab for any slicer, because it includes a Buttons and Size section.

Size lets you specify the size of your slicer. Buttons lets you change the size of the options in the slicer or timeline and also display them in multiple columns, which can be very useful when there are a lot of potential values, like here where I've changed it to show the values in two columns instead of one:

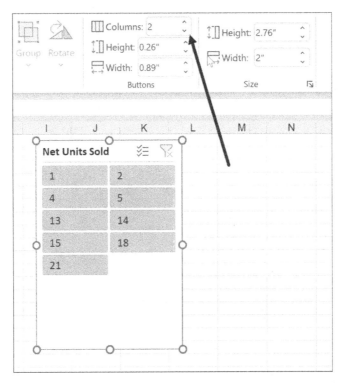

The timeline option does not allow that, it's very basic in terms of how it shows values. But you can at least change the size and the colors used if you want.

Calculated Fields

I will often want to take the values from a pivot table and do further analysis with them. Usually what I do is copy and paste that pivot table as special values, which gives me the data but keeps me from having to worry about the pivot table's dynamic nature which can move data around and is also very hard to reference from outside of the pivot table.

But my solution is not ideal, because sometimes you want to be able to look at your data over time and not have to rebuild your calculations every time. In that case, it's a good idea to build the calculations directly into the pivot table.

The way to do this is by using Calculated Fields. Let's walk through how to do that now.

Go to the Fields, Items, & Sets dropdown menu in the Calculations section of the PivotTable Analyze tab and choose Calculated Field.

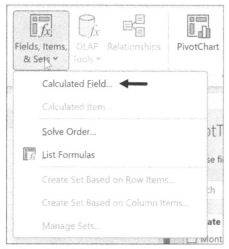

This will open the Insert Calculated Field dialogue box:

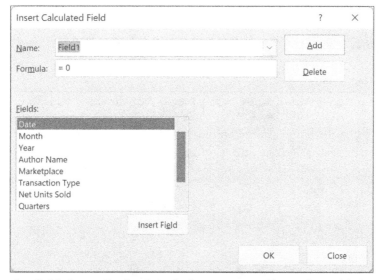

First step, name the field. I usually don't include spaces, so I'm going with RevPerUnit.

Next step is to build the formula. We're going to stick with simple math here. What I want is the Royalty field divided by the Net Units Sold field.

So I click into the formula field, delete the 0, go to the Fields section, find Royalty, double-click on it to insert (or click on it once and then click on Insert Field), type a / for division into the formula field and then go and do the same for Net Units Sold.

That gives me this:

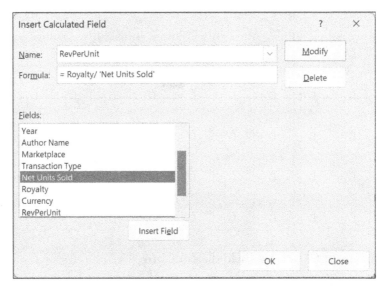

When I'm done, I click OK.

Excel automatically inserted the field into the Values section for me. But it's also now part of the list of fields I can choose from to insert into my pivot table, so I could use it as a filter, for example, just as easily.

Now, because I used division, some of my results came back as #DIV/0! results so it's not pretty right now:

	A	B	C	D	E
4	Sum of RevPerUnit	Column Labels			
5		2020	2020	2020	2021
6	Row Labels	January	February	April	January
7	AUD				
8	Author A	#DIV/0!	$2	#DIV/0!	$5
9	Author B	#DIV/0!	#DIV/0!	#DIV/0!	$5
10	Author D	#DIV/0!	#DIV/0!	#DIV/0!	#DIV/0!
11					
12	CAD				

But I can maybe modify that calculation. How to do so is not intuitive. What you do is go back to that dropdown and choose Calculated Field again and then for the Field Name you type in the exact same name as before. That will change your option for that field from Add to Modify. Type in the new formula you want, click on Modify, and then OK.

The formula I was able to get to work for this was:

=IF(ISERROR(Royalty /'Net Units Sold'),0,Royalty /'Net Units Sold')

It wasn't exactly what I wanted because I'd rather display a blank space than a zero value, but at least it got rid of those error messages.

	A	B	C	D	E
4	Sum of RevPerUnit	Column Labels			
5		2020	2020	2020	2021
6	Row Labels	January	February	April	January
7	AUD				
8	Author A	$0	$2	$0	$5
9	Author B	$0	$0	$0	$5
10	Author D	$0	$0	$0	$0
11					

(I know we haven't covered a lot of functions yet, but if you're curious about what I used there it was a combination of the IF function and the ISERROR function. Both are covered in the next book in this series or you can look them up in Excel's help.)

And, one more tip on this, if you ever need to see the formula you used for a calculated field, choose the List Formulas option. That's going to show you a new worksheet with all of your formulas in the order that they calculate.

It also has the added benefit of showing each formula so you can copy it if you need to make a small edit and don't want to try to recreate it from scratch. (I was unable to edit the formula directly on that worksheet, which would've been nice, but does not seem to be possible, at least not with fields that have spaces in their name.)

In general, I would recommend keeping your calculations simple in your pivot table, but again, you do you. If you can make it work, good on ya.

Conditional Formatting

While we're here talking about more advanced analysis, let's dip a toe in on applying conditional formatting to our pivot table entries. This is not something I have done a lot of in the past so I can't tell you how it will go wrong. But I can tell you how to do it.

Create your pivot table, select the cells that are in the main body of the pivot table, and then apply your conditional formatting like you would to any other cells.

I recommend that after you do that you go to Manage Rules and choose to edit the rule you just created. When you do so there will be an additional choice you can make:

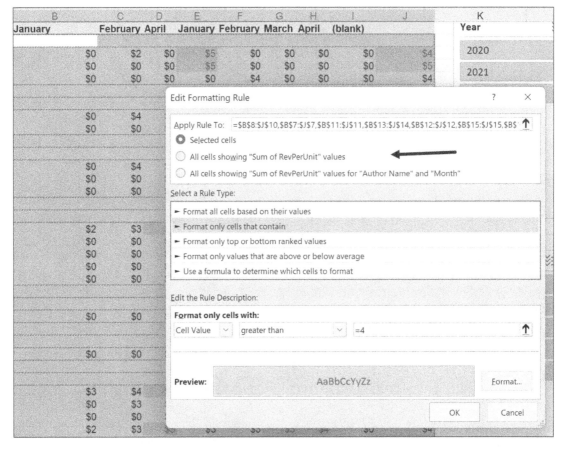

Right now if you look at the Apply Rule field you can see that Excel is using my selected data range. But I can check the box below that, which currently says "All Cells Showing Sum of RevPerUnit Values", to have it apply the rule to my field instead of those specific cells.

That way if the table updates I won't lose the conditional formatting for that field.

If I want to make sure the conditional formatting isn't lost, but also want to limit it to this specific combination that exists, I can check that last box which currently says, "All Cells Showing Sum of RevPerUnit Values for Author Name and Month". That way, if I use the RevPerUnit field in some other part of the pivot table it won't bring that conditional formatting with it.

Here I was able to add separate conditional formatting to two fields (Sum of Net Units Sold and Sum of Royalty) that I had in a pivot table:

	A	B	C
1			
2			
3			
4		Column Labels	
5		2021	2021
6		January	January
7	Row Labels	Sum of Net Units Sold	Sum of Royalty
8	USD	194	334.33
9			
10	GBP	16	38.22
11			
12	CAD	8	27.14
13			
14	AUD	5	25.05
15			
16	EUR	3	4.22

The trick was, or at least the way I got it to work, was to click into one cell in each column, add conditional formatting, and then edit the rule to expand it to all of that field not just that one cell.

It did take a little fiddling, so if it doesn't work the first time, don't give up. Alright, now let's talk for a moment about Pivot Charts.

Pivot Tables – Pivot Charts

Pivot charts did not always exist, so my default still tends to be old-school charts that I've been using for decades. But I've been experimenting enough with these that I feel comfortable mentioning this possibility to you.

What are pivot charts? They are the ability to create a chart straight from the data in a pivot table.

Here I have a very basic pivot table:

Row Labels	January	2021 February	2021 March	2021 April	2021 Grand Total
Currency USD					
Sum of Royalty Column Labels					
Author A	296.36	266.15	2934.47	1982.47	5479.45
Author D	22.08	50.85	128.46	61.22	262.61
Author B	3.44	6.88	5.59		15.91
Author E	3.47		11.24		14.71
Author C	8.98				8.98
Author F	0				0
Grand Total	334.33	323.88	3079.76	2043.69	5781.66

It shows four months of data for six authors for one currency. This type of data lends itself well to a column or bar chart, so let's try to create one of those using the PivotChart option located in the Tools section of the PivotTable Analyze tab.

Click on PivotChart and it will bring up the familiar Insert Chart dialogue box:

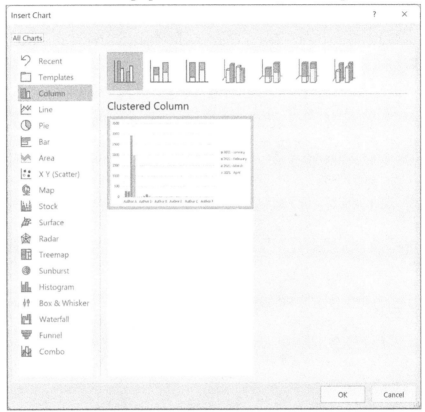

What I usually find at this point is that my pivot table is not set up the way that I want it to be for that particular chart. I don't know if you can see that here, but the Clustered Column chart it's showing has the four months for each author clustered together. But what I really want is all of the authors clustered together for each month.

I have two options here:

First, I could go back and fix my pivot table by swapping Author Name and Year and Month so that Year and Month are in the Rows section and Author Name is in the Columns section. If I want to do that, I click Cancel.

Second, I can go ahead and create the chart as-is and then fix it from there. I usually choose to fix it from there. So I click OK to go ahead and create my chart.

Once the chart is created, I can go to the Design tab and choose Switch Row/Column, which will fix the chart. *It will also change your pivot table* as you can see here:

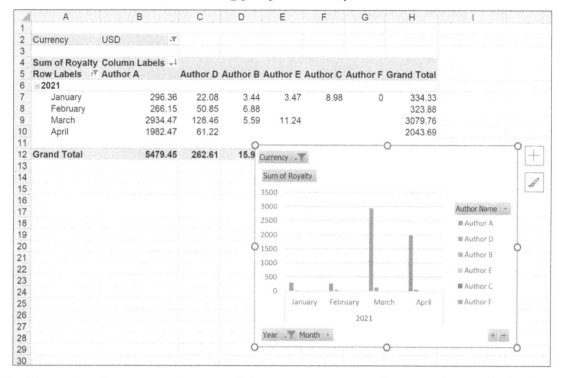

Looking at that chart, one author sort of drowns out everyone else so maybe a stacked column chart would be a better choice. At this point making that change is just like working with any other chart. I go to the Design tab, choose Change Chart Type, and then select my new chart type. Better.

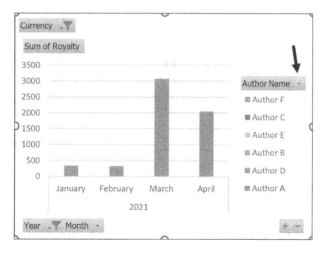

Or maybe I just don't need that author in the chart. If I click on the arrow next to Author Name (see the screenshot above) that will bring up a dropdown menu that lets me choose which values to include in the chart.

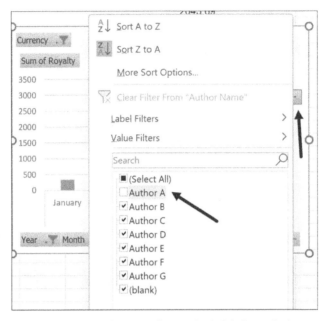

Above you can see that I unchecked Author A. Each field that's being used in the pivot table is available to select or not select. You can also use search, value filters, and label filters.

Here is the updated chart which shows far more detail for all of the other authors now:

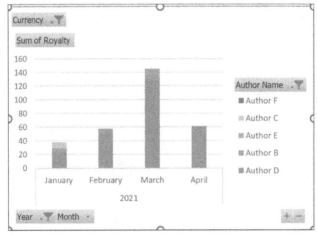

If you look at that chart you'll see that there are other fields you can filter directly on the chart such as Currency, Year, and Month.

Any changes you make to those filters will also be reflected in your pivot table. And vice versa. You can't change one without changing the other. You can, however, create a pivot chart, copy it, and then paste it as a picture to keep that chart you created without having it be impacted by future changes to the pivot table.

The same Chart Styles and formatting options exist for pivot charts as do for regular charts through the Design and Format tabs available up top when you click on your chart.

I find pivot charts to be more interactive than standard charts because of the ability to filter. So if I want to look at say, trend in sales over time for different authors or different series where I have too much data for one chart, rather than create six separate data tables and the charts to go with them, I can create one pivot chart and then quickly cycle through a subset of my data by using that filtering ability.

Just remember that your pivot chart is tied to your pivot table until you lock it in place as a picture. If the chart is being used for some sort of board reporting or regulatory reporting or something where it matters that it be fixed in time, do not leave it as a pivot chart. Lock it down. And, honestly, I'd lock down the data, too, but that's just me.

Okay. A few clean-up items and then we'll finally be done with pivot tables.

Pivot Tables – A Few More Items

Just a little bit of housekeeping before we wrap up this very extensive topic.

Move Pivot Table Values

You can move pivot table values around. So, for example, in my pivot table with Authors A, B, C, D, E, and F maybe I want authors A and E next to each other because they're the same genre.

To move a pivot table value, right-click on it and use the Move secondary dropdown menu to move the field to the beginning, up one, down one, or to the end. You can also use this option to move the field from columns to rows or from rows to columns.

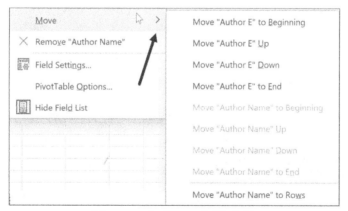

Name A Pivot Table

In the PivotTable Analyze tab there is a section on the left-hand side called PivotTable. You can name your pivot table there if you want to. I never have, but I do believe there are some advanced-level tasks in Excel that are easier if you name your pivot tables.

PivotTable Options

That same section also has an Options dropdown where you can click on Options to open a PivotTable Options dialogue box which contains a number of settings for that specific pivot table:

On the Totals & Filters tab you can turn off showing grand totals. On the Display tab you can choose the default sort order for data in your pivot table. On the Printing tab you can set print titles to select what prints at the top of each page or left-hand side of each page. On the Data tab you can set the pivot table to refresh each time you open the Excel file. And more. If you're curious, it's worth clicking through.

PivotTable Options is also available by right-clicking on the pivot table and choosing PivotTable Options from the dropdown menu.

Move PivotTable

In the Actions section of the PivotTable Analyze tab there is an option to move your pivot table. Click on that and you can either move the pivot table to a different location in an existing worksheet or to a new worksheet. Choose the new location based upon where the top left corner of the table will be. It doesn't take into account any filter fields you may have above that.

Recommended PivotTables

If you're not sure what pivot table you want to build or how to build one, there is a Recommended PivotTables option in the Tools section of the PivotTable Analyze tab. Click on that and it will take the data you selected for your pivot table and suggest various pivot tables:

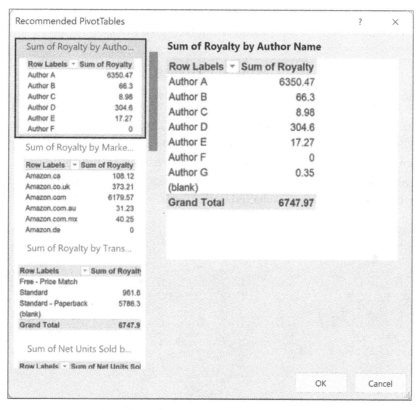

For basic pivot tables the suggestions are solid, but in my case they were all one by one tables. Also, the suggestions covered basically any numeric field combined with any text field which meant that towards the bottom it suggested combinations that made no sense.

But it does at least show you how a basic pivot table is built.

Show Options

At the very end of the PivotTable Analyze tab there are three options in the Show section. Field List turns on and off the PivotTable Fields task pane. Buttons hides or shows the expand/collapse buttons for grouped data or when you have multiple data levels. Field Headers hides or shows the Column Labels and Rows Labels text in the pivot table.

Linking Pivot Tables

It is beyond the scope of this book but Excel has in recent years been upgraded to allow for the linking of various data tables, which can create a data structure akin to what you do in Access or other database tools. That includes pivot tables.

If you want to explore that more, search for help on "work with relationships in PivotTables". It's not an area I've explored enough to give help.

Blank Entries

You may have noticed that some of the example pivot tables I showed you had a "blank" field value as well as the expected values. For me this usually occurs because I just selected the entire worksheet rather than a defined area that only had data in it. I usually just hide those entries or ignore them, but if they bother you the solution is usually going to be to be more careful in what data you select before choosing to insert a pivot table. Either that or to delete blank columns or rows from within your selected data.

Remove Duplicate Values

Alright, pivot tables were the last big topic I wanted to cover, but there are a few other intermediate topics that are easy to do and incredibly helpful. The first of those is how to remove duplicate values.

Here, for example, I have some sample data and I want to extract the unique author names from this list:

	A	B	C	D	E
1	Royalty Date	Title	Author Name	Marketplace	
2	2021-01-31	Book Title A	Author A	Amazon.com	
3	2021-01-31	Book Title A	Author B	Amazon.com.au	
4	2021-01-31	Book Title A	Author C	Amazon.com	
5	2021-01-31	Book Title A	Author D	Amazon.com	
6	2021-01-31	Book Title A	Author C	Amazon.fr	
7	2021-01-31	Book Title A	Author C	Amazon.ca	
8	2021-01-31	Book Title A	Author A	Amazon.com	
9	2021-01-31	Book Title A	Author C	Amazon.de	
10	2021-01-31	Book Title A	Author A	Amazon.com	
11	2021-01-31	Book Title A	Author A	Amazon.com	
12	2021-01-31	Book Title A	Author A	Amazon.com	
13	2021-01-31	Book Title A	Author D	Amazon.com	
14	2021-01-31	Book Title B	Author D	Amazon.com	
15	2021-01-31	Book Title B	Author F	Amazon.com	

They've made this option a little hard to find, but it's still there. Click on the column(s) with the data in it where you want the unique values (or combination of values) and then go to the Data Tools section of the Data tab. Right now Remove Duplicates is an icon with a blue bar, white bar, and blue bar stacked with a red X in the corner. It's located in the same section as Text to Columns.

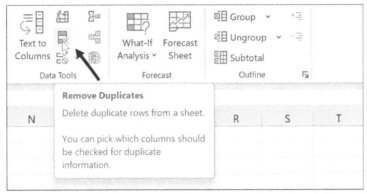

(You can hold your mouse over the image to make sure you have the right one like I did above.)

Click on that image.

If you have more than one column of data in your worksheet, like I do, and you only selected one column, like I did, then you will see a Remove Duplicates Warning that suggests that you expand your selection.

	A	B	C	D	E
1	Royalty Date	Title	Author Name	Marketplace	
2	2021-01-31	Book Title A	Author A	Amazon.com	
3	2021-01-31	Book Title A	Author B	Amazon.com.au	
4	2021-01-31	Book Title A	Author C	Amazon.com	
5	2021-01-31	Book Title A	Author D	Amazon.com	
6	2021-01-31	Book Title A	Author C	Amazon.fr	
7	2021-01-31	Book Title A	Author C	Amazon.ca	
8	2021-01-31	Book Title A	Author C	Amazon.de	
9	2021-01-31	Book Title B	Author D	Amazon.com	
10	2021-01-31	Book Title B	Author F	Amazon.com	
11	2021-01-31	Book Title B	Author A	Amazon.co.uk	
12	2021-01-31	Book Title B	Author A	Amazon.com	
13	2021-01-31	Book Title B	Author C	Amazon.com	
14	2021-01-30	Book Title B	Author B	Amazon.com.au	
15	2021-01-30	Book Title B	Author C	Amazon.com	
16					

Click on the "continue with the current selection" option instead, and then click Remove Duplicates.

Understand, however, that if you remove duplicates from one column within a range of data like I'm about to do, that it breaks the relationship between that column of data and the other columns of data in that table. It means that data table can no longer be used with that column of information unless you reverse removing duplicates by using Undo.

(I'll show you this in a moment.)

Next, you'll see the Remove Duplicates dialogue box where you can indicate whether your data has headers or not. (Excel will go right to this dialogue box if the column you selected was standalone.)

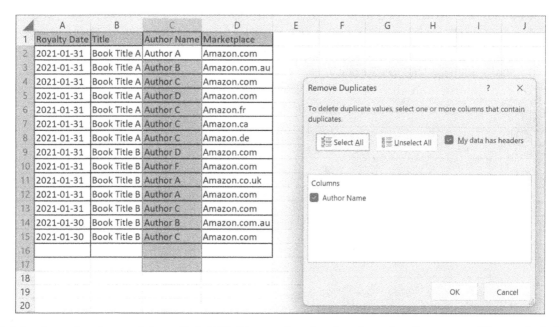

Make that selection and then click OK. If your data has headers, that first row will be excluded from the removing of duplicates. Meaning if my header were Author A and one of my entries were Author A, Excel would keep both.

Excel will then remove the duplicates from your selected column and display a dialogue box that tells you how many duplicates were removed and how many unique values remain. And you'll see that the column of data you used has now been reduced to just the unique values that were in that column.

If you selected the whole column like I did, one of your unique values will be the blank cell that you can see in Cell C7 here. So really there are five unique values in my data.

Note here that Row 6 used to be Author C, but because that was a repeat value, you now see Author F listed in that cell. That's what I mean by breaking the relationship between this column and the others. You can no longer trust that the value in that row for that column is the original value that was in that cell.

You can also use more than one column when removing duplicate values. This will give you the unique combinations across columns for your data.

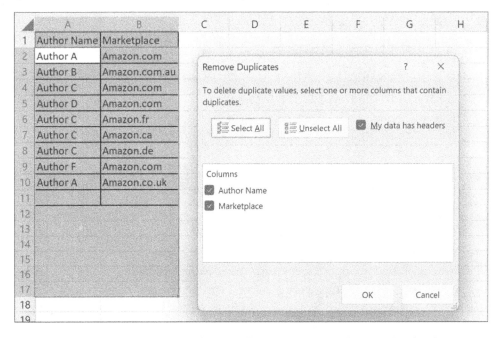

Here, for example, I've removed the duplicate values using both Author Name and Marketplace. (I reopened the Remove Duplicates dialogue box so you can see what that looks like when there's more than one field selected.)

Author C is now listed four times, but only once for each marketplace. When you Remove Duplicates using multiple columns what Excel looks for is unique combinations of the values in those columns.

Once more, be careful here if you have a larger data table. You really can't remove duplicates from some but not all columns in a table without destroying the relationships between the columns in the original table.

Because, once again, even though you're using multiple columns, it still has the same flaw, which is that it will pull up and list all unique combinations with no respect to how they relate to your other columns in your table.

Even if you select the whole table and then uncheck the fields you don't want to consider, it doesn't work. Here is an example where I did that:

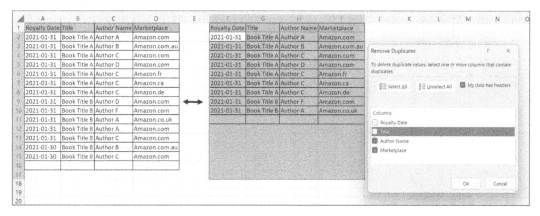

It takes until Row 9 to happen, but you can see that the data from the original table on the left is broken in Row 9 when it associates the data in that row with Author F instead of Author D. Because there was already a combination for Author D and amazon.com in Row 5, those values were deleted in Row 9.

If that sounds confusing, bottom-line: Take the column or columns where you want to remove duplicates. Isolate them separate from any other data. And then remove duplicates. If you always do that you'll be fine.

(I'm just too lazy most of the time to do so, which is why I walked through this in the way I did. I like to show others the mistakes I make so they won't make them, too.)

I love remove duplicate values, but this is one of those tasks that can permanently break your data. You can't rebuild a table where one column has had duplicate values removed and the rest haven't. You have to back out of that using Undo to get to the original table.

Which is why it is always a data best practice to keep your original source data somewhere untouched and work on a copy of it so that you always know there's a good version of your data somewhere no matter what you do wrong.

Okay. On to converting text to columns.

Convert Text to Columns

This is another one I've found really useful over the years. On a project a while back I was given a list of employees in the project that was written with the first name followed by the last name. So I had entries for "John Smith" in one cell.

Problem was, John went by Duke, so with the data organized that way no one could ever find him. They were looking under D and he was under J. But everyone knew his last name and could've found him that way just fine.

What I wanted was that same list of names, but sorted by last name. That's where the Text to Columns option comes in. It's very easy to take an entry like "John Smith" and turn it into two columns, one with "John" and one with "Smith" in it.

(I will note here that search, Ctrl + F, could've also been a solution to this issue but that required twenty-plus users with varying degrees of skill to be able to use an Excel file. By splitting the entries into first and last name and then sorting by last name, I could create a printed list of team members for those who didn't want to work with Excel.)

To use Text to Columns, select your cells, and then go to the Data Tools section of the Data tab, and click on Text to Columns.

This will open the Convert Text to Columns Wizard dialogue box:

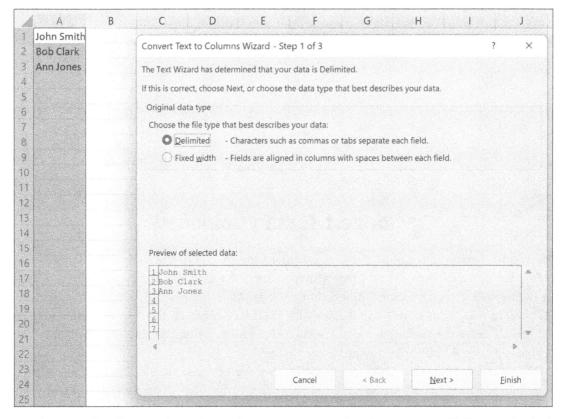

For what I'm showing you here the option you want on that first screen will almost always be delimited.

What delimited means is that the entries you want to separate all differ from one another in terms of potential length ("Joe Smith" and "Vernon McClarick" could be in the same employee list) but that there is a consistent separator between the values (in this case a space).

Fixed, the other option, is for when you're breaking down entries that are all consistently the same size for each section. For example, a social security number is always written as XXX-XX-XXXX so you know exactly where to draw the line each time to split out the first, middle, and last portion of that entry.

For delimited, which is what I'm covering here, click Next and you can then specify how to break the text out.

It will have Tab selected by default. Uncheck that unless your text uses tabs, which is the case with data in .csv files, for example. And then find the character or characters that are separating your text.

In this case, I want to check Space.

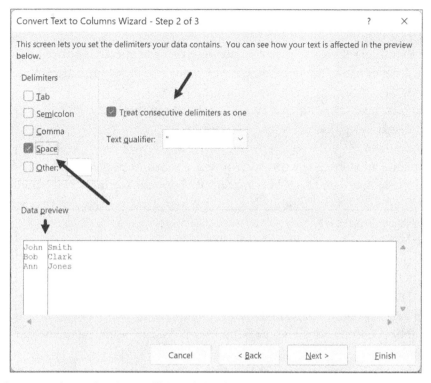

Excel will show you how the data will break in the data preview section at the bottom.

If you have something like "Smith, John" that uses two characters to separate your entries, just check the box for both of them. In this case I'd do so for the comma and the space. And then make sure that the checkbox for "treat consecutive delimiters as one" is also checked.

You can also enter a custom separator in that Other box. So if I have "John Smith-3" and I want to have "John Smith" separated from that 3, I'd want to use a dash (-) as my delimiter.

Whatever delimiter you choose will be deleted. So with "John Smith" I'm going to get a column with John and one with Smith and that space that was between the two words will be gone.

Click Next or Finish once you have your choices made and things look right in the preview screen.

If you click on Next there's a final screen where you can specify a format for each of your new columns. I never use it, but you could if you want to. Click Finish from there once you're done.

Excel will then take the data that was in that column and will split it out into as many columns as it needs using that delimiter you specified.

If you have data in the columns to the right of your entries that is going to be overwritten, Excel will generate an alert to tell you so. You can choose to proceed and overwrite that data or cancel and move that data first. (This sometimes happens for me when I think the text I'm converting will only take two columns but it turns out it takes three because someone has a middle name, for example.)

I find Text to Columns incredibly useful. But...

Not every situation will go smoothly. If you have entries for "Maria Teresa Valdez", "John Smith", and "Hubert Rockford, Jr." all in the same column you're going to run into issues splitting that data into separate columns. The first names will line up fine, but then the Teresa part of Maria Teresa's name will be in the same column as the last names for John and Hubert. And there will be a comma at the end of Rockford. And Jr. in that name will be in the same column as Valdez.

You need to look at your data before and after to make sure that the result you have is what you need it to be.

Also, you may need to combine this task with various Excel functions (like TRIM or TEXTJOIN) to get the final result you want. (Those are covered in the next book in this series, or you can just look them up using Excel's help.)

Additional Tidbits

In this section I'm going to run through a few additional tips or tricks I've picked up over the years.

Fix Number Stored As Text

There are going to be times when you're working in Excel and it gives you an error message or indicates that something is wrong. I cover the formula-related ones in detail in the third book in this series, but I wanted to cover here a different error message that I receive often working with my vendor reports, and that's when numbers are stored as text.

Most of my vendors provide me with .csv reports not Excel files. These days Excel can open those without you even noticing the difference. (In the past you had to have Excel convert them for you.) But sometimes due to the nature of those reports the numbers are not stored as numbers.

Here is an example from one of my vendor reports:

You can see that the top left corner of the cells in Column C all have a green triangle.

When I click on one of those cells, that error triangle appears. Hold your mouse over it and you'll see a dropdown arrow. Click on that to see the menu of options pictured above.

The first line in the dropdown tells you that the error in this cell is that the number is stored as text. You can fix that by clicking on Convert To Number.

If you don't want to fix it, and don't want to see the marks in the corner of each cell, you can choose Ignore Error.

If you're not sure what to do, you can choose to open help through that dropdown by choosing Help On This Error.

In this case, I don't want that value treated as a number. If Excel treats it as a number it will display in scientific notation which does me no good. But often I do need to convert an entire column of values from text to numbers.

To convert all cells in a column at once, select all of the cells first. You should see the warning triangle next to the top cell in the range. Click on the dropdown arrow and select the convert option. That will convert all of the selected cells, not just the top one.

Quick Access Toolbar

If there are tasks in Excel that you perform all the time and you don't want to be bothered to go and track them down in each separate tab, you can add them to the Quick Access Toolbar, which is located at the top of the workspace and always available to you regardless of the tab you're in.

The most reliable way to edit the Quick Access Toolbar is to go to File and then click on Options in the bottom left corner. In the Excel Options dialogue box that appears, click on Quick Access Toolbar.

The left-hand side will show popular commands that you can add to the Quick Access Toolbar. Select the ones you want and then click on the Add option, which will move them to the right-hand side. If you want to remove a task that's already been added, click on it on the right-hand side and choose Remove.

You'll also need to click on the checkbox at the bottom for "Show Quick Access Toolbar" or you won't see your tasks when you go back to the main workspace.

Click OK when you're done.

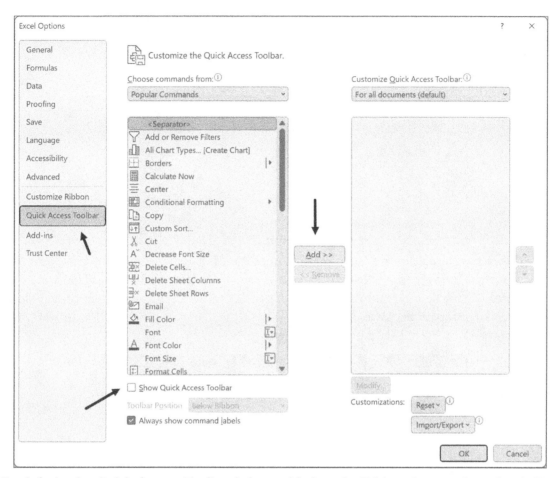

By default, the Quick Access Toolbar is located below the Ribbon (menu tab options). You can see here that I have a shortcut now for adding new charts:

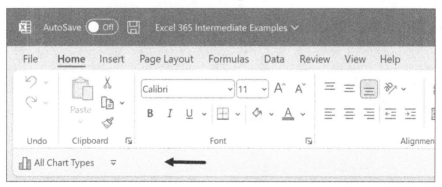

In the past, the Quick Access Toolbar was located above the Ribbon next to that save icon. That's still where I like it to be.

Just below the checkbox to show the toolbar in the Excel options dialogue box is a dropdown menu for Toolbar Position that you can change to Above Ribbon if you prefer that as well.

Here's what that looks like:

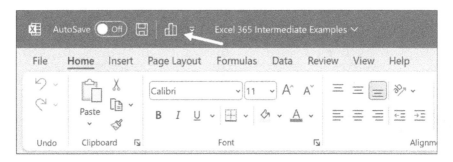

The quicker, but less reliable way to open the Quick Access Toolbar is to right-click on or near the save icon at the very top of the workspace. (I say it's less reliable because there were only about three spots where I could right-click and get this to work. But one of them does seem to be directly on top of the save icon.)

So right-click and you'll see a dropdown menu:

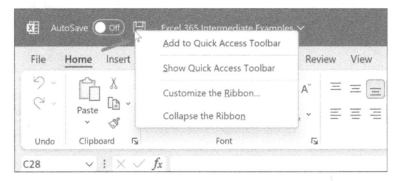

Click on Show Quick Access Toolbar. That will put a small downward pointing arrow that you can then click on to bring up the Customize Quick Access Toolbar dropdown menu

If the option you want as a shortcut is listed in that dropdown (New, Open, Save, etc.), click on it and its icon will be added to the toolbar. If you want more choices, click on More Commands to open the Excel Options dialogue box to the Quick Access Toolbar page.

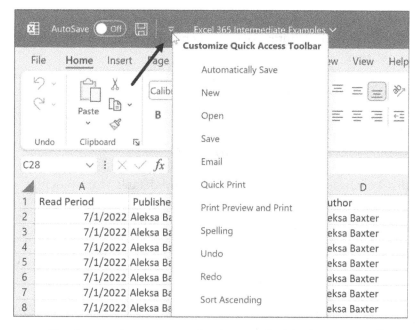

In Excel I personally do not keep any tasks in my Quick Access Toolbar because most everything I use regularly is there on that Home tab, but in Word I do have Page Break and Read Aloud.

I would recommend adding tasks here that you use often but that are kept on a different tab than the one you use most of the time, but not any tasks that you could do with a Control shortcut.

Options

We just looked at one of the things you can do with Excel Options, but there are a large number of ways to customize Excel to your personal preferences.

First, go to File and then click on Options in the bottom left corner to open the Excel Options dialogue box. There are a number of choices there on the left-hand side and then a number of options for each of those choices. (You saw above the page for Quick Access Toolbar.)

This is usually where you can go to fix any weird change that they make to Excel that you're not used to or don't like. And sometimes where you need to go to correct certain things that don't work for you, like me and using (c) for rule citations more than I use it for the copyright symbol.

The one caution I will give here is that the more you customize, the more challenging it becomes to work on a default version of Microsoft Office. (And, for me, the more annoying it is each time I get a new computer and have to set that all up again if I'm using the one-time-purchase versions of Office.)

If you think that you will work at a variety of companies with Office or that you may need to hop onto a colleague's computer to help them out, then I would recommend against extensive customization.

But if you're working for yourself and going to use 365 forever and ever and never need to use anyone else's computer, then make it work for you.

A few examples of what you might want to change on the various pages:

General

- LinkedIn Features section that is checked by default that somehow connects your LinkedIn to your Office account. (Nope.)

- Turn off the Start screen and go direct to a worksheet.

- Change the Office theme (as discussed in *Excel 365 for Beginners*).

- Change default font or font size.

- Change the number of worksheets that are available in a new workbook.

- Turn off the Mini Toolbar and/or Quick Analysis options.

Formulas

- Change Row and Column references to R1C1 format so that columns are also numbered. (Good for when working with macros.)

- Change when calculations are performed.

- Turn off error checking rules.

Proofing

- Add or modify autocorrect options.

- Change dictionary language for spellcheck as well as Spanish and French modes.

Save

- Choose default file format for saving.

- Set how often to AutoSave file.

- Choose default location to save files.

Add-Ins

- Add additional Excel functionality that's not available by default, such as the Analysis ToolPak or Solver.

Zoom

You can zoom in or out on an Excel worksheet. In the bottom right corner there is a slider bar that shows 100% by default. You can click on the vertical bar in the middle of that space and drag to the right to zoom in and to the left to zoom out.

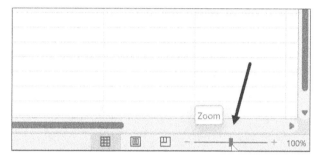

But this only zooms in or out on the cells in the worksheet. Your menu options will not change size nor will any dialogue boxes or dropdowns. To make those more visible you'll need to change your computer settings.

In the Zoom section of the View tab there are also Zoom options.

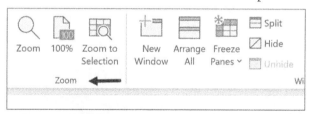

Click on the 100% icon to return your workspace to a 100% zoom. Click on the Zoom icon to open the Zoom dialogue box which will let you zoom to a specific zoom level.

Zoom to Selection will zoom by default to 400% on the cell(s) you had selected. If the selection is too large for 400% to show all of the entries it will zoom to whatever level will show all of them the best. Be careful using this with a really large selection because it will zoom to the point where the text is not visible.

Conclusion

There's a lot more you can do in Excel. I've dropped a few things from this version of this book that I covered in prior versions like spellcheck and limiting values in cells because I don't think most people need that. But those options do exist.

And there's a whole area of Excel that involves creating connections between worksheets and tables and importing data that I have never included in any of these books. Nor have I ever covered macros. Both are specialized and advanced topics that require a certain level of care or you can create a very big mess.

Also, my target audience for these books are not people who want to wade through that sort of mess. My goal with these books is to give you what you need to be a day-to-day user of Excel not a superuser.

But I do want to let you know that there is a lot more to Excel than I've covered in this book or that I covered in *Excel 365 for Beginners*. And more than I'll have covered by the end of the final book in this series *102 Useful Excel 365 Functions*.

Because if there's something you need, it may very well be there. Excel's help topics are excellent and you should definitely make use of them. (F1 to open the help task pane or go to the Help tab.) They often have videos to go along with the different tasks which are all very well done.

The benefit of these books is that I gave you a path to follow when learning this information. Start here, go there, add this, and here we are. But there's a whole wilderness out there to explore if you want and many knowledgeable sources to draw from.

Don't be afraid to experiment with Excel. Open a new file. Take a copy of some of your data. (Not the original.) And then try to figure it out. Ctrl + Z and Esc will usually bring you back from any mistake you make. But if they don't, close the file without saving, and try again.

Now, having said all of that, formulas and functions are a key part of how I use Excel and we have not covered them in depth yet. That's what the next book in this series is for.

So if you want to continue your learning journey with me, then definitely check out *102 Useful Excel 365 Functions*.

Alright then. That's it. Reach out if you get stuck. I'm happy to point you in the right direction. Good luck with it.

Index

About the Author

M.L. Humphrey is a former stockbroker with a degree in Economics from Stanford and an MBA from Wharton who has spent close to twenty years as a regulator and consultant in the financial services industry.

You can reach M.L. at mlhumphreywriter@gmail.com or at mlhumphrey.com.